The Moms

Stories of Sorrow and Courage
Following the Death of a Child

By: The Moms
Compiled by: Gerri Haynes

ISBN: 1508925461
ISBN 13: 9781508925460

TABLE OF CONTENTS

Dedication

To every parent who has loved a child and experienced the death of that child, we dedicate this book. May you find peace in the love of other parents who are living through this most painful reality.

To the mothers who courageously wrote their stories, a deep and unending blessing.

Introduction

This book is written by mothers, for mothers and for those who care about mothers. Each story is the personal journey of a mother who has experienced the unthinkable - the death of a child.

For more than twenty years, it has been my privilege to meet every other week with mothers who are seeking ways to survive the death of their child. These women are my teachers. No two women approach grief in the same way. No two women find the same path to continuing to live beyond the physical presence of a child. Here, you will read very different stories - yet you may recognize threads that unite these women and give them the strength to reach out to you with their stories - hoping that your understanding and compassion will grow as you read. And hoping that in reading of their journeys you will find strength in understanding.

Some of the children in these stories were very young. Some lived to adulthood and some had children of their own. All of them died "out of order" - no parent expects that their child will precede them in death.

The anthropological role of the mother is defined in many texts. As the female parent of a child, the mother is a sustainer of the species, nurturer, protector, provider of food, teacher, friend - generally spending more direct contact time with the child than the father. The father shares some of these roles, but often in differing expressions. The sense of purpose felt by mothers at birth is at least partially fed by the need for our species to survive.

When we birth a child or become a mother, most of us do so with the good intention to be the best mother we can. Nearly all of us, in our humanity, might have improved our work - but most of us have loved and cared to the best of our ability.

The death of a child brings the loss of primary purpose. Often, there is a feeling of guilt, perhaps a sense of failure to protect from harm or to adequately nurture. To continue living, the need to re-establish a sense of purpose can be a monumental chore. Lack of energy, inability to sleep, loss of connection with other family members, friends, the community can present barriers difficult to overcome.

The "first mom", Diana, attended a hospital focus group conducted to investigate community needs for bereavement support. Diana's son had died three years prior to this group meeting and she alerted me to a specific need that existed – the need for mothers to find each other. In bereavement groups that followed, the need was repeated and a mothers' support group was formed.

The same women seldom comprise The Mom's group for any two meetings. Women attend as they wish or can. Sometimes they attend for a series of meetings, don't attend for a while, and then perhaps return for more meetings. Some have attended regularly for long periods of time and help other mothers find ways to survive.

All of these mothers learn from each other, are able to be the mothers of their children in the presence of each other; cry and laugh together.

For more than ten years, members of the group have participated once or twice during the year in long weekend retreats. These weekends are hard work and gentle fun; times to concentrate fully on the sacred work of grief and on living with painful reality. Together, the Mothers walk an ocean beach – coming to group activities to consider the work of the weekend. This opportunity to have open time with each other can provide glimpses of wisdom and areas for further processing.

There are normal cycles of grief that these women could describe: the shock that comes immediately following the death of a child, the numbness and pain and reality and searching; the attempts to reorganize and reinvest in life, the pain that still visits them and the strength of learning to live with the wisdom that comes.

In grief following a death that occurs in "the natural order" – that is older individuals dying before younger - the grief cycle during the first year often occurs in approximately three month periods: the event of death followed by about three months of coping (the shock time), then a "down" time when the reality of death is stronger – followed by approximately three more months of coping. At six months, there tends to be a painful time when the reality of a death becomes clearer. This seems to reflect the experience of children who often don't have a concept of the permanence of the loss of the physical presence of their loved one for about six months. From six to nine months, people tend to function through their sadness. From nine months to one year, the rise in coping is blunted by the sense (generally without complete awareness) that the one year anniversary is approaching. The first year anniversary is an opportunity to create a life celebration – often, however, this opportunity is overlooked and the time is steeped with loneliness.

Special occasions of the year - birthdays, anniversaries, holidays that are special to a family – often also present challenges and may need deeper understanding from the mother and those who love her.

For mothers, aspects of shock tend to persist. The second year seems to bring more pain of reality. We have come to believe that this extended time of "numbness" is a gift – that the second year is clearly the earliest that many mothers can survive the pain. Mothers also report that the pain of grief tends to rise again at five year intervals. Five year, ten year, fifteen year anniversaries are painful. Knowing of these cycles may help to assure an individual of normalcy.

Some of these stories were written years ago, some were written recently. You will see that they are timeless. Let these mothers also be your teachers.

Gerri Haynes

Danny
7/23/70 - 8/18/86

Danny

Died in a Motorcycle Accident

By Diana

If anyone had told me one of my children would die young I would have said, "Get the straight jacket and the padded room ready." I did not believe I could live through such a tragedy and remain sane. Yet, here I am twenty six years later trying to put into words who Danny was, the way he died and how I have survived, so I may share it with you.

First, I would like to introduce you to Danny so you may better understand who he was. He was my first born and a very precocious child. He was usually in some kind of mischief but very honest about it when caught. In my exasperation one day I asked him, "Why do you continue to do the things you know will get you into trouble?" He replied, very sincerely, "My mind knows I shouldn't mom, but my hands just can't help themselves!"

As he grew, so did his curiosity, his desire for speed and living on the edge. In grade school he had a teacher who shared the concern that if Danny didn't slow down he would not live to see old age. I've wondered if that teacher was around when Danny died and remembers those words to me.

Danny never walked down a flight of stairs, he jumped. When he skied he didn't wait in line with his sister, Dina, to compete for a ribbon, he raced against himself and the wind. He continued through his young life at a very fast pace. In junior high school he decided being smart wasn't "cool", so he quit turning in his homework. When his teacher asked him to produce the work he pulled the papers out of his locker proclaiming his belief that school was for learning and he had, in fact, learned the required material. After I was fortunate enough to give up my career and become a stay at home mom Danny decided having mom at home worked in his favor. He started calling me when he arrived at school asking me to deliver some forgotten item; anything from lunch money to books for class. I finally threatened to deliver whatever he had forgotten in my jammies and robe. The day came very quickly when I had to carry out my threat. Danny thought it was hilarious and wasn't embarrassed at all.

As he went on to high school he continued to have lots of fun but certainly did not work up to his potential. He stopped hanging out with the A students and became friends with the group that only wanted to have a good time. Danny was very social and being tardy for classes was a daily occurrence. We both got to know the vice principle well. The problem was she could not stay mad at him. She threatened to suspend him several times but continued to give him another chance. Behind her back the kids called her Sarge indicating she was not normally a push over. She would admit Danny had her number and used it often.

During this time period I made another threat. I told him if he continued to be late for class I would be forced to bring his brand new baby brother, Skylar, and spend the day walking him from class to class. He thought it was a great idea and would actually welcome us being there. Danny loved his family and life so much he saw no reason why this would be embarrassing for him. He was such a charmer it was once said he could sell snow to the Eskimos and they would never question their need for it. My husband, Rick, used to ask me how I could be so mad at Danny one minute and be laughing with him the next. That's just the way of our relationship and the kind of person he was. Danny caused us a lot of heartache in the last few years of his life. Not only was the school work and being tardy an issue, he wasn't meeting his curfew either. I made the commitment to pick him up rather than let him ride with friends. He didn't mind at all even though I lost many nights sleep. He got caught stealing a $1.49 item when he had $5.00 in his pocket. With those kinds of things going on he ended up in a juvenile facility with a parole officer and doing community service. Six months before Danny died we sent him to Arizona to an Urban Wilderness training camp. It was quite an experience for him. He came back very grateful for his family, the opportunities he had and the comfort and safety of his home.

When Danny died he was riding on the back of his friends' motorcycle. They were going very fast and I'm sure he had a smile on his face and bugs on his teeth! They had come by the house to get some riding gear and helmets and to see his baby brother, Skylar. Dina, his younger sister, was at gymnastics and did not get to see Danny one last time.

As Danny left he gave me a kiss and told me he loved me. He was very affectionate, even giving me goodbye kisses and hugs in front of all his friends in the high school drive, so, nothing seemed out of the ordinary. In looking back on that night my husband, daughter and I have wondered if he knew, or had a feeling, something was going to happen to him. He and his dad exchanged a few words about being careful and then a moment in time was frozen as they just looked at each other. My husband had a "feeling" he didn't understand until much later when he allowed himself to really think about that one last look and those last words. Rick now believes he knew something was going to happen to Danny that night but couldn't have verbalized it or stopped it.

Danny and his friend had been riding the night before. Danny told me how fast they had been going and admitted they were not wearing helmets. I gave him the "mom speech" about safety. He promised they would not ride again without helmets. They didn't. They had ridden to see Danny's girlfriend in a town close by. She wasn't home so they talked to her mom for a while. Danny's friend told her how fast they had been going. Danny said it wasn't a good idea to tell her their speed because she would just worry. The mom said, "Yeah, how would you feel if you were going that fast, had an accident and killed Danny?" That mom felt some guilt because she made that statement only minutes before it actually happened. Within an hour of their leaving our house we got a phone call. It was from the guardian of Danny's friend, with whom he was riding. It was obvious she had been drinking and it was hard to understand her. Plus, the information she was giving me made no sense at all. She said, "I got a call from the hospital. The boys have been in an accident and one of them is dead!" I ask her to repeat what she had just said. She did, only adding, she didn't know which one was dead. Of course she did because, we found out later, that someone from the hospital had called her to come pick up the other boy. Her call was very cruel and started a chain of events and a period of waiting that seemed to go on forever.

I put Rick on the phone with her and he made her repeat the story. He then called the hospital. They refused to give out any information about Danny over the phone. I'm not sure how many calls he made asking for different departments each time hoping to get some answers that they wouldn't provide. When he finally called and asked about Danny's friend he was told the friend had been released to his guardian. When I heard this, I spun around and collapsed on the floor with only the words, "No, not yet." I guess, because of that statement, I too believed he would not live to see old age as his grade school teacher had predicted.

Dina cried, "Mom, pray with me!", as she threw her arms around my neck. I did pray, but not out loud and not what I believe she wanted me to pray, for it not to be true. I believed in my heart that Danny was dead and I didn't have faith that God would make it all go away.

Then the waiting began. We had to wait for someone "official" to tell us what we thought we already knew: Danny was the one in the accident who wouldn't be coming home. It seemed like hours before an officer finally came. We were all watching out the window, Rick, Dina, our nine month old baby boy, Skylar and me. When we saw headlights coming up the street we went out on the steps to meet him. His first words to us were, "You already know don't you?" It seems I replied, "We were just waiting for you to come tell us." And he did. When the terrible truth was finally verbalized Rick fell apart. I saw that same officer months later and he ask how my husband was doing remembering he took the news of Danny's death so hard. Rick told me later he wished he'd have taken and had more time to enjoy Danny's great sense of humor.

The officer strongly recommended we not go see "the body". "It was a horrible accident" and "You wouldn't want to see him that way." If I've had any regrets it is that I didn't insist on seeing Danny. I may have wished later I hadn't but I'll never know.

Danny turned sixteen three weeks before he died. Dina was just fourteen - the age for girls to be worrying about grades, boyfriends, zits and best friends, not her brother's death. The kids at school were criticizing Dina for not grieving properly. She finally challenged them asking, "Have any of you ever had a brother or sister die?" The answer was, "No". She responded with, "Then, don't tell me how I should be acting. If I were doing the things you say I should be my brother would tell me to knock it off!" That was a very brave, insightful thing for a girl of fourteen to say to her peers.

Five years later when our last son, Rylee, was born it was two days before the anniversary of Danny's death. I brought Rylee home from the hospital on August 18th, the same date Danny was killed. That is the first day Dina was able to verbalize her pain, talk about Danny and how hard the past five years had been for her. That's when she started to process through her grief. The night of the accident Dina called Erin Oldridge, her best friend since we'd moved to the area and they were in third grade. Erin's dad brought her over immediately and they stayed with us while we waited for other friends, Jack and Karen Benedict, which Rick had called. Everyone kept telling me to call my best friend, Miriam Burke. Actually, I just wanted them all to leave me alone. I had gone into a third person role by then and I remember thinking how very sad all these people were and wasn't it too bad but it had nothing to do with me. I finally did make that phone call just to get them off my back. I do not remember what I said to her. She tells me I told her Danny had been in an accident. I did not tell her on the phone that he had died. Not verbalizing it seemed to make it not be true. Thank God for our friends. They stayed and cleaned, fielded calls, organized, arranged and Miriam literally moved in until after the funeral. We moved in a fog from that point on for a very long time. There was a casket to pick, pallbearers to ask, so much to do and, who cared? What difference did it make what the casket looked like or who carried him to the grave. Danny was dead and it didn't really matter to me about all these minor details.

When we had the "viewing of the body" we went with a small group of friends. My friend, Miriam's husband, Terry, was sent in to make sure everything was ready for us. Terry came back and very quietly told us Danny wasn't there. He had not yet made it from the Bellevue funeral home to Redmond. To which, after a brief pause, I said, "of course he's not. He was never on time for anything in his life, why should this be any different!" I startled some people momentarily then they realized that was exactly the way Danny would have handled the situation, with humor. My sense of humor and the conversation I had with Danny a few weeks before the accident has helped me get through many days. Danny told me I shouldn't worry about his relationship with the Lord, he felt good about it even though some of his choices were questionable at that time.

My parents, Bob and Vera Huitt, helped raise Danny and Dina when I was a single parent living close by them. It just about broke their hearts when I moved my kids 2000 miles away from Iowa to Washington. But, the death of a grandchild was almost more than they could endure. That's the kind of call every grandparent hopes will never come. Ricks parents moved the 2000 miles to be closer to us after Danny died. It affected all our lives in many ways.

On the day of the funeral when the limo came to pick up the family, everyone was going out the front door; I was going out the back. I thought if I didn't go it wouldn't be true. Denial has always been an easy part of the grief process for me. Our friend Jack convinced me I had no choice but to go.

I loved having the kids bring their friends to our home. One of Danny's friends he had known since grade school ask if he could *borrow* Danny's suit and shoes to be one of the pallbearers. I told him he could certainly have them. Danny wouldn't need them any longer. We had lots of kids at our house before and after the funeral. Kids came, sat in his room, talked and took little reminders with them when they left. They shared stories, some I knew about some I did not. It was a healing time for us all.

It took us forever to pick a headstone and decide what we wanted printed on it. Again, the process of not acting made it seem not real. It was the last physical act we could do for our son and prolonging and procrastinating seemed to help keep the reality away.

I found out I was pregnant a few months after Danny died. It was the worst and best year of my life. The two most extreme feelings a mother can have the birth and death of her children. I was so afraid our new baby would be a boy, remind me of Danny and the pain would be unbearable. A few months before my delivery date I did a complete turnaround hoping that we would have a boy and he would remind me of Danny. Our baby boy's name is Brick JorDan (BJ) after his big brother. He has Danny's sense of humor which they both got from my dad. It's great and I get to enjoy it every day.

Each child, Dina, Skylar, Brick JorDan, and Rylee remind me of Danny in different ways at different times. We have been truly blessed with wonderful children. No matter how many children you have, they are each special and not one can take the place of another. Danny's girlfriend, Kim, has kept in touch all these years. She still sends me mother's day cards and comes to visit when she can. When she married our whole family went to the wedding. Kim married a wonderful man who understands her relationship with us and has accepted us as part of their lives.

For Christmas we have had a potted tree at the grave and Danny's friends were invited to decorate it. We now have that tree planted in our yard and decorate it every year. Most of the decorations his friends brought are weather beaten but we still have and use them.

On Danny's birthday we have had little ceremonies with balloons and notes. The brothers have colored pictures and attached them to the helium balloons and sent them to heaven. Now that the kids are older we celebrate Danny's birth by meeting for dinner. Dina suggested we put Danny's story in a bottle along with notes from each of us and send it out to sea. The first year we did this Dina included our phone number. We got a call weeks later from a family who found the bottle, read its contents and called to tell us they were suffering from the loss of a young boy in their family and how much they appreciated being able to read about Danny. Danny's birthday is In July, he was killed in August. I once voiced to a friend, Becky Cox, how every summer I start getting antsy and unhappy and I didn't know why. She said, "You just don't get it do you? You do this every year right before Danny's birthday." I hadn't realized it but knew she was absolutely right. So, over the years I tell my kids or the students I am teaching to give me a little extra kindness and understanding during this time period because on Danny's birthday and death day I have my moments of being sad and lonely. There is a void in my heart that can never be filled. Your children fill your heart like pieces of a puzzle; they all interlock to make a whole. When one piece is lost no other can take its place nor can your heart ever be whole again.

My cousin, Debbie Whitie, was concerned I would never be the same. She was afraid I wouldn't laugh and be the fun loving person she had grown up knowing. She has seen that I do still like to have fun but my world, as I knew it, has shifted and things will never be as they were before Danny died. Miriam became concerned that I was holding all my emotions in and not processing. She told me that one day I would be standing in line at McDonalds and just fall apart. My response to her was, "Well then, I just won't go to McDonalds!" That pretty much sums up me, my sense of humor and how I continue to cope with life and all it throws at me.

One of the things I was told by another cousin, Harold Wilson, after having lost two brothers to tragic accidents, was this, "God knows all things. God sits up on the tallest mountain while we struggle down here in the valley of life. Only God knows what the future of our lost loved ones would have been. They may actually have been saved from a fate worse than what we have had to endure." This statement helped me to begin to accept Danny's death.

I was told parents tend to smother the remaining siblings. When I heard this I decided I would not be a statistic and fall into that trap. To overcompensate, I was too lenient with Dina and allowed her too much freedom. She is thirty nine today and we are best friends. The fear of losing another child paralyzes me at times. But I make a conscience effort not to smother them because of my fear. Grieving is like raising children, no one tells you how to do it "right". That's because there is no right or wrong way. There are the steps of grief and those can be felt and experienced in any order and you may redo the same step again and again.

The first Thanksgiving after Danny died, Rick wanted to have his family close and invited them for dinner. I wanted to be alone. I also wanted to respect his needs but didn't see how I could entertain. That day I began to learn to take care of myself. I told everyone they were welcome to be in our home but to have no expectations of me. If I left the room or the house any time during the day, let me go and not to take it personally. Because I made that statement and gave myself that freedom I was able to stay with the family for the entire day.

In the beginning I resented every car of teenagers riding by. I walked through stores and wanted to shout at the people, "How can you possibly be acting normally? Don't you know my son is dead and my life and this world will never be normal again?"

I did not attend his class graduation even though we were invited by several of Danny's classmates. It would have been too painful to be there and not fair to the families that were celebrating that day.

Each "first" is the hardest, birthdays, holidays, but God gives you the first year in shock. The second year the reality starts to set in and the pain gets more real. By the third year I realized Danny was not coming back. The pain was immense all over again.

Rick and I had gone in the first year to a group for grieving parents called Compassionate Friends. It got us through some rough times but was not the long term answer for me. It was the third year I went to a grief group at a nearby hospital. The group was for anyone grieving a loss; spouse, child, parent, a job, house or divorce. Gerri Haynes was the facilitator and ask everyone to state their name and why they were there. When she came to me I told them my name but that was all. Gerri asked me why I was there. I told her because my husband *made* me come and I did not choose to or want to be at, "this damn group." I suppose by this statement you can see I was into the angry stage of my grief. Gerri realized the need for an extension of this group, one for grieving moms who had lost sons to an early death. Unfortunately our group continued to grow finally including the mothers of lost daughters as well. The sharing between other grieving moms was deeper than anything I had experienced so far. No one understands a mom's pain as well as other moms. There were bonds made and friendships established. The strength of the group grows as new moms come in and the "old" moms comfort and console. What we offer each other is a realization that it will get better and helping someone else is part of the healing process.

Our lives have gone on. There are good days and the not so good days. Most are the good days now. I've watched my three smaller boys as they've gone through the school programs and experienced their teenage years. I remember when Danny was doing all those things and I get a bittersweet feeling. My life is filled with memories of Danny and that is all we have.

Danny is with me daily. Sometimes that brings a smile and sometimes tears. Either way, it's ok.

DANNY
Part II

Twenty-seven years later: the rest of the children are grown and out of the house. Their dad and I have divorced, which is a common statistic for couples who have lost a child. We actually survived together for fourteen years after Danny's death. I thought we had passed the point of concern in this area. Who knows if we belong in the statistics or if it was destined to happen anyway? I do believe living through the loss of a child does, indeed, change us as people, families and couples. Some people survive intact, some do not.

Danny died August 18, 1986. The first holiday without Danny was Thanksgiving. Denial and anger were the two easiest emotions for me. In my opinion they are the two steps of grief that leave you the least vulnerable. I chose to ignore the holiday, pretend that this wasn't a time to give thanks because, at that time, I didn't believe there was any reason for gathering with the family and thanking God. My husband however wanted to have his family, mom, dad, sister, brother-in-law, niece and nephew come to our house for Thanksgiving. I realized I was not the only one grieving and I needed to allow him, and them, to do what they felt was best to get through their holiday.

The only way I could participate in a Thanksgiving at our home was to set some ground rules for myself. I called my in-laws and told them they were welcome to come, BUT, if, at any time, I decided to leave the room or even the house they were not to take it personally. I ask them to understand my feelings and to accept them as what I needed as a compromise for the day. It all went well and, surprisingly, I did not have to leave at any time. It is very important to take care of yourself, your needs and your feelings while allowing those around you, who are also grieving, to do the same.

When Christmas came we bought a potted Christmas tree, took it to the cemetery and invited all Danny's friends to help us decorate it. We continued this tradition and re-decorated a new tree, at the cemetery, every year until we moved. After leaving the area we bought a potted Christmas tree, planted it on our property and decorated it every year with the original decorations.

For Danny's birthday, while the kids were small, we would have a little party/picnic and invite their little friends. The kids would color pictures for Danny which we would attach to balloons and then send them to heaven. Over the years, when the kids became older, we started going out to dinner to celebrate Danny's birth. In the past few years my daughter Dina came up with the idea of a message in a bottle. She brought a bottle and a copy of my original story of Danny, pens and notepaper to our dinner. She asked Skylar, Brick and Rylee, their brothers, to write some of their thoughts about Danny. We then put all of our papers in the bottle, went out to Ediz Hook on the Olympic Peninsula and, with some ceremony, tossed the bottle into the Straits of Juan De Fuca. My son Brick whispered to me, "Mom, that bottle is going to sink as soon as it hits the water. The seal isn't good enough to survive rough seas." I told him to keep that thought to himself because it was so important to his sister.

Weeks later my daughter got a call from a family who had been camping some twenty miles from where we had launched Danny's bottle. They found, and fished out of the water, the bottle, carefully removing and reading Danny's story and the comments from the kids. They then shared their families' heartache. A young boy had been run over and killed by a parent in their driveway. Their family was trying desperately to come to terms with the tragedy, find some peace and move through their grief. They told Dina how much our letters meant to them and that they believed the bottle didn't come to them by accident. I, also, believe Danny's birthday bottle was meant for them. We have launched bottles since without any response. But, I believe, once was enough. What a blessing.

There are as many different ways to honor our children as there are different children themselves. Whatever works for you and your family is what you should do. I have purchased Danny's favorite McDonalds meal, taken it to the cemetery, sat and eaten my meal while I talked to Danny. Something that silly can be a comfort. As I said, whatever works.

There is no right or wrong way to grieve or to make any day special and tolerable for you. Take care of yourself so you can help take care of the other people in your life that you love.

To live in this world
You must be able
To do three things:
To love what is mortal;
To hold it against your
Bones knowing
Your own life depends on it;
And when the time comes
To let it go.

Mary Oliver

Luke
June 2, 1999 – February 17, 2007

Luke

Died Suddenly and Unexpectedly from a Bacterial Infection in the Lining of his Heart

By Jill

Luke
"The Memorial," an excerpt from *Grief Cakes*

There will not be a graduation,
a wedding,
a retirement,
or a happy event to commemorate the effort
and celebrate the work of his life.
So all those memories and milestones?
They simply led to this afternoon,
a Friday at the beginning of March,
seven and a half years after his birth.
His last ceremony.
His funeral.

Two weeks earlier, Luke died
from a rapid and devastating infection
in the lining of his heart.
It left us staggering for sense and futilely searching for solutions.
I had never even heard of pericarditis,
whose flu-like symptoms
deceived even the doctors .

Incited by Death's dishonorable advantage,
the urgency for something *worthy*
summoned a collection of effort
to speak our sadness and injustice;
to show that someone beautiful and big
is gone and we will never be the same.
So we will meet somewhere.
And sit close to each other.
We will share emptiness.
We will demonstrate epic love.
We will extol his existence.
We will validate our despair.

The first step in our preparations
was to find perfect space.
It would need to be warm and sweet, like a child;
quite big, for such grief;
familiar and uniting;
a place for stories;
a place to bridge our worlds;
a place where Luke had been.
We finally decided to meet at the Seattle Children's Theater.
This had been Luke's summer camp for two years
and where together we saw
Mrs. Piggle Wiggle,
Sleeping Beauty,
and *Jason and the Golden Fleece.*
But this time, the entrance will read:
"Memorial, 2:30."

In preparation, painstakingly precise details
were recorded on long sheets of paper
tacked ceiling to floor.
Uncapping red markers,
friends soldiered through the list:

guest book, check
parking, check
catering, check
music, check

We made a program.
My uncle and aunt splayed colors across the table
designing lizards and frogs and snakes
to surround a picture of him
in a white shirt at the park.
Underneath the photograph,
we wrote his name: Luke Evonuk Deasy.
and his dates: June 2, 1999 – February 17, 2007.
Inside, a collage of him
with Gus, who will play the guitar,
the Halls, who will eulogize him;
and the Collerans, who will tell a story.
On the last page rests a picture
soft and silent,
blue water catching the light of the late afternoon,
and Luke standing on a dock,
just a silhouette in the distance.

We professionally printed our design
on smooth, thick, white paper,
the quality and quantity assembled
as for a dignitary.

Flowers, check
Ushers, check
Photo boards, check
Microphones, check

We knew immediately
that no priest,

reverend
or rabbi
would lead this service.
For this was not a day of heavenly rewards,
eternal rest,
religious salves,
or images of fluttering cherubs gathered "home" by God.
Instead, we chose our friend Piper to officiate.
She spoke the language of tragedy.
And she knew there was no cure
or reprieve
from this suffering.
She acknowledged that defeat
was an appropriate response
to the thieving of our family
and that a stoic resistance to pain
would cause the greatest sting.
She had been with us daily
since the day he died,
offering water in our desert,
movement in our inertia,
and direction in our daze.
In the evenings
she would tuck his little brothers into bed,
take a dark, brisk jog with my husband,
and rock me into the night while listening to my wailing.
She knows it is okay to want to die.
She said I could.
She was an oasis of permission
when everything I was allowed was gone.

So, in a darkened theater,
at the center of the stage, behind a podium,
near a single vase of flowers, in front of 400 people,
Piper spoke.

She welcomed the crowd.
She welcomed the courage.
She welcomed the tears.
She welcomed our love for Luke.

Then to the stage,
others approached
to recount seven years of memories
and a catalog of qualities.
They underlined his enormous presence,
his passion and emotion,
his sweetness and resistance,
his untamed spirit,
his favorite color.

And I spoke of him.
Confronted with the fear
of Luke in some realm
or dimension
impossibly far away,
I relied on the dreams he had,
the stories he enacted,
and the games he played
with knights and dragons and swords.
I told how, often, his imagination
took him to the bounds
of our familiar world
and then into the unknown
where he battled with adventurous companions
against fearsome creatures
within invented dark forests.
I concluded that
if there was anything scary
or uncertain
in his new journey,

then Luke was among
a kingdom
at last aligned with
his bold and courageous spirit.

When there were no more words,
we closed with 120 pictures
and watched his life projected,
magnified
and resurrected
on a screen that descended from the ceiling:

Luke swaddled in a blanket.
Luke in a high chair
Luke in a penguin costume
Luke on a park swing . . .

Savoring every feature,
we merged with his lost existence:
The earthy perfume of his mitten warm skin,
the complexities of his hide and seek smile
and especially his windy, wilderness eyes.
These eyes were drenched in ancient forest greens
with flecks of brown and streaks of golden rays.
Deep, contemplative eyes
reflecting patience and insistence.
Mischievous, exploring eyes
seeking a bit of thrill.
Penetrating eyes that could wait and watch.
Eyes that would challenge and goad.
Eyes that could beckon and inspire.
Eyes for books under the blankets.
Eyes for movies cuddled together.
Eyes for discerning the best baseball card trade.

And his crazy hair.
I can't find curls like that
to touch and comb anymore.
One lock could unravel several inches.
It could wrap around my finger, like a ring.
Soft and brown, spiraling down;
his forehead crowned with locks.

Luke with his arms around Maddy
Luke catching a snake
Luke on Santa's lap.
Luke and his birthday cake . . .

I watched the images appear and fade.
All the stages of his life together, before me, at once
He was seven and a half . . .
and he was six . . . and five . . . and two . . . and one. . .
he was eight months
and he was, once, just a day.

Now he is every age.
And I want those moments back. I miss every one.

Luke riding Grandpa's tractor
Luke splashing in mud puddles with Gramma.
Luke in line on the first day of school.
Luke surrounded by a team of friends . . .

Watching the images on the screen,
while surrounded by everyone we knew,
I recognized the enormous vacancy in the room.
My son was gone. But there was more.
Matt's son was gone also.
And Tom's brother.

Ray's brother, too.
And for Maddy, her best friend.
Oliver's best friend.
Kelli's godson.
Ms. French's student.
Our parents each lost a grandson.
Deanne, Jake and Joe, a nephew.
And Morgan and Dillon's cousin.
Gone.
The tears in that room were for hundreds of deaths,
hundreds of relationships,
hundreds of Lukes.
The emptiness was exponential.

Luke watering the flowers.
Luke holding his baby cousin.
Luke decorating heart-shaped cards.
Luke stirring cookie dough . . .

As the final image disappeared,
the lights came on,
and Piper closed the ceremony,
"We embrace birth.
We celebrate life.
We deeply and devoutly honor death.
Luke's family invites you to gather in the foyer after the closing
song.
This concludes the service."

His college savings paid for it.

"WHAT IS TO GIVE LIGHT MUST ENDURE BURNING."

VICTOR FRANKL

Bradley
January 20, 1966 – April 9, 1988

Bradley

Died by Suicide in a Beautiful Park Near Seattle

by Vicki

Saturday, April 9th, 1988. It was a beautiful day! We had taken a much needed mini vacation to Vancouver, British Columbia. On that beautiful sunny day, in one split second, our lives would be changed forever. We would never again be the family we had been and it would be a long time until we saw sunshine again. I have learned since that there is a gift from all this pain. Over the years, I have come to realize this gift has made me a more compassionate person. I now have the ability to deeply connect with others with an empathy I never thought possible. Life is fragile. I live for today for no one ever promised me tomorrow.

Bradley James McDivit was born on January 20, 1966. He was a beautiful baby and he and I were inseparable. We spent so much time at the zoo, the wading pool at Green Lake and taking long walks in his stroller. Ironically, one of our favorite spots was the beach at Golden Gardens where twenty two years later he would tragically end his own life through suicide. We have numerous pictures of him in his shorts laughing and playing on the beach. I believe he chose this place because it had wonderful memories.

I bring us back to April 9th. Jim, my husband and Brad's father, and I were staying at the Westin Bayshore. Many stressful events had happened in our life. Over dinner we talked and believed our lives were turning around. That Saturday morning we went to the beach and enjoyed the hot sand and delicious blue skies. The ocean and beaches have always played a monumental importance in our family's life. The water sparkled in the sunshine. We went back to the hotel room. There was a light blinking on our phone indicating a message was waiting for us. Jim returned the call to our brother-in-law. When he got off the phone he said simply, "Brad shot himself. A jogger found him on the beach at Golden Gardens. He is dead." He said "Can you get your things together to get home?" I said "I'm fine, I feel like I'm watching this on T.V."

Years later I recognized this as the blessed cocoon of shock wrapping itself around the pain to protect me from a truth that takes many years to accept as real. We went downstairs to check out of the hotel. The management had been informed, but not one person said anything about it to us. I said we were leaving and could we please have a refund. They handed us a cash refund and we got in our car. I am still embarrassed by us asking for that refund. This is such a perfect example of how shock can make us so normal. I do not judge people on T.V., etc. by how they react in trauma. Somehow we drove back to Seattle by ourselves, experiencing a myriad of emotions as we drove. We still look for blinking lights in hotels.

We had a beautiful memorial and accomplished all the necessary tasks. But as time moved on and life continued for others, I began to feel isolated, confused and hopeless. I couldn't eat or sleep. When I felt weak and dizzy, I drank raspberry seltzer to quench an incredible thirst. I would take a few bites of frozen yogurt. For some reason, my body could tolerate this and no other food. I lost 30 pounds in six weeks. I felt an incredible lack of confidence. It was my job to be Brad's mom and I had failed! I didn't care about anything.

I have been privileged people to have "visits" from Brad. The first one was Sunday April 10th. I was wide awake and Brad was standing beside my bed. He was wearing his grey Levis and the vision of him was more powerful than if he were there physically.

He came again in the same place one year later. He also appeared in the car beside me.

Five years after his death I had one of the most moving experiences of my life. It was the anniversary of his death day. I went to Golden Gardens. As I walked toward the beach, I saw a most astounding event. Brad's face and shoulders filled the sky. Rainbows radiated from him on all sides. This vision lasted a few seconds and is etched in my memory forever. I have never had another visit. I believe he was telling me he is peaceful and I have other work to do here on this earth.

I like to remember with fondness and no regrets the last time I saw Brad. I was at his apartment and left to do a little shopping at a nearby mall. I bought some market spice tea. I returned to his apartment to say good bye. Something in me told me to stop the car, go back into his apartment I gave him some tea. I pulled out a jar and I filled it. I said, "I love you." I didn't know at that time it would be my last time to see Brad. I have since learned to never leave a loved one with unkind words. My every good-bye is said as if it will be my last.

How has our family survived? At the time of Brad's death, our daughter Shauna was 17 and our son Christopher was 16. We began a lifetime journey. I reached out for help immediately. I now know this is what saved my life. I called my counselor and Compassionate Friends, a group for bereaved parents. I also belonged to a group of survivors of suicide. One year later I met a beautiful lady who has been so instrumental in my healing. Gerri Haynes was one of my lifelines. She offers so much hope and is very wise in helping the bereaved on this most difficult journey.

After Brad's death, my son, Chris, rode a roller coaster of emotions for many years. Chris was in high school when his brother died. He was and is a brilliant, kind, sensitive boy. He had been a model child and had a 3.9 grade point average in his junior year.

On Sunday one year after Brad died, Chris took several of the pain killers he had obtained when his appendix was removed. To our surprise, Chris was a substance abuser.

On a very dark January in 1996, he called Brad's best friend in Minnesota and said he was planning to die. He drove his car deliberately into a semi-truck going 85 M.P.H. He had Brad's picture with him. The car was so badly wrecked it was simply a piece of metal. The engine was pushed into the front seat. Chris had many injuries but he survived. He was in the hospital for 14 days. I believe Brad was with him in that car. Chris has now had successful treatment and has been clean and sober for a year and a half. We are so proud. He knows that he can survive and he can teach others. Chris is a very successful young man and had learned what is really important in life. We are so thankful he is still with us.

Our daughter Shauna gave birth to a beautiful baby girl in 1990. She is a wonderful mom and Alexa, our granddaughter has taught us to love again.

Why? Why did our beautiful, sensitive son choose to leave us? We have spent many years searching for the answer to this question. The search for the answer is a very important part of our healing. Brad planned his death. He cleaned his apartment and bought cyanide. As he watched the sun rise he took cyanide and shot himself in the head.

After years of searching we have come to the conclusion that we will never know for certain why. We have many theories but there is one person who had this answer. He can't tell us and we have learned to accept this. He didn't write a suicide note. He had a very small piece of paper in his pocket the day he died. It said "a broken wing." Our children chose Brad's favorite song, "Free Bird", for his memorial. I like to think he is now free and at peace to fly unencumbered. I prefer the phrase "died of suicide" rather than "committed suicide". A person "commits" a crime. The connotations are so negative.

Our family has struggled with guilt and some shame. We have learned that Brad made this decision. If we had made a decision for him, he would still be alive. Although I have never heard of a person using a gun and cyanide, I know that Brad chose both methods to be certain his decision would be final. I do not pretend to understand this. I cannot!!!! But I now find comfort at Golden Gardens. Our son is here. We visit often and bring flowers and always, a candy treat. Oh, how he always loved to eat!

The ocean has been an instrumental part of my healing. I go to the beach to breathe. Grief is like ocean waves. Early in the process the waves are huge and oh so powerful. They are incessant and there is very little peace between the painful waves. As time goes on there are moments of laughter. Sunshine begins to peak in and moments of hope shine through the tears. Eleven years into this journey I no longer experience the monstrous waves. I have reinvested my life and I like who I am. The waves are softer and gentler. They will always be here but I have learned to live with them.

A very important part of my healing was my reaching out to help others. I volunteer at Children's Hospital and I lovingly go three hours a week to rock and cuddle babies. I have been on the board of Compassionate Friends and continue to work as a facilitator. I am blessed to have a career as a first grade teacher. My days with my children help bring me peace. I can have hugs as needed. I have learned to nurture myself and do what I love. I never for a moment forget what it was like at the beginning of this excruciatingly painful journey. I can only hope that I can listen to others and know of their pain. This has helped me make meaning out of Brad's death.

There is no end to this story, but there are beginnings. When I remember Brad I remember the things I love about him. Brad was extremely intelligent. He was sensitive, introspective and very caring to animals, children and older people.

Brad, we miss you so, but are so grateful for the 22 years you were with us. I now know this gift. I treasure every moment, every ray of sunshine, time with friends, laughter and the joy of my family and grandchildren. Rainbows are brighter, sunshine is warmer, hugs are plentiful and feel so so good! You are with me always, not beside me, but in my heart always. I love you! We live for today for no one ever promised us tomorrow. This is the gift I received.

Love,
Mom

Excerpt from "The Summer Day"

I don't know exactly what a prayer is.
I do know how to pay attention, how to fall down
into the grass, how to kneel down in the grass,
how to be idle and blessed, how to stroll through the field,
which is what I have been doing all day.
Tell me, what else should I have done?
Doesn't everything die at last, and too soon?
Tell me, what is it you plan to do
with your one wild and precious life?

Mary Oliver
"New and Selected Poems"

Rick
December 8, 1958 – March 9, 1994

Rick

Died From a Cardiac Arrest in his Home

By Marilyn

In memory of Rick and for my Family

You never expect your child to die before you. It just isn't the way it's supposed to be.

It has been seventeen years since my son Rick died of a cardiac arrest at age 35. In some ways, it seems like a lot longer. Yet, in an instant, we can be back to the day he died or (in our case) when we found him.

My husband and Son worked in the same office and every Thursday they had lunch together. On this Thursday, Rick wasn't at work and he hadn't called my husband to tell him he wasn't going to lunch. When my husband told me that Rick hadn't come to lunch, I thought it was odd, so I called and left a message on his answering machine. On Friday, my husband came home and again he said Rick wasn't at work, so I called again and left a message. I also called my younger son, *Steve*, but Rick hadn't called him either. Steve said not to worry because he knew Rick had a few vacation days coming. Still, it wasn't like Rick not to call.

On Saturday, we decided to drive to Rick's house to see if he was there. I thought I had the back door key, so we went around to the back. We could see him lying on his side on the couch. I pounded on the glass hoping he would move, but he didn't. We tried the door and it wouldn't open. My husband called 911 from our cell phone and then we went to the front door. We got the front door open and my husband went over and touched him. He was dead.

We went outside and waited for the Medics to arrive. I started to scream and the neighbors came running over. We told them something had happened to our son and that he was inside. When the Medics came, they told us to stay outside, so we went and sat in our truck. Because Rick was in such good physical condition, the Medics thought someone might have killed him, so they called the police. We were in shock. My husband called our daughter, Debbie, on the cell phone. Our son-in-law, *Marty*, answered the phone and my husband told him Rick was dead. We couldn't contact our younger son, but Debbie and *Marty* were able to contact him later. Our son-in-law and our daughter called our friends and our families. My husband called Rick's boss to tell him Rick was dead. Rick's boss came immediately to Rick's house and sat with us the entire time we were there. Some of our friends called us at Rick's house but got the answering machine, so they didn't know what was going on.

The police were in the house for a long time. After they completed their investigation, they said they were going to take Rick's body to the Coroner's Office to perform an autopsy to determine how he died. The police asked each of us to write a report and bring it to the police station. They asked what funeral home we wanted Rick to be taken to and we told them. . We waited for someone from the Coroner's Office to arrive and when she did, it took a long while before they told us they were going to leave. They said it would be better if we weren't there when they took Rick out of the house, so we drove around a short while and when we went back, they were gone.

I will always regret not going back into the house to hold Rick and say good-bye. When we got home our younger son was there. A little while later, our daughter and her family arrived. Everyone was upset and in a state of shock. Friends came over and brought us a meal. We could hardly eat. Our friends were there for us then and continue to be very supportive. Some people who experience the death of a child feel that their friends have avoided them or want nothing to do with them but this has not been our experience.

We had three children, one daughter and two sons. Our daughter is eleven months older than Rick was and our son, Steve, is two and half years younger than Rick. Rick was not married.

Our kids lived with us while they were going to college and didn't move out until they were in their mid-20s or so. After they moved to their own homes, they would often have Sunday dinners with us at our house.

The last time I saw Rick alive was a week and a half before he died, when we all had Sunday Dinner together. The following weekend we were going to the Olympic Peninsula. The kids told us to have a good time. As usual we called them when we got home to let them know we were back. Rick wasn't at home so I left a message on his answering machine. Several years later my sister and her family came out and we went to the Olympic Peninsula. We didn't want to go there by ourselves because that was where we were just before Rick died. So we took my sister and her family and having them there really helped us.

There were so many things to do after Rick died. In our state of shock, it was hard to know where to start. We had to find a cemetery plot. We drove around to different cemeteries trying to decide where to bury him. As we drove into one cemetery, I saw the mountains of the Northwest. Rick loved the outdoors and liked to hike so we decided to have him buried in sight of the mountains. Then we had to make all the funeral arrangements and wondered how we would get through it. We were numb, but functioned. The numbness protected us, so we could do the things we had to do. When the numbness wore off and reality set in, we knew that our child wasn't coming back.

Looking back, I don't remember some things, but I know I experienced all kinds of emotions. One minute I was sad and then I was angry. Then I would laugh at something and think, "How can I be laughing when I just lost my child?" I would see someone who looked like Rick and think it was him. Certain times of the year are harder than others. Around his birthday, the day he died and the holidays. I'm more upset as the day gets closer and then after the day has passed, I calm down again. No matter what I do around these days, I need to feel comfortable doing it. Everyone is different in the way they handle these times but as the years go by these "special" days do not affect me as much.

I cried a lot immediately after Rick died and then when it got harder to cry, I became tense. I ask myself the same questions over and over again. I think, "If only I would have done this, he would be alive." At first, I grieved constantly. As time has passed, I actively grieve less, but then something triggers a thought or memory and I am right back to the beginning again. The times when this happens are not as frequent as at the beginning and they don't get me down as much. Everyone grieves differently. Some people go back to work right away, while others can hardly function. No matter how you feel, you are not going crazy. It is the way you deal with things now and grief can last for a long time. I found that I needed to go back to my normal routine. My husband and I went back to work two weeks after Rick died. We also went back to swimming and walking-activities that are good stress relievers. Working out in the garden helped me a lot.

Rick had a house we had to sell but when we went over to his house, we had trouble getting started with clearing out his things. Finally, our son-in-law came over and helped us get started. It was hard to get rid of anything, so we packed up clothes and personal items and brought them to our house. After seventeen years, we still have many boxes of Rick's things.

After Rick died, a friend arranged for our family to go to a cardiologist who could help us go over the autopsy. I was upset over the fact that Rick was by himself and no one was there to help him when he died. The doctor told us that Rick had had a cardiac arrest and that death had happened very fast. He also told us that his wife leads a group of mothers whose children have died. She has helped me and the other mothers in my group tremendously. Although these groups may not be for everyone, ours is a place where I have a lot of support and I can talk about how I feel without being judged.

About three and a half months after Rick died my husband and I were about to go for a walk when the phone rang. The call was from our younger son's health club, telling us that he was having a cardiac arrest. A doctor there and another man had given him CPR until the Medics arrived. When we got the call, the paramedics were stabilizing him and taking him to the hospital. We jumped in the car and got to the hospital before he did. All the while, what was going through our minds was, "How can this be happening again?" At the hospital, tests that showed some partial blockages in Steve's heart arteries, but no damage to his heart. Still, he needed by-pass surgery. In surgery, the doctor could not re-create what had happened during Steve's cardiac arrest, so they put in a defibrillator to protect him from another arrest. I just do not know what we would have done if Steve had died. I know that the percentage of people who survive cardiac arrests is small and the fact that he is mentally and physically OK is a miracle. For these things I thank God every day. I will always be grateful to the person at the health club who was watching the cameras and monitors so they could see my son and realized that something was wrong.

All my children have high cholesterol, but are otherwise healthy and active. After Steve had a cardiac arrest, our daughter wanted to be sure she was all right. She had some tests done and everything was fine – for which I am thankful.

Because of what has happened to our sons, I know I should not take anything for granted. We never know what's going to happen.

Life can be going along just fine and then something happens that will change it forever. I know that Rick would want our family to be happy again and we are. I would give anything to see him walk through the door again but for now, we have to rely on all the wonderful memories we have of him and know that someday we will be together again.

What I have learned:

1. You know that in one split second your life has been changed.
2. You know just how important your family is.
3. You go on with your life, and you will always miss your child.

Keeping Things Whole

In a field
I am the absence
of field.
This is
always the case.
Wherever I am
I am what is missing.

When I walk
I part the air
and always
the air moves in
to fill the spaces
where my body's been.

We all have reasons
for moving.
I move
to keep things whole.
Mark Strand

Carly Rae
7/23/84 – 1/31/01

Carly Rae

Died in a Motor Vehicle Accident Near her Home

By Richelle

Here it is again – another New Year. This year, there are no expectations, no goals, no resolutions. Today is today. Live in the moment. We have a new president. I am divorced. I will work on my health.

January 16th is my 55th birthday. My daughter, Jenae, and her husband, Chris, take me out to dinner at a Greek restaurant that I picked out. Chris' friend from work joins us for dinner. Amy, my youngest daughter, takes time off from work to join us. This time, this year, I have relived the day and weeks before my birthday as if it were 2001. But this year, there is no anxiety, no tears, no sadness – just gratefulness for the time I spend with Jenae and Amy and Chris.

January 23, 2009: spent with thoughts of Carly. No anxiety, no sadness. But I have another birthday dinner to think about: mine. I will celebrate this birthday at the home of friends, Mary and Skip. I have chosen Mary's famous chicken enchiladas for dinner.

January 24, 2009: I have written my remembering thoughts. I was afraid of this month because of all the memories that are my last ones of Carly. It has taken eight years to get to this point. Today, I have cried because I do miss her – everything about her. Even the not-so-nice things about her. But today is the 24th and still no anxiety – just the feelings of loss. I will relive this month of

43

January for many years to come. Some years will, and have, been better than others.

January 1, 2001:

The start of a new year with all the promises it holds. All the resolutions that I make and the goals I want to achieve all sound so attainable. But, each day comes, bringing its own "to do" list and Life gets in the way. Most days are so busy that by the end of the day, I forget exactly what I did that day. But my memory of this January is different. I can tell you what happened each day. Of the days of that January, a few stand out.

January 9: Meeting with lawyer again to start divorce proceedings

January 16: My birthday – 47 years old. Lucky for me, I had already lowered my expectations. My goals were realistic. We were going out for Chinese dinner – a family favorite. Dinner was very late because my husband, Toby, was completing my birthday present – flower boxes for the living room windowsills. Carly was hypoglycemic and cranky without food. Jenae had homework that remained unfinished. Amy was missing – out somewhere. Toby and I were separated, but he made an attempt at a nice family dinner. We weren't the "happy family" inside, but we can fool most people. I don't have a family photo from that meal – even though I thought about taking one. I wish I had that picture.

January 23, 2001: Jenae and I were planning a surprise 16 ½ birthday party for Carly. Carly was in Hawaii on her 16th birthday and she had told us she missed having us give her a party. Trust me, she didn't miss out on anything. Jenae and I did some shopping and planning and put together a party with cake, presents and friends. Carly got into her PJs to do her homework. This was finals week – like all good students, Carly was studying. When her friends came by to say, "Surprise" and "Happy Birthday, 16 ½!" Carly see seemed a little annoyed – visible in her picture. Not all of her friends could attend this gathering, but the ones who did were happy. We had her favorite dinner: ground turkey soft tacos.

January 31, 2001: Late arrival day for school. I left for work before the girls left for school. I woke them up and made sure they would get ready for school in time to catch the bus – bidding them "Good-bye" as I left. Jenae was driving to school – I didn't worry about her being on time. Carly was getting a ride with a friend – or taking the bus. If she ran late, Jenae would take her – but Amy had to get ready for the bus!

Carly had after-school plans. She had two jobs, but was going to miss work that day. When I awakened her, we talked about her after-school plans. She was going to a friend's house, to dinner with co-workers from one of her jobs (to celebrate the birthday of one co-worker), then to a church youth group and then back to the friend's house to spend the night. She had clothes to pack for each event. She wasn't planning to work for the next few days. Since one of her jobs was for my boss, I agreed to explain Carly's absence to them. I remember Carly lying in bed, sleepy eyes, just waking up. Little did I know that would be the last time I saw that.

After my work that day, I needed to run some errands, then to attend a Graduation Night planning meeting. In the gym at school, I saw one of Carly's best friends and asked if she had seen Carly. She hadn't seen Carly, but reminded me that Carly was planning to attend the youth group meeting with two other friends. It had been a long day, and I needed to go home. Jenae and Amy were home in their rooms. I sat at the table facing the pile of bills and tried to make the available money stretch to cover all of those bills. At 9:50 PM, the phone rang. It was Carly, calling to tell me about her day. She said she almost forgot to call me, but wanted to say, "Good Night" and to tell me she would be seeing me after school the next day. She was planning to miss work again. I told her I couldn't believe I was letting her do two things like this – spending the night away from home and going out to dinner on school nights. Carly laughed her Carly laugh and said, "Good Night and I Love You, Majah." Majah, the name she always called me instead of Mom.

Twenty-some minutes after 10, Carly was gone. The mother of the friend Carly was staying with let the girls do something else unusual for a school night – in addition to having friends spend the night, she gave them permission to drive to a neighboring town to watch a movie or to visit with friends. On the drive into town, they were involved in a car accident. Two of the girls, including Carly, were killed.

That night, an angel came to my house to let me know what had happened to Carly. The local medic chaplain (???), he had to convince me that he didn't have the wrong house. I told him I knew Carly was staying overnight with friends. He had first called on the phone to introduce himself and tell me that he would like to talk with me about my daughter, Carly. At first, I thought she must have had another asthma attack and was, perhaps, re-hospitalized. No, that wasn't why he was calling. He came to the house and helped me tell Jenae and Amy about what had happened. Then he stayed with me while I made phone calls, trying to find someone to stay with me. I didn't want to wake people up in the middle of the night to tell them the bad thing that had happened to Carly. I called my mom. She didn't answer. I don't remember who else I tried, but I did reach some friends and they came to my house. I remember calling Carly's friends to let them know what had happened – so they wouldn't get this information at school. Other people also arrived. One drove to Toby's to let him know what had happened.

At 6 AM, I started calling my family members and telling about what had happened to Carly. Then the shock set in. I think I went into "auto pilot." The following days were filled with making arrangements and decision – decisions no parent ever wants to make! Some of those decisions were good, some were not.

January 24, 2009

Beginning to put on paper what happened eight years ago was very hard, but once I started writing and remembering, the thoughts flowed. I'm not sure about all of the details. I know I wish I had written sooner or kept a journal as someone suggested.

This day was a busy one. I had many commitments. I gave myself permission to cry for a short period of time – then got on with the day. I hadn't cried for a while – it felt cleansing.

January 25, 2009: Anxiety tried to creep in. I went outside to get fresh air.

January 27, 2009: Mom's only group. I shared my Carly story with two new moms. It was good to be at Gerri's before the anniversary.

January 31, 2009: I had lunch with co-workers and on this, Carly's anniversary date, I opened up about Carly. At work, I shared Carly's picture and received lots of support from my co-workers.

January 31, 2009: In completing this writing about Januarys, I know this has been a good week. Three years ago, I was drunk every night after work. This week, I drank in control and moderation. On this day, I drank not one drop…not even wanting to drink. I woke up wondering how I was going to do today. So far, so good – it's sunny outside. The day started out well. The morning was good. I had some alone time to think about Carly and lit a candle. Amy came home and we "hung out" together. I asked her if she wanted to go the accident site and she said, "No." She didn't really care that much." I tried not to let that comment hurt my feelings, but it did.

I went to the site by myself and placed one white rose and some tulips there. I picked up some trash and was spending time there when my neighbor arrived to be with me. She cried and I held her and we talked for a while. She was little when Carly died. Now she is 17 years old.

When I got home, it was time to take Amy to work. After I dropped her off for her 3:30 work, I was alone again. Being alone, I wasn't sure what to do with myself. I didn't want to go home until Jenae came home from work, so I sat in a parking lot and talked on the phone. Many people called me to make sure I was doing ok. Then I stopped at my Mom's house to stall for time. She wanted to make sure I wasn't going to be alone later.

When I did get home, Jenae acted as though it were any other day/night. There was not one mention of her sister, Carly. I spent some time talking to the mother of Carly's best friend, and then I went to my room to watch TV and monitor the clock. Finally, it was 10:20 PM and it was over for another year. I wrote these words several years ago and the only thing I can come up with is that I was numb for most of that first year.

What I have learned:

1. The death of a child can happen to anyone.
2. You can survive.
3. My life has changed; I am not the same person I was before.

How could I have come so far?
(And always on such dark trails?)
I must have traveled by the light
Shining from the faces of all those I have loved.
Thomas McGrath

Shaun
12/14/1972 – 8/4/1996

Shaun

Died Following a Motorcycle Accident

By Cheryl

Shaun, one of the joys of my life, was Baby B in my set of twins. He was the smaller of the two, weighing 5 pounds, 12 ounces. Throughout his life, we knew what he wanted. He set his goals and attained them as he grew.

This story starts on October 7, 1995, when my husband and I met Shaun and his twin brother, Chris at the I-90 Motorsports to co-sign for their twin Yamaha 250s. When we returned home, I received a telephone call telling me my older brother had been found dead. What devastating news! Even though he was 15 years older than I, we were so close! I thought I would not survive that loss. My parents had died years earlier – I told myself I was a "pro" at grieving.

The following May, Shaun fell while he was racing his motorcycle at a Motocross track. He was unable to move out of the way quickly and another rider rode over Shaun's left leg, fracturing it in two places. One week of caring for Shaun in the hospital and then being able to care for him when he was released from the hospital gave me the feeling of again being a needed mom. By that time, he was 23 years old and was living on his own. One month later, Shaun's twin, Chris, was riding at the same Motocross track. As he was going over a jump, his foot landed ahead of the motorcycle. It took thirty-seven pins to hold his foot together. This was a scary accident – we did not know whether or not his foot could be saved – but it was.

When the boys healed, they were excited about Washougal – another big race. They had attended an outdoor Motocross together for several years. The twins did everything together: boating, riding, camping – all of their activities.

We were planning a 20th birthday party for my youngest son, Jesse. His birthday is August 3rd and we had scheduled a big Sunday afternoon dinner. Shaun and his fiancée, Tara, came over early that day – Shaun was working on replacing the interior in his boat. We had lunch, then Shaun called a friend to see if he could come over to finish putting his motorcycle back together. He was about ready to be released to ride again. He was so excited to ride – I begged him not to get on that bike.

About 6:00 as I was leaving for the store, Tara called and said that Shaun was hurt and that the aide car was on its way. I asked Tara, "How do I get there?" She said she did not know, but that Shaun was awake and talking. As I ran out to my husband's truck to get his cell phone, Shaun's life passed in front of my eyes.

On the way to his friend's house, I saw Chris' truck in front of his fiancée's home and I called to talk with her Mother (Linda) to let her know that Shaun had been hurt and please not to tell Chris. I could not find the house, so then I did call Chris and he told me where to turn – then the cell phone went dead.

Shaun was already in the aide car when I arrived. I ran to the back of the car and looked inside. A fireman pulled me away, but not before I could see the medics intubating Shaun. Right then, I knew he was not awake and breathing on his own. The fireman said they were taking Shaun to Harborview (trauma center) and that it was just "a bump on the head and some scrapes on his back." He also told me we could see Shaun in about one hour at the hospital.

Shaun's friend drove me home so that I could get my husband. We drove to the hospital and waited. Meanwhile, family members were called and started arriving at the hospital. All I could do was sit there and remember Shaun as a baby. Everything was moving in slow motion. I could not comprehend what was going on. When a social worker approached me, my worst nightmare was confirmed.

The doctors spoke to us about the seriousness of Shaun's injuries. They said they could remove the back of his skull and then he would have a five to ten percent chance of survival, but he would be a vegetable. My husband said, "No, let him go." I reacted with a scream and told them to do the surgery – that I had enough medical knowledge to take care of him for the rest of his life. But if you had known Shaun, you would know this would not be what he'd have wanted. Shaun set his goals and lived life on the edge. Earlier that day, he had told me he would never live to see forty.

Shaun's heart failed on the operating table. He was revived. The doctors came to see us at about 5 AM to tell us that Shaun would not survive. My husband talked with them about the donor program. I could not even think of someone taking apart my baby.

We left the hospital and dropped Tara and her mother at their home. As we pulled into the driveway, Tara's father came out to tell us that Shaun had "crashed" as soon as we left the hospital. It seems this is a common thing that happens. We went home to sleep for a couple of house, then returned to the hospital to meet with the donor people and to say, "Good-bye" to our son.

Soon after we returned to our home, family and friends began to arrive. I sat and stared – not knowing what to do. I just wanted to go with him. I found then that I was not a pro at grieving and that I would not ever recover from this.

My husband and his brothers took care of all the funeral arrangements. My doctor gave me medicine to help me deal with the horror of what had happened. There are no words to explain what a body and mind does when thrown into the sheer panic and terror that seems will never end. Nothing made sense. Everything was in slow motion.

My daughter-in-law was about five months pregnant at that time. The night Shaun died, she went into labor. Chris had to spend the night at the hospital with her and could not be with us. The labor stopped, the baby was fine and he is now three-years-old and the light of my life.

I returned to work after only two weeks. I did not want to be alone. I would not go to bed alone. I would not go the store alone. Someone had to be with me at all times – I could not bear aloneness. Many of my family and friends thought I would kill myself. I would not and could not eat. Work was ok – it kept my mind busy. I concluded that if I stayed busy, I could stay alive.

Then I started having panic attacks and found it hard to breathe. Panic attacks are awful – the more I fought to breathe, the more I panicked.

In December, I finally called the Grief and Bereavement service at our local hospital. I interviewed on the telephone and then in person for the Sudden and Traumatic Loss class. When I entered the first class, the feeling of so much sorrow in the room made me want to run. The class was weekly for six weeks and we had to commit to completing the course. How different it is to be in a group of people that are all grieving. Only one other person in the group had lost a child. After the classes were over, the class facilitator gave me the telephone number of the women who would save my life.

Days turned into weeks – weeks turned into months. I was still counting. The first year passed very slowly. I functioned. People would say, "You sound like your old self again!" I thought, "Did my voice change?" My friends would say, "Time will help heal you." I would look at them as if they were crazy. My husband tried to comfort me, but I wanted to be left alone with my grief.

One day at work, Chris said to me, "Mom, now I don't have any friends anymore." He meant that with Shaun dead, he was alone – even though he was married and had a son. That drove me straight to tears. I had to leave work – that was something I could not fix for him.

My youngest son says he no longer wants to celebrate his birthday – it reminds him that that is the day we lost Shaun forever.

As time went forward, I waited for things to return, as much as possible, to normal. Life was a rollercoaster. Up and down, week after week. At the one-year anniversary of Shaun's death, I stayed home and spent time with my grandson, Corey. The day passed. The first year was so hard. But it came to the day that I had to start living my life again. When I started going places, I found if I got too far from home, a panic attack would start. I was afraid to be out of reach from my living sons. I would have to turn around and go home. I would call my sons. They were always okay. They would try to get me out of the house, but it took a big effort. I went to work daily, but doing other things was too hard. I would look for Shaun in passing cars or think I heard his voice calling me. Then I would cry and need to go home and shut out the world.

By the second anniversary, I was starting to go out and being okay. I could laugh and not feel guilty. I found that people connect to others who have lost children – there is something in the eyes. With these people, there is an instant feeling of comfort – an ability to speak freely and not scare them away. Most people do not understand and cannot until they walk in the shoes of one who has had this experience. Most people will run away – they seem to be afraid that if they talk or listen, this tragedy might happen to them.

But during this time, I have attended a support group for Mothers whose children have died. There are several women who are dear to my survival. These women can relate to what each of us feels and to the trials we experience. All of us except the facilitator have lost children. But this woman opens her home to us every other Tuesday night and there we feel safe in talking and crying – or in being angry and screaming. There is so much support there. Once or twice each year, our group also goes to the ocean together – there, we are ourselves. It is peaceful and we can think about trying to go on with this life without our children.

On the third anniversary of Shaun's death, I had to work away from home. I found that I was okay during the day. My family called me that night. That day came and went. I think now that it has been more than three years and I wonder if I will ever be able to make it through a day without tears.

Time has a way of getting away from you though. In December of the third year, Shaun and Chris and my niece, Tammy share the day they were born. That year, I invited the boys over for dinner – we still need to celebrate Chris' birthday. Jesse, my youngest son, was fine until he realized what day it was. He knew it was Chris' birthday, but had placed Shaun somewhere else in his mind. We all cried. But at least we can talk and reminisce about the past and talk about what Shaun would say or do if he were still here.

The holidays of 1999 were very hard. For some reason, they were harder than other years and other holidays. I am, though, a survivor and I will go on. I have reduced the mind-altering medicines. I now take only one that helps me sleep and I am amazed at how clear my mind is again. I still cry every day and I have asked the Lord for some peace in my heart.

Each day is new and I make the best of what I have been handed. I hold in my heart a fear of this happening again to one of my children, but I must go on with life and with love for my family and friends. I truly hope this helps in your time of need and that in time, the pain will lessen and you will have joy in your life again.

An invisible thread connects those who are destined to meet, regardless of time, place, or circumstance. The thread may stretch or tangle, but it will never break.

(Anon)

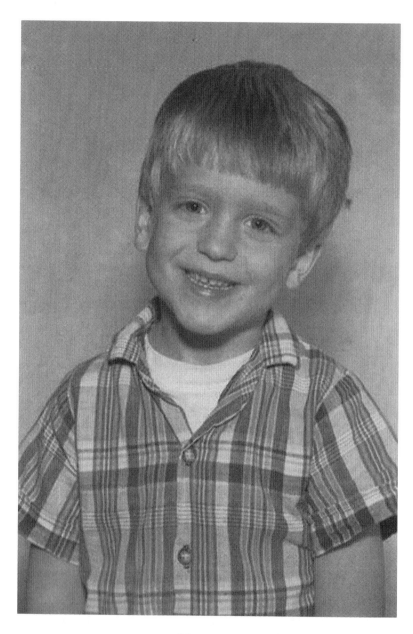

Shannon
April 27, 1982 – January 7, 2001

Shannon

Died as a Pedestrian on a Freeway

By Debra

"The end is in the beginning, and yet we go on...."
Samuel Beckett (Endgame)

The preceding quote is on a small brass plaque on my son Shannon's memorial bench at Point Robinson Lighthouse on Vashon Island. I did not put the date of his death on this memorial because my son continues to make his presence known, as if he were still next to me. I have no doubt that he continues to exist beyond the death of his body. I have seen and experienced things I cannot explain.

Shannon died accidentally. It was unexpected, and I never saw his body because of my state of emotions on the day he died. Possibly this was for the best, as I may have never stopped screaming if I had seen his body. It has allowed me to fantasize about him returning. I will keep the home he lived in, not just for the memories he and I shared, but because he will know where to find me.

His ashes are in a water-blue pottery jar created by a local artist. I can lift the lid and touch them with my fingers. Sometimes I look for something I can recognize of him. There is not much to recognize, really. It looks like white gravel, but I can still lift him up in my arms and place him in bed with me, warming his ashes with my body, or place his urn on the bedside table. Most of the time, his urn is in front of a west-facing window with a view of the forest. The sun can shine on him there. I could not put him in the cold ground. He was trying to come home when he was killed. This is his home.

Shannon was eighteen years old when he went to a club on the waterfront in Seattle with friends he didn't know very well. They attended a private party where there could be a lot of drugs. As he went out the door, I asked him not to go and cautioned him to be careful of the drugs that would be there. He said, "Don't worry Mom, I won't do anything stupid." I told him how handsome he looked and that I loved him so much. We hugged each other tight.

Eight hours later, around 4 AM, Shannon crossed the Interstate I-5 just north of the Convention Center in Seattle. He was on foot and under the influence of LSD when he was struck by two cars at high speed. An ambulance happened to be passing along at that time, and the ambulance personnel tried to revive Shannon at the scene before taking him to Harborview Medical Center. He was treated there by an excellent staff, but his body was too broken to survive.

When the police chaplain came to my door later that morning to tell me of Shannon's death, I was pretty sure they had made a mistake. I dropped to my knees on the ground outside my front door and told them they were wrong, but they took me inside to make a phone call. I talked to the medical examiner on the phone, confirming that Shannon only had four fingers on his left hand. He had been arrested for a minor offense a couple years before, and fingerprints had been on file to identify him. When I asked for drug testing, they found he had overdosed on pure LSD. There were no other drugs or alcohol in his system. He had been robbed of his ID, his backpack, and had 35 cents in his pocket. If he had been able, I know he would have called me to come get him. I don't believe he was in his right mind at the time. I pray that he was not cold and scared and that he didn't suffer.

It is very difficult to put these words on paper. Each time I tell Shannon's story, I tell different parts of it, but not all the details. I am very protective of my son and don't speak of all his actions that night. Some people are judgmental about how he died, but most are kind. In the Mother's Support Group, I often withhold some details if there is a new mother there because this was not a "nice" death. It is not the kind of death that is easy to describe.

During his middle school years, my son was very intelligent, able to survive his own mistakes. He loved to live on the edge at times, trying new things and meeting new people. Shannon enjoyed getting down on the floor and playing with children at family gatherings. He enjoyed opening gifts with his father's children, putting together their toys and playing with them.

I often found Shannon chatting on the Internet with friends. Some of these friends looked up to him for support in making decisions, and sometimes I overheard him give sound advice. This helped me feel that I had raised him with good values.

He created models of ships and cars. He was very knowledgeable about the Titanic. His father's ancestors built ships and Shannon loved ship history. He planned to follow in his grandfather's footsteps and join the Navy.

He enjoyed history and government, and he was thrilled to be able to vote in the Presidential Election in the year 2000. He and I sat in the parking lot before we went in to vote, and reviewed the issues we would be voting on that morning. He was thrilled to participate, and he was excited to go back to his government class to tell them about it.

Shannon loved music and had a large number of CDs in his backpack that night. He was robbed of his entire Korn collection and most of his Nirvana CDs. He loved to go to music events in the area and hear new groups as they became popular. He was friendly with several of the DJs from The End radio station and hung out near them at some of the events.

I'm so grateful no one else died or was injured with him.

Almost immediately after Shannon's death, I noticed crows coming to me, staring at me, and I began to watch their antics. They reminded me of my son, so smart and wily. I feel they are symbolic of him. In fact, my spiritual practice has been enhanced by my son's death and I feel he is one of my teachers.

This state of mind placed me in a reclusive, almost hermitlike existence, where I was able to explore my beliefs, receive spiritual information, and learn about the power of love. If I had continued my life as it was, I might not have gained this insight. Some people would say I have lost my mind and that I am crazy. Well, I maintain that there is freedom in being considered crazy. I can be myself.

After he died, I was more reclusive and more anxious. I became impatient easily. It's difficult to listen to people complain about their living children, when I wish I could have my son back. I wish I had more children of my own. It is hard to listen to people be cruel to each other about petty grievances. They can't seem to recognize the gift they have in the presence and love for each other. We have no guarantee we will have another day to say the things we feel in our hearts. We should not waste this day. This moment is all we have for certain.

Currently, I've come a long way in controlling my emotions through meditation and daily spiritual practice, being kind to myself, living in the present, and living my life as impeccably as I can. I'm not living perfectly, but I want to live as if my son can see what I am doing because I think he does see me, and checks in on me from time to time. I can accept that I am human and get angry or impatient, but the next step is to try to figure out how I contributed to that situation that made me angry. I want to find a way to live in the present, enjoy the life as it is. I want to feel happy again. I've been getting glimpses of that happiness.

It has been eight years since I last saw Shannon in his body, but I still see him in dreams and meditation sometimes. Since his death, he has come to me in dreams, telling me of what he is doing now. He teases me, showing me his loving spirit and intelligence. He and I were very close in life and I feel very close to him still. I don't remember my dreams very well, so I'm very greedy for more when I remember one of him. He usually appears to be an older or younger man than how I saw him last. Sometimes, he appears to be a toddler, at other times an eight-year-old, much as in the picture with this chapter.

Always, there comes a time in the dream when we have to part ways for a little while. Once, I had a dream of windsailing with him over a sea of warm water and moon light shining toward us on a still sea of indigo blue. We were laughing and looking at each other, when I looked down and noticed the hole where my sail should have been. I said, "Shan! We forgot our sails." He laughed and said "We don't need them." Suddenly a booming voice from above said, "She has to go back now." Somewhat sad, we turned around and went back to shore, but he and I vowed we would do it again.

Sometimes he leaves me coins, most commonly pennies. For instance, I recently had a consultation for a tattoo of his name on my arm. While I arranged the down payment for the future appointment, it seemed that pennies were flying out of my purse and falling to the floor. I found a penny on the sidewalk as I returned to my car where there had been no penny before. These pennies tell me my son is excited and pleased that I will have his name tattooed on my arm. Below his name is a crow feather.

One of the first dreams I had of my son, was within two weeks of his death. I was at my grandfather's home, when a cat chased a small dog out of the house toward the road. I became alarmed, afraid that the dog would be struck by a car and killed as my son had been. Suddenly, I saw Shannon walking across the grass toward me with the little dog in his arms. The dog was happily licking his face and wiggling for joy. My son spoke to me with his eyes, words that came to me clearly. He said "My first job is to take care of the dead animals." I said, "But Shan, the dog is not dead!" He replied, "Neither am I." I like it that he has a job there. It seems appropriate with the way he died and his love of animals. It is true for me that he's not really dead.

Speaking about Shannon helps keep him alive in other people's memories. Sometimes people feel uncomfortable talking about him. My family and friends avoid the subject, mostly because they don't want to cause me pain. No one can make me feel any worse than I do. It brings me joy to speak of him.

Sometimes, as an ICU nurse, I am asked if I have children. Depending on the situation, I'll answer that I had a son and he died accidentally. It opens up conversation, especially for other mothers and fathers who want to talk about their fears and feelings. I rarely give details, but let the discussion focus on their feelings and circumstances. It seems to open communication when I speak about my son.

Flashbacks and the memories bring my day to a grinding halt when they come: the night of the accident, the way his body looked in the photographs, and the ways in which I wish I had changed the outcome. Whenever the memories and visions become too vivid and I start to obsess about what I could have done differently to prevent this tragedy, I just push the eject button on the video that is tormenting me. I pretend it is a VCR tape in my mind and that I can eject the tape for now and get back to it later.

I was divorced six months after Shannon died. That was not as difficult as one would think, as I was about to clear my life of things that were not working for me. I swept my house clean of things not useful or that had a negative impact on me. I went back to my job three weeks after Shannon's death. All I had to do was maintain what appeared to be a normal life, such as brushing my teeth and keeping the cats fed.

But a year later, when I found myself planning my own death, I remembered hearing about the Mother's Support Group that Gerri facilitates in her home. I called her on the phone, and she encouraged me to join the group right away. Every other Tuesday, mothers who have lost children gather around a coffee table, eat snacks, drink tea and talk about how the last two weeks have been for them. They take turns talking and listening to each other. Crying is totally acceptable and encouraged. Sometimes that is the only time I cry. Occasionally, there is a new mother with a recent loss and raw, painful grief. These mothers can barely speak, as they tell their stories. Each of us can recall being in that place, and we welcome them. There is no requirement to return and sometimes mothers attend only a couple of times a year, but some of us go every two weeks when possible. It is the place where I can still be Shannon's mother.

Our retreats to the beach house in Southern Oregon are times of healing and renewal before returning to our challenging lives. She feeds us nourishing food and we talk about our children all day if we want to. I love to hike the beach and the woods, communicate with the osprey and raven, collect heart-shaped stones and feathers from the beach, sun in the little creek, throw roses into the waves. Gerri's Mothers Group has saved my life and possibly other lives as well.

There is something unique about a mother's loss. There is no "moving on" or "getting over it." This grief is a life sentence. Some friends thought I should be moving on and doing better than I am. My closest friends are the members of the Mothers Group. We can talk with each other about anything with complete trust, accepting each other as we are.

In conclusion, Shannon was born at home, within two miles of Point Robinson on Vashon Island. He was born on an April morning in 1982 with the sound of pheasants and a view of red tulips. When he was small, we went to the beach at Point Robinson to play in the sand and build houses among the driftwood. It seemed appropriate to dedicate a bench in the grove of trees on the beach at Point Robinson. Near the bench, the Fearey family also arranged to have eighteen cedar trees planted to represent his eighteen years.

The bench is made of driftwood and cedar in Shannon's memory. It is a place for his friends and family to gather and leave a flower or a shell. It can be a place as well for visitors to the beach to have a little picnic and watch the ships go by. I like to sit quietly for a few minutes, listen to the birds and think of Shannon's voice saying "I love you, Mom".

Samuel Beckett's words seemed an appropriate quote for a plaque on his bench. This quote reminds me that what seems like the end is just the beginning. He and I were able to talk about nearly anything. I can still talk to him and watch for him in my dreams.

What I have learned:

1. I have learned that I'm stronger than I thought. Surviving this most difficult thing, the death of my child, has prepared me for anything life can throw at me. I have experienced the worst thing that can happen to me.

2. Not to sweat the petty stuff. Arguments based on history are rarely of meaning to me.
3. I am more in touch with the unexplained in life. My spiritual practice has become stronger.

Forever Justin
12/25/88 – 7/25/98

Justin

Died from Wounds Inflicted by his Teen-Aged Babysitter

By Juli

Justin was born on a very stormy Christmas night in 1988. It was not an easy birth for him or me, over 30 hours. He spent the first 12 days of life in and out of hospitals. When he was four days old he was flown to the Intensive Care Unit in Medford where he stayed for eight days before getting to come home. He was unable to nurse until he was ten days old but once he was able it changed our world. The bonding was strong for us both. Now that we were together, nothing would tear us apart. I remember taking him for a walk once. He was still an infant so I carried him in a front pack. I walked into the woods and sat on a log to feed him. He looked up at me while nursing and gave me the biggest "life is great and I love you Mom," grin that anyone has ever seen. His eyes sparkled. I will never forget his face at that moment or the amount of love that my heart felt for him. What a gift. What a joy.

Because he was an only child, Mom sometimes doubled as play-mate. He would often come in from outside feeling a little frustrated with trying to play with the boy next door. The two of them were very different people and had a hard time getting along so he would ask me to come out and play with him. We would sit in his tree house or play catch or go for a bike ride. For Christmas one year my parents, Papa Joe and Grand Mom to Justin, gave us each a pair of roller blades. Well lucky for me the house was in a state of construction so we were able to practice in the house before venturing out into the big outdoors. I'll never forget how hard he laughed at me when he finally got me outside. Once I was coming down a street with a slight downward slope. I got going pretty fast and did not know how to stop so I had to crash on someone's grass. I didn't think he would ever stop laughing.

Another time when he was about three, for fun we dressed up as the king and queen and paraded around the house in our royal attire. One February he was complaining of nothing to do. I know it was February because that was his dog Squirt's birthday. So we gave her a birthday party. We made cupcakes and party hats and invited the cat, Pierre, and the bird, Pickle, to sit at the table and eat cupcakes with us. I have some great pictures of that day.

He loved his pets and besides the ones I have just mentioned he also had two ducks, a goose and at different times, two rabbits. His first rabbit, Bun Buns, lived outside in a hutch but would come out to run around with Justin. If Justin was sitting on his tree swing Bun Buns would come up to him and stand on his hind legs with his front feet on Justin's leg as if to say, "Can I ride with you"? I would sometimes try to catch Bun Buns to put him back in his hutch. After chasing him around the yard for half an hour or so, I'd give up and ask Justin to go put him in. All he had to do was walk out there and the rabbit would run up to him. Justin would bend down, pick him up and take him to his hutch. He once found two baby quail that another dog of ours had separated from the mother. He tried all day to find the mother so that he could return them to her but he never found her. So, we took them in and tried to feed them, but they would not eat. They later died and that broke his heart. He seemed to have a way with animals.

Justin was a very happy child and grownups found him very likable and easy to be with. He loved making people laugh, sometimes telling the same joke over and over as many times as it took before people stopped laughing. However, he didn't think school was a place he wanted to be. His first day at kindergarten proved him right. At 10:00 recess his right index finger was smashed in the door jamb of the bathroom door while waiting his turn for the restroom. It was quite a severe injury and as Randy and I were driving him home from the doctors after getting the finger repaired, with tears in his eyes he blurted out, "I told you I didn't want to go to school".

After a few days of R & R we took him back to school. He started to settle in and although he wasn't the most academically minded child, he loved the social life. He made friends easily and loved playing wall ball and other sports with his friends. Teachers gave him nicknames like "social butterfly" and one teacher told me that she would give anything to have a room full of students with his attitude. Nothing seemed to get him down or alter his happy go lucky disposition. In third grade he started wrestling and although he never won a match, he ended every one with a smile on his face.

There were things that bothered him though. He did not like the thought of people killing animals. He did not like litterbugs and it bothered him that he had a hard time remembering things he was taught at school. I found that to be so insightful for such a young child to realize that about himself. He was very connected and aware of the world around him.

He collected things like rocks and bird nests and loved to climb as high as he could to the tops of trees and wanted to be a rock climber when he grew up. He loved his family and our extended family of friends. He and his cousin, Weasel (Joey), were more like brothers than cousins. Although we lived miles apart, when they were together they were inseparable. I was pregnant with Justin when Weasel was three. He was fascinated by my pregnant belly and was convinced that there was a chicken inside.

One of my fondest memories of them was when we went to visit Aunt Toad, Cousin Weasel and Uncle Steve, and Justin, after many hours of begging me for permission, got his hair pruned down to nubbins by his Aunt Toad to look just like Cousin Weasel. He couldn't stop rubbing his own head which provided some relief to Weasel, whose head he had been rubbing prior to the pruning. Another special person to Justin was his Aunt Jill who took him horseback riding.

Once, after spending a day at the barn with Aunt Jill, she gave him some money to spend in town before coming home. Justin spent his money on a present to give to the lady whose horse he had been riding. That's the kind of person he was. Always thinking of others. Some other people that were a big influence in his life that I feel should be mentioned are, his Step Dad Randy, Uncle Doug, Aunt Terri, Uncle Billy, Uncle Brad Aunt Leslie and Brie, and the Meszaros family.

In July of 1998, he went to visit with his Papa Joe and Grand Mom. He and Papa Joe made a birdhouse shaped bird feeder and with his Grand mom he painted a vase of blue and green. My two favorite colors. These were both gifts for me. My birthday was coming up. He gave them to me when his grandparents brought him to where Randy and I were camping and where the three of us stayed and camped for a few more days together. While sleeping in the tent one night he told me how much he had been missing home. Before going to his grandparents' house he had been at his dads for 4 or 5 weeks. I didn't have the heart to tell him that when we returned home he was supposed to go back to his dads to finish his summer time with him. When we returned home I called his dad and asked if he could stay with me a couple more days, so he did.

The day before Justin was to return home, he was brutally murdered by the 17-year-old, male babysitter his dad had hired to watch him while he was at work.

We had a beautiful celebration of life for Justin outside in front of the school garden that Justin and his classmates tended under the helpful guidance of a wonderful man and teacher the children referred to as Mr. V. After the ceremony, some of us planted agates in the garden in his memory. For the children of his school we had a day for them to share their thoughts and feelings. It was such a gift to me to hear their stories of how they felt about Justin. I remember one little girl telling me that on her first day at that school, Justin was the first one to ask her to play. Another child standing by said, "Justin played with everybody".

My son did not have an easy time coming in or going out of this world, but I am thankful to be able to say that for the most part, everything in the middle was fun and enjoyable. He was surrounded by people that loved and cared for him. We ended every day with a bedtime story and a hug and kiss goodnight.

I hope I have painted a clear and just picture of the wonderful little child that was a part of my life for a short nine and one half years. Memories are all I and the other moms who have shared their stories have of these wonderful little gifts we were given for however long we were given them. I am a better person for having loved and shared with my son, Forever Justin.

The family and friends that continue to love and mourn the loss of Justin are many. Thank you for taking the time to read his story.

I'll love you forever Justin, Mom

What I have learned:

1. Never pass up the chance to tell loved ones that you love them. It may be your last chance.
2. Forgiveness, forgiveness, forgiveness.
3. Our relationship with others defines who we are. Love and laugh as much as possible.

Aaron
July 19, 1984 – July 23, 2006

Aaron

Died in a Motorcycle Accident

By Lisa

AARON MY BEAUTIFUL GIFT
Today I see you here. But here it is not the same…
Gone is your smile, although only for a while.
I can see the brown of your eyes no more
and it hurts to my core.
Then suddenly I realize as I hold your face in my hands that as sad as it
must be, I know I hold only the package of such a precious gift.
Twenty-two years nine months ago. My Lord started to make me some-
thing very special. It formed in me for nine months and when he was born
OH WHAT A JOY!!!
I was only holding the package God wrapped Aaron up so beautifully in.
The real best of him was yet to be seen.
Now I understand
You are here NO-MORE
I am only left with such a beautiful wrapping just like a gift, when some-
one takes the time to make it look so pretty.
The real gift is inside
That was OUR Aaron. He was wrapped so beautifully. What a handsome
young man he was, with that bright smile, eyes the color of dark cinna-
mon, his brown hair he kept so very perfectly.
God blessed me for twenty-two years and now the package after twenty two
years has been opened and SET FREEE

I always knew he wasn't mine forever. But as I hold him I realize more than ever, that we all had a part in making him who he was.
God had trusted us. It seems so unfair a short twenty two years, but then I think of the life he lived and how he lived it and realize more than ever…
"…It is not the years in your life that count, but the life in your years"
(Abe Lincoln)

I DON'T UNDERSTAND

I don't understand! You're not here!
I am left with all this fear.
You're not here and I'm left with all this pain in your place
Could it be that as you left to that beautiful place something else
Settled in your place
That's what I feel—It's a pain so great--that which is left in your place.
It comes over me sometimes slow and sometimes quickly—None the less it consumes me.
Taking over my body making it churn and twist. I never felt such pain.
It's hollow, empty and scary. It's hard, cold, empty and lonely. This pain I feel Could it be that as you left this world you were replaced with only pain.

Just maybe now that you're gone to a beautiful place I am the only one in pain?
You my Ron are at peace and joy without the worries of this world as I, your mama.
Are these the labor pains of your re-birth to a different place. I don't understand. What is the pain It is a four letter word P A I N It strikes with anger with a blow, hard just so hard. It consumes me, twist me makes me feel Hopeless, it feels like a vomit needing to come out with tears and screams or silence and stillness. Yet when the tears and twisting subside I know it's still there that four letter word that I don't understand. It is not gone It is what has come to replace you the beautiful you My Ron

SOMETHING ABOUT THE NIGHT

It's quiet
It's still and no-one knows I'm up
Thinking, praying, crying and hurting
Something about the night it's peaceful It's painful it's my time
sh-sh-sh don't wake anyone Only those in that special place know I am up
They can share my feelings in the night

OVER THE HILL

As your body lays still
just slightly over the hill
Your spirit had run

As your body lays still
Ours is consumed in pain
As your spirit runs free
ours Stands still,

Our minds or hearts our very spirit
No longer what it used to be
Before that day your body lay still

Your pain was gone, vanished, done
Ours had only just begun

HOW DO YOU KEEP GOING

No recipe
No instructions
No process
YOU JUST GO
One foot in front of the other

One breath at a time one minute at a time
Tears pain and fear you just do

It seems so ironic that a story begins from the end. That is what it feels like since he left us. My beautiful son Aaron is gone. GONE, GONE from the physical touch of my arms, from the sight of my eyes, and the sound of his laughter and call of "Mom" to my ears!! It is ended. That is what goes on in my mind every day. Just days after he did leave, I somehow told myself I would see him again. Yet the pain is so overwhelming I can't dismiss the thoughts that come with THE END. Why? He was so much more than the exit. I'm looking at the ending of a beautiful orchestrated life. There was joy, happiness, there was sadness, there were triumphs and failures and everything was beautiful, good or bad. The story showed gratitude, dreams, joy, love and promising future then suddenly WHACK. The script ends horribly. Not the way the story was going at all.

Those living life with us felt the same and we all stood in protest slamming our fist. The sound of protest and hollering out WHY!! WHY!! Some even waved their fist in the air, pain shown on their faces. As the hollering of their voices start to subside...I am still giving it my all, harder and harder I scream PLEASE!! PLEASE!! PLEASE!!! This is not FAIR!! NO! YOU CHANGED THE WHOLE STORY-- NOT WHAT WAS SUPPOSED TO HAPPEN!

Those around me look at me compassionately and hold me kindly and lovingly. They discuss the story and tell me it's wrong and that it never ever should end this way. I feel so comforted, then slowly life goes on for them, but they too slowly drift away to live their lives, accepting the fact that Aaron's life is over. Now, I'm the only one left standing pounding my fist screaming, screaming and screaming out for the story to go on, to pick up before that sorry ending. It can't end this way NO!!! NO!! NO!!!

NO! I can hear in the background things like: He was such a great guy, he was a good friend, we will never forget. These words only make me scream louder. I just won't let up. This was MY life. It wasn't supposed to end in this way, for me it's DESPERATION. My Heart is Raw bleeding now. And my voice has gone silent from the pleading. No words…they have all been said. I don't want to believe it could happen this way. I feel left alone in an empty room. The bright lights have gone dim. And I sit, Me, Mom of Aaron alone. I can't stop pleading, so in silence I cry out. I cannot accept it, but its real, the story is over Aaron's story. Aaron has died. I really don't have a choice. No One asked me. He didn't ask me, God didn't ask me. How could this be? I thought I knew the ending. I was just living this beautiful story. The details were what made my life so beautiful and most of all joyful. It was wonderful.

As I sit in this place that marks an end and I know I have to move. Get up, pull myself up. It's me, I have to. How? I hear voices of people that love me…then a voice says… "Listen to me! Look at me! This is our son, our pain, no one can get us better but ourselves. You and I, we have to get ourselves through. He was our son, only we can get ourselves better." I am being held firmly and I feel pain of someone other than my own. The words work their way through my own pain and somehow I know that this is strength, that this is what I must hold onto and grasp tight. Pain, confusion, hopelessness, despair, and whatever else that is in me, I can't find words that are adequate to describe what is inside, I must hold on to the strength behind the voice. I'm not sure how but I know.

I question over and over, how could this happen. I question my life and what I did or didn't do. But mostly I am just thinking that Aaron left. How can life ever go without him, he was such a huge part of our lives; our family cannot be without him. My mind tries to think of how life will be and it just can't. I stay sitting in this chair thinking, "Will I be able to always remember what happened for the last 22years?" I want to stay in this dim room just sit just think to remember, but again I hear "_ONLY We can get ourselves better._" I'm trying to understand what it looks like because, it will never-ever be better. HE is GONE! SO GONE! NEVER TO BE AGAIN. HOW COULD IT BE BETTER? HOW? How? How? I have no strength, no will. Sickened and scared to live and afraid not to because I have other children; my beautiful boys Jacob, Matthew, Nathan and Raul. How about Joe – how could he ever be left without me? How could I leave them the pain I have at this moment. That is what it means not to walk to leave the pain, to drop it for someone else to bear. So to whom? To whom do I leave this unbearable pain? Yet knowing, I continue to think of just not walking out of the dim room. I know I have to push these thoughts away – far away. But it's loud. So I think of my boys, I try to, I try hard. I hear sounds again of people around me. I try to just hear, then slowly it turns to listening. But everything around is different. So Gray. so dull, so cold, so slow. So very sad, so very empty and lonely. But it's there all still there. Aaron Oh My Aaron is not there! NOT in this world with us, with me! I am left here with the rest of what held him so lovingly, in the same world that held him and our lives with him.

Where do I start? How do I start? It's hard to breathe, to think, even to fully open my eyes. I have never ever known such emotion and don't know what to do with it. So I sit. I sit and I sit. I can hear the world around me HOW COULD IT KEEP GOING? Don't they know what just happened AARON died!! He died!!! I can't feel anything but immense sadness I don't feel...I really don't feel anything but a deep heavy sadness, so very unfamiliar.

Wait, I feel scared, like nervousness. My whole body is so scared. Is this a part of being so sad? It's a feeling of fear I recognize it. Fear, FEAR I know you. Aaron I'm PETRIFIED to live without you! I can't let this defeat me Aaron! Who could possible know or begin to understand how scared I am to live without you. You were my first born. You taught me Life of love and understanding, sacrifice, happiness. You made me a mom. What Gift could be greater? You made me the person I am. My life began with loving you. And now life is asking me to go on without you. Can I really? Help me my Ron. You trusted me and now I find myself seeking trust in you – that somehow that boy who made me a mom can still help me.

We taught our children faith in God and now I don't want God. He changed the story. He deceived me. I can't understand God anymore. Where is he? Aaron, I believe you would never leave me, leave us. So I will trust that. God he took him just took him. Aaron must be here. I think how very precious he is. How he loved me, loved us, loved everyone. How he loved the gift of life. You have been unwrapped. Your spirit has been freed to soar the heavens. That is what I can trust in God for. Right now losing you is just too much. I can't lose GOD. I need to believe you are somewhere. I will just ignore GOD…I will… God, you let me down. I have to walk but if you're there, really there, just walk with me out of this room this space of such sadness. Aaron and your mother the Virgin Mary are the go-betweens…after all, she suffered the same. I don't want to deal with you God. I can't, just can't but please if you really are, then hold my son, may all that I trusted before be real for him.

I slowly stand with strength I didn't know was there. All I can do is stand for a short brief moment enough to tell myself I must walk, weak or broken. I realize I don't even care that I take full steps. That perhaps dragging myself is where it will start. I must get myself better. For those who believe I can, my boys – for Jacob, Matthew, Nathan and Raul. ME, I have to believe that Aaron's life is worth living for.

Almost three years have gone by, and I'm still trying to hold myself up over the chair that I was sitting in. The story plays over and over. The good times, the sad times. The things we did to-gether. I realize that the story the memories are there whether I'm trying to stand or not able to move. I sometimes wonder if I have taken steps and don't even know because some things are different. My children are older and life is moving in so many di-rections. I can see it, but it has a different shade now. I still call for an Encore. I still pound till my hands are raw. I don't know when I will stop. But I can hear Aaron telling me to try. God has not left, I feel his power, but he is still respecting my request. I do call his name more often then I care to admit. But I still feel like I don't want to be in the same room. I feel a glimpse, just a sliver of under-standing, a sense of we agree to disagree. Much like when I had to discipline Aaron and my other beautiful children. Love had to be bigger than the disagreement. And what could possible compare to taking my child.

I'm beginning to notice my thoughts changing or trying to be-cause the thoughts are not all the same. The thoughts shift by the moment sometimes. I can say to myself the show might be over but the show is in me, or in part of me; the story is my own. Or one I really like is some day, somehow I will get the strength to walk strong! Not out of the room like I thought I had to but ONTO the stage and continue the story. Because of Aaron, Life must keep go-ing. I must believe.

Aaron is soaring through us and among us. He has been set free. Now I have to figure it out. Walk onto the stage of life, it's hard, it's excruciating, but only I could choose to try. With the world going as it may around me my beautiful son is part of me forever. Aaron, "My Ron."

People that don't know you, how do I tell them how beautiful you are or the person you are. You were our first True Love. The one who has shown us the meaning of life and now teaching us death to a life well lived. You the thought of your life truly began when dad and I meet way back when we were in High School. We dreamt of getting married, having children and living happily ever after. We married and just a few years later had you. You were a healthy and thriving little boy. I still remember the pain of your birth. I still can feel you in my arms as I nursed you for the first time knowing that my life, our life had truly changed and we were overjoyed. A joy I had never ever felt. From that day forward, I began to understand love.

I remember how challenging you were and how when you were hungry I had to drop everything and feed you, change you or play with you. I remember the faces you made with new foods we'd introduce and you pulling up to peek over the crib, and your first steps and even your falls. I remember the pride I felt seeing you in your cute little outfits that I would take you out in. I remember taking you on a bike ride in your seat behind me, the parks and the stroller rides, the books we read and songs we sang to you. I can remember the preschool chick-a-dee as you called it. You just cried every time I left you. You always thought it was much more fun to stay home with me and your little brothers. And really in some ways, that never ever really changed

I remember how you would come over and give me "luvys" as you called it. Your sweet little hands, holding my cheek, and how each time we brought home a new baby brother you'd cuddle him and hold him giving him luvys. You'd just talk and play for hours. You were so proud!! I of course remember naptime. I remember it was never long because you were ready to jump back on that bike and race down the block to grammas singing GI-GI -JOE-----JOE! JOE!

The best time of your day was when you'd hear the sound of that truck rubble out around the corner and suddenly the house would explode with DADDDY!! DADDDY!!! DADDDY!!!! You would be the first one down the stairs. I can remember hot summer days with sprinklers and slip in slides and neighbor kids running and laughing playing kick the can and how could I forget all those frogs and salamanders you brought through the house and even those pet RATS! Or on snow days you pushing your brothers down the snow-covered hill in the back yard. I remember all those sports you played basketball, flag football, soccer, wrestling, baseball, track, tackle football. I remember how you began to blossom and your character began to come alive. That little shy boy not so much anymore.

Going into Middle School brought us alarm until you hit 8th grade and were on your way to High School, now that was a call for panic, our first going into the **well-known** world of a Teenagers. You proved to continue to grow in character and in spirit.

Looking back to those teen age years, what a fine young man you were. Sure we had our hard times. I remember teacher conference, late assignments, or the prerecorded message A STUDENT IN YOUR HOUSEHOLD WAS ABSENT ON…We always trying to protect you from the world, always trying to keep your mind, your spirit and most of all help you with your faith in God, hoping your choices in Life would be Christ centered.

One of our many found memories of High School is Mariner football. Not only the thrill and excitement of every game, but what it taught you Aaron, and what we learned about you. Sports, but in particular football was a place where you could continue to come out of that shy boy, where everything in you said I CAN! Where the will inside you proved its force. In trying to discover who you were and what your place was in this world you took what you learned in your workouts and in your dedication and applied it to how you continued to live.

On one occasion, you went fishing with some friends and came home so upset because as I understood you had cast out the entire brand new fishing pole into the lake. You begged me to go back out there to get it out of the water. I could not IMAGINE how you thought you were going to do that. Your friends were done trying but not you, you just kept saying I know where it is MOM. Just go with me. So there I go and in the dark with my headlights facing the water, after so many attempts, you got it! It was unbelievable sometimes the will you held it was always YES I CAN in so many aspects of your life.

In reminiscing those last years of your young life I remember your love most. I remember how you loved us and always spent time with us.

On your 17th birthday you wanted a car so bad. You already had a job at Cost Cutter and didn't like walking there. I think you were hoping we were going to surprise you because we asked you to come to the garage but much to your surprise we had hidden your gift in the truck of the car. It was a bike not exactly the wheels you hoped for.

I remember what a hard worker you were and how it annoyed you if we were doing something together as a family and you could not be there. Then that day came when you wanted to move out. We didn't want you to go but you did anyway. I still remember how weird that felt. Then once you spread your wings about as far as they could go you admitted that you really missed being home. So you figured it out, come over EAT, do laundry, beat up on your brother then leave so you can be out late with your friends. You moved out but you never really left home. You were usually home for dinner and if not you'd always check in. Most of the time, I woke up to you on the couch.

Something that Aaron was truly about was Love and kindness. In so many ways Aaron let us all know that he loved us. Aaron was one that was not scared to Love. He made it so simple by little things like thinking about you at the store and getting you a candy he knew you liked or going out to play catch. For me it was calling me when he would go somewhere he knew I was uneasy about or just to say what's up mom or love you. He told us he loved us so often that there were many times where we would respond, "Yes Aaron we Love you too." In a rather, *I know it all ready.* His response was **you sissy.**

Aaron your physical life here on earth came to an end but the part of you that lives on is the Love you so freely shared. Your kind words, your pats on the shoulder that gentle and silent, luv you. All those good times and Lord knows we shared so very many. You were my first, the one who made me MOM. You taught me so much about the joy of life and now here I find myself in a place that only nightmare are made of. Your life, our life with you has ended. But how could I ever begin to understand. Maybe the answer lies in the fact that **everything** we ever based raising you and your brothers is now here and put before me. We raised you to have faith, and now faith is asked of us. Faith that your life and mine is here for the purpose of everlasting life. I know you loved God. Your loved showed it.

I remember going to your condo on the morning of your death. Walking in, it was surreal. I guess it was hope in finding you. As daddy and I walked in, words cannot describe our hope. As the emptiness of the room overwhelmed us, I walked into your bedroom. I pulled your blankets to your bed and next to the pillow, there I found the cross dad and I had given you the day you moved out of the house. I stared at it for a second and suddenly everything in me grabbed it. I held it close to my heart.

You had moved once again and this time it is back home. YOU ARE HOME MIJO. Home is where we are all going, some sooner than others. Aaron, I cannot understand why so soon. And perhaps the pain I feel from the loss of your physical life is no different from the pain I remember the day you made me your Mom. That pain will never subside until the day I see you and hold you again. You gifted me US with so much love you told me you loved me and hugged and kissed me enough for a lifetime. Yet it still does not seem to be enough. I LOVE YOU MIJO

Aaron's spirit will always be a part of me, of us, whether it is his smile we remember, his friendship, his thoughtfulness --or it may be helping others as his loving memorial scholarship has already done. I do not know where the love he left us will lead us.

I am here only because I know just like with his birth there is an **unimaginable** joy to follow…. and it is for eternity.

What I have learned:

1. **Strength:** I use to feel like a strong mom. I was able to face anything concerning my children with such strength and courage. When Aaron was born, it was so symbolic to me that I gave birth without pain medication and did so with all his brothers as well. To me it meant I would do everything and anything within my power, setting aside my own pain, weakness, and especially my own desires, to give them my best. In other words, I vowed to love them selflessly and unconditionally. I remember feeling strong and powerful, knowing that I was a pillar for my children. For 22 years I loved Aaron and his brothers in this way. Then the unimaginable happened. Aaron was killed on his motorcycle.

   Suddenly the woman of strength was NO-MORE. The strength I had demonstrated vanished. I couldn't imagine ever having strength to go on. Or to love and care in the same way I had before. I felt so lost and confused. I was so weak and helpless. I remember the feeling of desperation and not caring about anything! Sadly and truthfully, even finding joy in our other children was difficult. This truth made it so much harder because there was ABSOLUTELY nothing in my universe that could mean more to me than any one of my children. Yet, I the woman of strength and courage was depleted of every ounce, and nothing around me seemed to matter.

I didn't believe I would ever feel anything but sadness until one day I realized that years had gone by and I was still breathing, my heart was still beating and I was still actually alive. I had managed to continue to live!! Strength. It could only be STRENGTH that is keeping me here.

I have learned that I am so, so much stronger than I could have ever fathomed!! I learned that I alone am in control of how I will deal with my pain and sadness. I never thought it was possible that I could face a world without any of my children. I had found strength within ME to somehow keep going and to stay alive and slowly start to emerge back in my world. I learned that the strength I need has to be found inside of me. As insignificant as things may seem, it's important to get out and doing what you really don't want to do. These things do matter. I learned that gradually, choices made over time do make a big huge difference in my healing. I learned that my measure of strength was measured by me because NO ONE could possibly know my pain and how deep it feels. If all I could do that day was breath, I was STRONG. I have learned that I must define my strength every day to help me heal every single day for the rest of my life.

2. <u>Understanding</u>

I think most of us want to be understood. No matter what we are going through, we like to have someone validate our feelings by understanding us. But the pain I feel every day of my life because of the absence of Aaron is one thing that I DO NOT want anyone to understand.

I learned that people say and do things that hurt. I have learned that people are always trying to say the right thing to make me feel better, to ease my pain, yet many times it is so very far from comforting that words meant to be consoling are painful. I have learned that people cannot truly and wholeheartedly understand unless they have lost a child. Plain and simple. This is one of those things I DO NOT want them to understand because that would mean they too would have to lose their child and experience all that I do. I have learned I have to disregard the comments that come from people that hurt me. I have learned that they are trying to say the right thing, the comforting thing, but if they don't, I will forgive them and be grateful that life has not brought them the knowledge I have regarding the loss of my son.

3. **My husband**

I have learned that if there is anyone that could feel closest to the pain I feel over losing my son, is my husband, who is Aaron's dad. As ironic as it may sound, his reaction to his pain is totally different from my reaction to my pain. It sounds contradictory; however, I have realized that although we both absolutely loved Aaron, we both had a different relationship with our eldest son. I have had to learn to accept that we both grieve differently and that loving Aaron in our own special way is what makes the grieving process for each of us distinctly different from one other. There is so much confusion that goes on with the loss of my son that expecting my husband or even my children to feel exactly what I feel is just absurd. Things that totally make my heart explode with grief may not have the same impact on my husband, and most days I expected him to know what things would set me off. Over time, I have learned that my husband is definitely the one who experiences pain to the degree I do for the loss of Aaron. That knowledge has opened so much more understanding and compassion in us to one another's pain.

It is only with the heart that one can see rightly
What is essential is invisible to the eye.

Antoine de Saint Exupery

Chelsea
August 28th, 1982 – August 9, 2008

Chelsea

Died as a Result of a Fall from the Roof of a Home
By Ginger (Chelsea's Mama)

In Chelsea's own words:

"I love laughing and having fun. I love my job. I love my friends.

My favorite colors are leopard and magenta, I love being a social butterfly.

I have a good heart and like to do nice things for other people.

I know what I want out of life and don't let lame people rain on my parade.

I think it's wonderful how a smile can be contagious.

Traveling is my fave."

My hope is that by writing this, I can help other Moms who have lost children. Without the support of other Mothers, family and friends, I don't know if I would be able to function well enough to write about my journey of grief.

How do I explain the worst day of my life? On August 9, 2008, I lost my only daughter, best friend, confidante, travel partner and shopping buddy. I will never forget that night when

I was planning to travel back East for a family reunion and I talked her into going with me. I told her that I thought it was important for her to meet her relatives on my side of the family. I so regret that conversation. I thought it would be a loving and safe place to go because I was born there and my grandparents had the family farm. I visited there every summer while I was growing up.

Little did I know that this trip would turn out to be a parent's worst nightmare. Who would have thought I would get "that" call in the middle of the night?

Chelsea was invited by her second cousin to attend a wedding 40 miles away from where my relatives live. That morning, she decided to go. I thought it would be an adventure and she would be taken care of. The police report said there was drinking at the wedding. She had just reached the condo where she was going to spend the night. She was on the back deck with her cousin's best friend and the report said that she climbed over the balcony, so she could see the lights. She lost her footing, fell, and received massive head trauma, which lead to her death.

As you can imagine, it was a very traumatic night being in a strange city, being asked a lot of hard questions, and told about the trauma that lead to my daughter's horrible death. I have a lot of questions about that night because, you see, my daughter was careful about drinking, afraid of heights and was a "girly girl" wearing a dress! Not the type of person that you would think of climbing over a balcony that was half her size. I may never know what happened that night because the last two people she was with have refused to talk to me. They haven't taken any responsibility, have never said they were sorry for my loss, or have ever checked in with me. They seem to have no remorse. Since my daughter had been drinking, the local police ruled this to be an accident. One thing I can tell you is that alcohol killed my daughter. I hate the fact that her death was so unnecessary and senseless!

My daughter had a beautiful soul. Her smile was so bright that she would light up a room when she entered it. I miss her so much! I feel so fortunate that she chose me to be her mother. You see, I had a dream of a blond little girl when I was 16 years old and knew in my heart that we would meet some day. That day was August 28, 1982 and one of the highlights of my life! It was a privilege to be Chelsea's Mama. Raising her wasn't always easy, but she taught me unconditional love. We told each other everything and sometimes I would have to say to her, "too much information." I've been told by some of her friend's moms that they wish they had the same kind of relationship we did. Our relationship was always up-to-date and I feel good about the fact she knew I loved her and I know she loved me. I have such a broken heart.

As devastating as her death has been, I knew from the start that she would have wanted me to do my best and keep moving forward from here. So, after her "Celebration of Life", I went to my first support group for parents who have lost a child. I also went to my doctor and found a good counselor. I'm blessed that I was invited to join a group of other moms. It's the most kind and supportive group of ladies I've ever met. They support me in ways that nobody else can because they understand the ache in my heart. I don't know who I am now or where to go from here and this is the hardest situation I've ever been though. I don't know where it's taking me, but I'm hoping with support from others, I can continue putting one foot in front of the other.

I can feel my daughter's spirit and know she is with me. Sometimes I wish it had been me that died that night.

For me this is what four months looks and feels like:

C – Confused. Where and what do I do now? I have a hard time remembering, planning and lack the energy to care. My perspective of life has changed.

H - Heartache. I will never see my daughter get married or have kids. I will never be a grandmother.

E – Encouraged. By listening to other Moms that have walked further into their journey, they give me hope that I will live through this and be able to walk through my own grief journey. Someday, I hope to be able to think of the positives (the 26 years I had to enjoy my daughter) instead of the negatives (the last four months).

L – Losses. Too many to count. Besides the loss of my Daughter, the loss of focus, passion and a reason for living.

S – Sad. I miss my best friend. I always told her that I "didn't know what I would do without her" and now I need to figure out how I'm going to live without her. This makes me sad.

E – Emotional. Being true to the pain and grief and not holding back. Knowing that if I don't release my emotions I just may go mad, or be an old, mean lady that can't give back to society or help others.

A – Anguish. There isn't a day, hour or minute that I don't remember the horrid feelings from that night and the weeks that followed.

What I have learned:

1. That I'm stronger than I thought I was, the body is amazing, it can withstand so much grief and pain, more than you could imagine. At 6 months into my grief journey I had to make the decision of moving forward or ending the pain. It's not part of me to give up, so I choose to move forward, doing the best I can to help others and not to be a miserable

person that takes their pain out on others. I'm coming up to my daughters 6th anniversary of the last day I saw her, I don't give that day much energy but every year I remember the first day I saw her (her birthday)!

2. I've learned tolerance, for others that don't get what I've been through and wonder why I can't seem to "get over it", and patience within myself that recovery will take as long as it will take. I'm a different person, today if I don't feel like doing something or being with someone I'm honest and don't do things that don't feel right.

3. It's okay to let others help you, it's good and helpful to talk to others about your feelings, especially someone that understands, and there are great organizations out there with people just like me. I have joined them and have close friends that understand, and help keep me going.

I know that just because I lost my daughter it doesn't mean that she is gone, she is still in my heart and thoughts, and dreams….oh, and I love the dreams! I feel like I don't have a future, it died with my daughter so I truly live one day at a time, and sure I plan things but don't have a clue what tomorrow will bring.

Remember you are not alone in your journey! Chelsea's Mama

My Only BJ
April 9, 1988 – August 26, 2006

BJ

Died in a Motor Vehicle Accident

By Jenny

It has been four and a half years since my most precious son, BJ, died. By some innate drive to live I have survived. I know that I appear to function more normally than one would, which makes it more comfortable for those to be around me. But, because of the immeasurable bonds we form with our children I am just as broken, sad and lonely as anyone could be. I have read parts of many books and the entirety of a few books that speak of grief and loss, some resonate with me and others do not. I write nearly every day in a journal I started a week after BJ died in an attempt to understand my own grief. What I understand is that I will never be the same and I am forever changed. To honor my son I strive to capture BJ's energy and spirit, and yearn to live as richly as he did in his young eighteen years of life. Due to some cruel twist of fate I've survived my son. Given that sentence, I feel compelled to carry his ability to "live and love out loud" (Tina Sellers) forward - that is both my privilege and responsibility as I remember him. I want to be "more like BJ" because of who he was and because he is no longer here.

BJ, was the second born of my two children and my only son. BJ peacefully entered the world at 11:20 p.m. on April 9, 1988. He was quiet and so beautiful (well, actually, both of my kids were born with squinty eyes and were quite hairy…but, he WAS beautiful). His name, Jeffrey, means "God's peace" and that interpretation fit his personality. I counted on BJ's easy going, "it's all good," peaceful nature every day. However, the actual name, Jeffrey, was never a good fit for him. Perhaps it was too formal. His sister, Rachel, who is 23 months older called him "baby Jeff," as we had named him Jeffrey, Jr. after his father. My sister said you can't call him "baby Jeff" forever, what about "BJ?" When BJ entered junior high he wanted to be called Jeff so we enrolled him as Jeff Brown, but, his friends, classmates, and soon to be new friends and teachers continued to affectionately call him BJ, and that is the name that stuck with him. To me, he was always either BJ or Beej.

Like many parents I became a composite of my kids. To be a parent has been, by far, the most rewarding piece of my existence. I didn't have the opportunity to work from home so I pursued the career that would be most in line with the schedules of my children and became a teacher. Time with my children was what I lived for, they were certainly my greatest pleasures and treasures – and yes, I can say that having met and learned from the challenging years of adolescence! The time invested in loving and understanding my kids has come back to me ten-fold – I am fortunate to have been a mother and a friend to my children. I am sad that I will not hear BJ call me "Mom" again, except in my dreams. Still nothing can ever change the fact that I will always be "BJ's Mom."

Rachel called BJ the "golden child." I have to say he was worthy of that label. BJ has been described by many as someone that was nice to everyone. He was always happy, smiling and laughing, and lived each day to the fullest. He made an effort to become friends with everyone he met, and treated everyone with the respect they deserved. It was evident at an early age that BJ had the gift of selflessness. He was generous with his time and took pleasure in seeing other people excel. He biked with me, hiked with his Dad, hunted with his step-Dad, and was the most loyal person imaginable to his diverse group of friends. He would show up for his friend's court dates to support them. BJ gave Rachel roses on Valentine's Day the years she didn't have a boyfriend and he always got me malted milk balls (a favorite!). When he was preparing to climb Mt. Rainier with his Dad he was disciplined, focused and determined. If he was heading out for three days to camp with his friends he could kick back with the best of them and will be remembered for building legendary bonfires! Lastly, BJ was as comfortable l learning new skills on the jobsite, with his summer Construction job, as he was spending a summer night watching an entire season of "House" with his girlfriend.

BJ graduated from high school just as he lived – quietly humble while receiving many honors. He graduated in the top 5% of a graduating class of over 650 peers and was set to go to the University of Washington to pursue a career in Construction Management in the fall. I often refer to his last summer as "the summer of a lifetime." BJ had purchased a 1999 Porsche Boaster in April of his senior year. It was a silver convertible with a navy blue soft top. I can still picture him as he would leave for work or a date with the top down, music up and smiling...what an amazing smile BJ had! He had started dating a lovely young woman in April and they seemed to be very much in love. They were nearly inseparable during the four months they shared. They had some wonderful weekend experiences and talks that were deep and mature about a future they wanted to share together. He had joined the Laborer's Union and was learning the trade of concrete work. He worked as a laborer so that when he received a degree in Construction Management he would have actual experience and would make a better manager. He was always on the go, filling his days and nights to the fullest.

Looking back on it now, it is almost as if there was something pushing him – was he destined to have a short, though rich life? I remember his last week as if it was yesterday. Is that because I ran through those days so many times in the wake of his death? Is it because with the stress of losing him those days were imprinted more deeply into my memory? I don't have answers to those questions, but I am glad that my memory is clear about those last days.

The last time I saw BJ, he was returning from a full day spent with his girlfriend. They left early in the morning and drove to eastern Washington – they had time at Crescent Bar where they floated on mattresses on the Columbia River. They also drove to Lake Chelan and took in the sun there. When I called him, at about 9:30 p.m., he had just dropped his girlfriend off and asked that I stay up so that he could tell me about his day. I will always be glad that I was awake and we talked for about ten minutes before his phone rang, it was his girlfriend, and so I went to bed.

The next day I left early to start Day One of the Three Day Walk for Breast Cancer. The walk that year was through our old and present neighborhoods, and at nighttime the tents were set up at BJ's first elementary school. The two days that I walked it was like a walk down memory lane because the things I walked by (including our old house and the place where he bought paint ball supplies) brought thoughts of my children's lives. I spoke with both of my kids the first night when we got back to the tent and heard of their days. I was so excited to tell them where we were camping and where I had walked. The Second Day was another beautiful sunny day as August is such a wonderful month in the Pacific Northwest. I called BJ in the morning and though the call was brief, our conversation ended as all of them, with "I love you" and "I love you too." When I got back to the camp area at the end of the second day I tried to call BJ, and just got his voice mail.

At about 7:30 p.m., his girlfriend called and said she hadn't been able to get a hold of BJ since about 11 that morning and she was worried because he always returned her call if he couldn't pick up at the time. She knew he had gone to golf in a tournament with a buddy from work but he was going to head home when the tournament ended. We agreed to let each other know when we were able to get a hold of him. I started to get anxious. I had the oddest and most uncomfortable feeling that something had happened to BJ.

When I went to bed at 8:30 on Saturday night, I felt as if I should be calling hospitals or law enforcement to see if he'd been in an accident. I was woken at 1:41 a.m. by the ringing of my cell phone. My husband said he was going to pick me up because "BJ had been in an accident." I gathered my things and despite the warmth of the tent and the summer morning I was shaking. As I walked out to where he was picking me up I was thinking, "what would be the absolute worst thing that could happen?" I figured if I thought of that then anything would be better. I thought that he might be at Harborview Hospital, the lead trauma hospital in the Seattle area. When I got in the car, I asked Mike where we were going…I'll never forget his words and how they took all of the life out of me – "we are going home, BJ is dead." I remember screaming, crying and hitting the inside of his car…I hated him for saying those words to me. I hated that he told me in that way – but, I've since realized there is absolutely no good way to hear that your child has died. And thus began the beginning of hell.

When I was thinking of the worst possible thing that could've happened to BJ - never once did I consider that he died…that was impossible. Even now there are moments in a day when I feel it is impossible that my son has died. But, when I went to bed feeling something had happened to BJ, he had already died. BJ died at 7:41 p.m. Saturday, August 26. The days that followed were a blur of trying to understand what had happened and making plans for a service fitting BJ. We would learn later that he had gone to play golf with his mentor from the Construction Company. His friend, 25 years his senior, had bought him beer during the tournament in which they'd taken second place. After the tournament, they went to a local Tavern for steaks and celebration. They left the tavern and six minutes later both died in a crash. As the story would unfold, BJ's blood alcohol level was .12 while his friend's was over .2. They took the car out on a road that BJ was unfamiliar with, but one that he would've loved – what he most enjoyed about the Porsche was how it could corner and take turns. The speed they were going was in excess of 65 miles per hour on a road that posted 35 miles per hour. Alcohol was not a big part of BJ's life, but it was part of his death. Speed was not a big part of BJ's life, but it was part of his death.

There are dozens of "what ifs" surrounding that day. "What if his friend's golf partner hadn't cancelled at the last minute?" "What if the weather had been windy and rainy (as it was the same day in 2008 when I returned to BJ's cross)?" "What if he hadn't been able to save for the car" and so many other unanswered questions. I kept myself awake many nights spinning through the unanswered questions, but I realized that answers wouldn't change the outcome. BJ died on a beautiful, sunny night in August with the top down and music up.

As I have attempted to navigate through my new, forced reality, I come up with a lot of analogies to explain how I feel. One of these ironically has to do with driving. Before BJ died, I was really feeling good about where I was in my life. My kids were doing great, I was proud of them and savored my time with them. I enjoyed teaching and shoot, it was summer time! My health and life were very good. So, four years ago I had the perfect ride. That "perfect ride" would look different for each of us. We would each choose a different car, road, music to play, destination, and companion in the car. For me, the ride was a 65 Mustang convertible, white with a black top. The weather was warm enough to have the top down without getting chilled by the wind or burned by the sun...The music was a mix, but definitely a lot of country especially Brad Paisley...I was driving into the country away from the city, away from traffic, crowds and congestion...the road was brand new asphalt – smooth, quiet, without any irregularities. So, there I was driving along, comfortable, confident and enjoying where I was going. Then, on August 26, 2006, when I came around a gradual curve that should have been easy to negotiate I dropped into a sink hole and my drive came to a grinding halt. BJ died.

It has been well over four years since BJ's crash and I'm not sure if I've even hit the bottom of that hole...I know I dropped really far and then found myself on an unknown road that was all torn up, really rough and had a lot of detours. I have had days of feeling as if I'm getting a little bit of traction - only to be spun in a different direction, or to hit a patch of ice only to be spun uncontrollably in yet another direction...It is difficult to believe the road will even out and become at all predictable and I know without a doubt the ride will never be the same because I lost my most precious passenger on that day, my young son and best friend.

I have likened myself to a tapestry – a perfect blending of colors, textures and threads woven from the different personalities of my two children. In losing BJ, it is as if someone grabbed a loose thread of mine and yanked it, leaving the entire fabric of my being completely unraveled. There are many sections that to the naked eye appear intact, but in fact, on closer inspection, there are gaping holes and I don't know how to mend myself. I love my daughter dearly, I've always been close to her and I am most certainly closer to her than ever but she cannot be two people. She is a beautiful, caring and warm young woman and being with her is as comfortable as I can be but it cannot be expected that she could also be her brother. My memories of BJ are sweet and warm. I am fortunate to have been blessed with a son that spent time with me in many meaningful ways to give me the gift of such memories...but, oh, I long for his voice, his laugh, his radiant smile and the life so evident in his beautiful brown eyes.

For over two years, I had been trying to capture what BJ meant to me. I wanted to explain the love I have for him and to start approaching the pain of losing him. I've worked weekly with a woman counselor who has the gift of being able to walk WITH me on this journey into the unknown. Just recently she told me of a colleague's loss – the death of a wonderful Brazilian friend of 28 years that had been like a second father to him. The friend said the recent death "was teaching him depths of what the Portuguese word, *saudade* means." He said it was "not an easy word to translate - for what it's worth, several years ago an international organization of translators rated *saudade* as the 7th most difficult concept to translate into English. *Saudade* is the feeling of simultaneous pain and joy at the memory of someone or something loved that is now lost or gone. It is pain because of the loss; it is joy because of the love. Brazilians would say that there is never one without the other and that the only way to be truly human (i.e., to love) is to be willing to enter into the pain. Thus, much Brazilian music, poetry, literature is about *saudade* - the joy of the pain. So Brazilians seek to remember even when the memories bring pain, because to forget is to truly lose that which was loved. This isn't masochism (enjoying the pain); but it is willingness to bear the cost of pain in order to love. Saudade is complex and it is not something that I ever understood with my mind. I'm finding that I am learning *saudade* in steps as I experience it. For me, the helpfulness of having a word for what I am experiencing is that it teaches me not to look forward to losing painful memories, but to accept the

on-going pain so that my heart will remember the loved one."
(Kevin Neuhouser) And there it is – the most accurate written
expression of what I feel with BJ, the way my heart will acutely
remember BJ. The pain and the love, and in feeling the pain
remembering the love...love you infinity BJ.

In loving memory of

Joshua Gunnar Seather

June 7, 1990 – February 28, 2007

"For I consider that the sufferings of this present time
are not worthy to be compared with the glory
which shall be revealed in us."

Romans 8:18

Josh
June 7, 1990 – February 28, 2007

Josh

Died by Suicide at his Home

By Julia

I lost a child and I lost my mind: I have been in groups for mothers who have lost a child - groups that nobody wants to belong to. When life has given us these challenges that we now must face, and with this it helps my mind get through another day. I used to say inside my mind, if I lost a child I don't think I could make it through. My worst fear came true, the exact nightmare, the horror, of losing a child became my reality. I looked the darkest kind of life straight in the eyes. How could this happen to me? On February 28, 2007 this became my reality.

I lost my Dad when I was ten-years-old. I always felt as if, "What did I do wrong? "After my father's death came the death of my brother, my best friend, my mom, my grandma, who was my second mother, another one of my dearest brothers, then my son. I continue to wonder, how this could happen? How can I even fathom to live with this?

Joshua Gunnar Seather born June 7, 1990 was 16 years and 8 months old when he died. Standing at 6"2 yet still on his launch upward, big crystal blue eyes and a smile that could light up my world. He was outgoing, goofy, crazy! He would scare me with his outgoing personality, his "live and let live" motto. He snow-boarded, water-skied, played football and basketball, always going for the gold. He was never in slow motion, if anything in fast forward. I cannot truly capture the person my son was, because he was one of a kind, my baby, my friend, my son. I can only even begin to articulate who he was and who he stood for. February 28, 2007, after worry had taken over the night before, I found my son motionless, breathless, lifeless. My whole life had taken a left hand turn into a sadness I know I will never recover from.

I have six children. Joshua was my third child. I had been married three times, I had my oldest beautiful children, Paris Nichol and Richard Benjamin from my first husband who was physically and emotionally abusive. In my second relationship I wasn't married, but we were together seven years, when my blessing of Joshua entered and then my daughter, Jazmine. In my 40's, I married again and a beautiful baby girl Jizel was born. At 45, yet another blessing, my last child, Xeriza, was born!

My son, Joshy and I had a good relationship. We could talk about issues that bothered him. He didn't talk to me about everything but as his mom, he and his friend knew that we had a special relationship. Joshy was having difficulty in school; he had fallen behind, going from one home to the another. We attempted home packets but it was hard to keep him on a schedule. He said he had trouble sleeping. That should have been my first clue. He transferred to a different school, yet he had no motivation for getting up, he felt "why try?" The school wouldn't let him do alternative school and he got behind in regular school. Joshua wanted to go to a doctor and I took him to see a physician who stated Joshy was depressed, I thought, "No way! This kid has a constant smile, an ongoing laugh, he loved to go to his friend's house, he was always busy playing." But he never had the motivation to discipline himself about school work. The doctor decided to put Joshua on a drug, Prozac. About eight weeks after starting the medication, Josh took his life.

Josh never let his family know his plan but he did consult with a volunteer at the church a week before he made his decision. Joshy, had recently given his life to our Lord Jesus Christ. This volunteer was at the church Josh had been attending for six months. During prayer time, Josh told the volunteer that he felt demons after him and that he felt suicidal. He hadn't mentioned this to the young pastor, so the volunteer decided to write him a letter, to share in the youth group the next week. We didn't attend that group and Josh died by suicide. It is so hard to believe I didn't lose my faith, I know there is a plan bigger than I know. The volunteer asked Joshy why he felt that way, was it home, parents etc. Josh stated it was bigger than that – almost as though he knew a plan.

I never got to say "good-bye", never got that last hug and kiss, I miss him with a yearning pain that will never cease. I long for his touch, his smell, his smile. From that day my whole life had changed, the way I feel or look at things. I now reside with a never ending feel of broken. I know without a doubt, if I didn't have two younger children I would not be here writing this chapter. I believe in Our King, Our Lord, and Savior Jesus Christ. I know my son with no longer having pain and hurting went home to Jesus Christ. Still it doesn't take the pain away, it is still very real. My family will never be the same, we will wonder what he would look like, what he'd be doing, but I do know if I continue in the faith I will see him again and I cannot wait.

I started reading many books on other families who have had to go through a loss of a loved one. Reading these books, along with the bible, have allowed me to keep my faith strong and not allow the demons to entertain my head with more lies. I believe the demons attacked my son in his thoughts and the Lord took him home.

One of the churches staff members would record the teens in their various activities, well he had caught Joshua on film many times, but at one in particular. Joshy 6 months before he passed from this world to a new life, the video where he stood up on a large stage at the church summer camp holding over 350 kids, giving his life to the lord. The night before he got on stage he had a dream of Jesus coming to him and he wrote it on a note pad the church had provided him. The following evening Joshua stood to read what he wrote and dedicated his life to the Lord. He wrote:

"OH Dear God, Yor Holy Spirit is in me I can feel it. I remember the dream last night. I remember coming towards U and coming out of the Darkness and into the light. And Satan wouldn't let me go. U kept saying fight him my son Fight him. He has no power over U. U are strong, U are my son. U kept urging me to come forward…and I could feel ur love. And U said Drop ur Guilt, Drop all ur sins. I forgave U when I died on the cross. Let go of them my son. And right then I let go and was launched towards U lord. And I thank and praise U lord for ur holy spirit that is within me. I can feel you, lord. Ur Pressence is strong and I know as long as I Believe and love U, No matter that U will not leave me cause I can finally grasp ur love for me lord. I realize these last five years I have been in Darkness. Shadows have cast over me and my life has been in Darkness without U lord. So I devote the rest of my life to you."

I'm to stay here and continue to learn lesions humility, boasting, patience the list is endless. If anyone would have ask me where I thought I would be in 10 years It would be with all my children watching them grow to adults and have a life of their own but my life changed into a direction I never want to go in but I'm here and I'm powerless I can only go forward into the lie that was handed me I'm not happy about it I heard someone say they now know what it feels like to really be sad and happy in the same body but I know what it feels like to disappear but I am visible Through pray and mediation it seems clear my purpose here. One of my friends stated I help prepare Joshy to move on, that was my job. He out of the other 6 children had fallen away from the Lord, he wouldn't go to church after age 11 he states in his writing he was in darkness for the past 5 years and that night on stage he saw a light he started going to youth group, church, he was meeting new friends, the spirit was visible.

I sat in the pews at church with all 6 children Christmas of 2006, all six kids and I had a lite candle in our hands our eye twinkling, singing and praising in celebration of Jesus' birth . I looked to my left - there were Jazmine, Richard and Joshua. I looked to my left there were Paris, Jizel and Xeriza, two months before he passed. I will never be able to sit in church with all 6 of my most precious gifts again, not in the physical body at least, but I still feel Joshy around. When I look at his picture it feels as if he is still right here, I hear him talk to me, saying "Mama it's okay. Hang in there Mama."

I have changed my view of life, I want to be close and support other families. I have gone to crash sites, 1 year anniversaries 2 years, 3 years the vicious, endless cycle. With these other mothers we didn't meet accidently, I feel our kids connected us and for that we need to share and support one another. My inner body aches and hurts to meet new moms just to know there pain is unbearable I pray all day and all night talking with our Lord and Savior praying for all the mothers and families. I have to turn it over to God and I get periods of comfort, rest and reassurance Joshy is truly home. Whatever dark demons were in him they cannot bother him any further. He is safe. He is home. Though I can't wait to go home too, I will wait. I know God has revealed to me it is not time yet.

For me the journey continues the ups and the down I continuing on feeling broken but by continuing to reach out to others whom have suffered the loss of a loved one makes this journey a little more tolerable I ask God help me through this journey because I can't do it alone.

Joshy sister wrote a letter this is her letter. from Jazzy its call A Boy Named Joshua

A Boy Named Joshua

Unfairness, be trail, the fact that it all ended before it even had a chance to begin. Trying to make it in a world that rejects you. My biggest fear was always the minuet things in life. Now the bigger picture has revealed itself to me, either you make it in this world or you don't. Either you face the pain and the suffering to get to the top or you crumble under the pressure. Is trying even enough anymore? Is rejection something you can avoid? For all of you who think that it is a yes, you are truly wrong.

He seemed so strong, so brave so ready to face whatever he came across. I wish I could have seen through the cloak he hid under. I painfully wish I did. Or if not myself then others who loved him. Which to him felt like no one. He had so much love but we all hid it. He slipped through all of our selfish eyes.

If you saw the smile that lights up the room and bought a smile to so many other faces. The deep baby blue eyes, that we mistake for happy. The slinkish body that was in a 6'2 frame. The little arms with too much power. The manly hands that had no yet been grown into. The skin so fair it was enough to envy. A personality to adore. His humor, his sensitivity that only few got to see, and his respect towards others around him. Everyone has flaws, but now looking back I can't find one that I don't now completely love. He was one that anyone could miss, and fall in love with.

Many talents he portrayed, basketball, football, snowboarding, jet skiing, cliff jumping. From now till the day I to leave I can picture him eloped in all of these things, Seeing every spot of enjoyment on his face. I cannot even begin to articulate the kind of person he was, because he was one of a kind, my brother, my friend, my defender,

The kind of brother any little sister could hope for. But I didn't realize that till the end had embraced me. He comforted me in emotional ways, and was always there to make a scene. Though we had your typical big brother, little sister relationship, it was more. He knew me, and I knew him. We knew each other's little tricks, secrets, never the less, for open blackmail. Now I'm trying to hide those kinds of things. Because it's just a reminder, of how truly close we were.

But now all of these qualities are slowly fading into the back ground of our lives, for me it's still a secret struggle, for weakness is not my strong point. Whenever someone mentions death, or whenever I have too much time to think. It creeps back up on me. Like someone on a continuous enragement, to the point of annoyance. Like a stab in the back. Sometimes I forget that he's gone. That I have no one here holding onto my hand telling me that it's all going to be okay. My life was so complete; I owed all of that to **A Boy Named Joshua.** (I love you bro, Love Snoopy)

What I have learned:

1. When someone mentions suicide, consider they might be serious,
2. Material things do not compare to the time you spend with your children and being emotionally available for them,
3. Volunteer; never get so busy that you forget about other's needs. Life has gotten so busy, I forgot about the most

important things in life, like loving other people and volunteering. For example, volunteering for worthy causes like suicide walks, breast cancer walks. Show compassion for other people's heartaches and struggles.

How could I have come so far
(and always on such dark trails)
I must have traveled by the light
shining from the faces
of all those I have loved

Thomas McGrath

Toni
July 28, 1988 – March 27, 1997

Toni

Died from HIV Disease

By Dawn

She was such a sad-looking thing when she arrived at my home—
she weighed ten pounds and was covered with sores and scabs,
unable to sit alone, her wispy hair plastered to a pinched, little,
oddly sallow face. Although she looked like a two-month-old baby,
Antonia was almost ten months old. She was placed in my home
by Child Protective Services because her young mother was unable
to care for her, a very sick baby suffering from AIDS. She had the
sweetest smile, and when she looked at me with her big brown eyes,
I loved her immediately.

That April day in 1989 started as days usually did for me and my
house full of kids. I had been a foster parent for nearly 18 years. I
had quit my job as a registered nurse to stay home to be a full time
parent to foster children. The "medical" kids I took allowed me to
use my nursing skills and at the same time be with my youngest as
she grew up. That day, I had my own daughters; Amy, almost five
and Beth,18; three-month-old Sam, a crack baby;' and my teenage
foster daughters, Sheilah, Jessica, and Karen. Around dinner time,
I got a call from Children's' Services, asking whether I would accept a nine month old with AIDS and her two-year-old uninfected
sister. I didn't really have an opening, but I told them I would take
the baby if they couldn't find a place for her. At midnight, they
called to say they had been unsuccessful in finding a home. If I

would take the baby, the mom would take the sister home with her. Looking back, I realize that the child was meant to be mine—and how close I came to never knowing her.

In 1989, awareness of HIV/AIDS was pretty limited. There was a lot of confusion about how it might be spread. Many people were sure the government was covering up important information; others were sure that the information about risks and transmission were inaccurate and feared that children biting each other, mosquito bites, and other means of casual contact might spread the disease. I taught HIV/AIDS training courses for some time for foster parents and for the Red Cross. I also worked as a volunteer for Northwest AIDS Foundation, so I felt confident that we would be OK and our risk of infection was low.

When I first saw Antonia, I was taken with how thin and sick she was. She looked as I expected a child with AIDS to look. I was sure all infected children looked like her and certainly this was how the only other child I knew with AIDS looked before his death. Sores and scabs all over her feet and legs made her look as if she had boots on. There was so little area that wasn't covered with sores that it made my heart break. She also had scars from past bouts of chicken pox and scabies. She had drenching night sweats and suffered from chronic diarrhea. In spite of how awful she looked and what her body was putting her through, she was very happy and smiled and laughed easily.

The next week, I took Antonia to the HIV clinic at Children's' Hospital. The medical staff was thrilled that she had been placed in foster care. They had been concerned about the lack of follow through with her medical care but were hesitant to have her removed from her mother. For one thing, there was little that could be done for kids with AIDS; and second, if the mother and baby were both going to die anyway, why not let them remain together? The dilemma was resolved when the mom voluntarily placed her baby in foster care because she was so overwhelmed by the baby's medical needs.

At the clinic, we had a long discussion about whether Antonia should be in a home with fewer children, therefore exposing her to fewer to infections. The doctor said she doubted the baby would live much beyond her first birthday, so it would be good for her to have a somewhat normal life and be able to play with other kids. The child was also enrolled in a study that allowed her to have the drug, AZT, the first drug to fight the AIDS virus. The drug still wasn't available to many adult AIDS patients, so it was wonderful that she would be able to be on it. So Toni settled into our house and became part of our family.

The change in her was amazing! Her skin cleared up, she gained weight, and began to catch up on her developmental milestones. The combination of AZT, good medical care, and lots of love and nurturing made her into a pretty normal toddler by her first birthday. The grim prognosis was almost forgotten. I knew that AZT had a limited effectiveness and eventually she would become resistant to it. I was sure that by that time there would be more drugs available. It became easy to forget that she was a sick child. Certainly no one would be able to pick Toni out of a crowd as someone with AIDS. We celebrated her first birthday surrounded by adoring friends and relatives at our favorite park. Toni was very busy and quite an imp!

A few months after Toni was placed in my home, I was asked to take Kayla, a 19-month-old with AIDS. Kayla was a beautiful, blonde child with a round face and rosy cheeks. She was the opposite in coloring from dark, Native American, Toni, who had a thin face and body. Toni, Kayla, and Sam were all close in their development, so it was a lot of fun dancing with them to music from The Nutcracker and playing baby games. They thrived on the competition for attention and waited eagerly for their turn to spin in the air to the music. They were like a little pack as they roamed the house in their walkers. Toni was much more active while Kayla spent more of her time staying near me.

I hoped that Kayla would have the same positive response that Toni had to AZT but she was far sicker. She had a number of hospitalizations before she died at the hospital in my arms, nine days after her second birthday. It was absolutely devastating to our whole family. It was difficult to find comfort. I struggled to find a meaning in the whole thing. How could this be allowed to happen to such a sad, beautiful young child? Why did she have to suffer? Every time I thought about her, I cried, and because she was all I could think of, I cried constantly. The kids got used to me having tears running my face and quit asking what was wrong.

The children seemed to handle her death well. They cried and were very sad. I wanted to get everyone signed up for counseling, but none of them felt they needed to go. They said it was OK and fairly quickly went on with their normal everyday activities. I know they all think of her from time to time and were affected by her death. Karen named her first child Kayla Marie after our little angel.

During that time, I was lucky to have a volunteer from Shanti, an emotional support organization for people affected by AIDS. Marie Annette was wonderful and was there with me for the good times—the positive milestones Toni was making—as well as for the loss of Kayla. She was at the hospital with me when Kayla died. Marie Annette, the HIV social worker, Kayla's doctor, and I sat for a couple of hours as I held the baby after she died. We talked about the tragedy of it all and cried out of frustration and loss.

Marie Annette and I planned a beautiful memorial service that helped the family, friends, the professionals who had been involved in her care, and me deal with the loss of that sweet baby. We made it as personal and meaningful as we could. Examining her life helped the process of grieving. I cried daily for months because I could only think about what a tragedy it was and what a sad, short life she had. I searched for a meaning to it all. I looked for anything I could to find something positive in her loss. Knowing she was loved and that she had happy times in her short life was comforting. Gradually it got better, and I found I wasn't crying myself to sleep every night. As a year passed, I found that I cried less and less. It still is a tragedy. I miss her and think of her often and still cry for her.

Life for us went on and Toni thrived! Some of the foster kids left and were replaced with new ones, an ever-changing combination of personalities and problems. Toni loved them all and with her feisty disposition, she was usually the center of attention, although not always for positive reasons.

When she was two, Toni took the wallpaper off the bedroom walls. I mean ALL the wallpaper! She climbed on things, and it didn't take long before she mastered getting out of her crib. The only way we could keep her in bed to get any rest, was to put a harness on her or give her sedatives...we chose the harness. She really needed her rest whether she thought so or not!

Because HIV-infected children lag behind in many areas, it was important to get as much help for Toni as possible, so we started her in developmental preschool. She loved it! The school had a combination of normal developing kids and handicapped ones. It was perfect for her. The staff knew that Toni was HIV infected, but they were loving and supportive; they treated her like any other kid.

For her third birthday, Toni got a tricycle. It had 101 Dalmatians on it and a basket on the back to put things in. She filled it with toys, rocks, dirt—whatever she fancied that day. Toni definitely was not a girly girl. She looked funny in fancy dresses and seemed to be a dirt magnet. She loved rocks, sticks, trucks, and cars. She had baby dolls that she liked, and she played with a toy kitchen, but given a choice, she would prefer to be outdoors in the dirt. Fortunately, she also loved baths.

The September after her third her birthday, Toni started Seattle Public Schools in the Early Childhood Education Program. Again, she had a loving, accepting teacher. We didn't tell everyone her diagnosis, just the teacher, nurse, and principal. There was a lot of discussion about who needed to know, but I felt that what we were doing was adequate and stuck to that. I felt that everyone should be using universal precautions in handling body fluids; all people are treated as if they are infected, in a universal-precautions regime because so many people don't know what their status is. If Toni got hurt, the staff should be handling the wound appropriately to prevent the spread of HIV. Concern about how other parents would react to the news that there was an infected child in their child's class was the major reason I felt we should limit the information; mostly it was to make life easier for the school than fear for Toni's safety.

Her health was good and monthly trips to clinic were about all we had to do besides give her medications. I was sure she was beating the HIV. Our biggest problem was keeping her in the yard and off the tops of tall things. It didn't take long for her to get away from the yard when whoever was watching her turned his or her back. We got a fence, but we had to constantly check to make sure that people remembered to latch the gate. By the time she was four, however, she could get the gate open and be out of sight on her tricycle in seconds.

Once, she was found down the hill at the neighborhood grocery store with a cart of food and no money to pay for it. She was so disappointed that they wouldn't let her have the stuff! We had a talk about money and its purpose. A few weeks later she got three-quarters of a mile away to the neighborhood shopping area, where she was attempting to shop again. This time, she had two pennies to pay for her groceries. I went out in the car to look for her and found her on a street corner with a store employee, who was waiting for us to show up. In spite of our attempts to keep her from getting the gate open, she continued to be an escape artist. By far the scariest time was when she disappeared and was found by a policeman as she was heading down the very steep Magnolia Bridge in an attempt to go to town. If he hadn't been passing by at that time, I don't know what would have happened to her.

Eventually, Toni was diagnosed with Fetal Alcohol Effect and ADHD and at about age five, started on Ritalin. It made a big difference, and it was obvious to everyone when she missed a dose. The drug didn't mean she became a docile, quiet child—it just made her more capable of paying attention to the way she was supposed to behave and to be more compliant. In spite of the improvement, she continued to be a challenge and needed constant supervision.

By the time Toni was four, the AZT had lost its effectiveness and her T-cell (CD-4) count fell. Toni was started on a long list of drugs that each had a progressively shorter period of effectiveness. They tasted awful and it was a wonder she could get any of them down. Because her T cell counts were low, she had little immune response to disease. She constantly had thrush and started to have fairly frequent bouts of chicken pox; she had more than 30 episodes in her life. Toni became so matter of fact about having them that it didn't faze her; she just hated missing school.

Because I saw her every day, I didn't notice she was getting thinner and thinner until I got some film back after her sixth birthday and realized how awful she looked. She ate well and drank a nutritional supplement, but the virus consumed so many calories that there was no way she could eat enough to grow. Eventually, the doctor decided Toni should have a feeding (gastrostomy) tube placed in her stomach so she could be given extra calories at night as she slept. The day she came home from the hospital, she ran into the bedroom where another child with a G-tube was. Toni pulled up her shirt and said, "Look, Andrea, I have one, too!" She was so amazingly adaptive, and things just didn't get her down. The tube feedings worked for a while. She gained a little weight but was still painfully thin. Finding clothes that didn't look odd was difficult, and she really looked worse than ever in "foo-foo" clothes. At least with the tube in place, she didn't have to taste the awful medication.

I remember how difficult it was for me when she first began to have frequent hospital stays. It wasn't too bad in the beginning, when she felt well but had to be in for IV antibiotics or some other minor thing. She had a pretty easy time because she was so friendly and she loved having volunteers at her beck and call. But it was difficult for me to give over her care to someone else because I wanted to make sure everything was done the right way. I felt that if I gave up the routine I had for things, that if a dose of her medication was late, it would give the virus a stronghold and she would die. I got into some battles with staff over that. Toni had done so well for so long, I just didn't want to tempt fate.

Just before she went to first grade, we moved to a new neighborhood. It was difficult because we had been so secure knowing Toni was accepted at school. Now we didn't know whether we would find the same with the new neighbors and school. I talked to the school nurse and told her about Toni and her diagnosis. Toni was in the hospital and therefore would start school late. The nurse, in her enthusiasm to make sure things would go well, told a number of other staff members, violating school policy as well as state law. Again, as in the past, I felt it was important to limit the number of people who knew. Now that she was sick, I also wanted everyone to know her for who she was, not just as a kid with AIDS. I wanted them to judge her for being Toni, nothing else. After a number of meetings, we settled on a list of need-to-know people, which included the ones that had been told without permission. The list certainly included more people than I wanted and fewer than the school wanted. But when Toni finally started school, it worked beautifully. She had a great teacher that she adored.

That October, Toni was in the hospital for an infection. She was happy as usual and felt quite well. We had just come back from the playroom when her Infectious Disease doctor and the HIV nurse practitioner came to talk to me. They were very somber and asked to have someone take Toni so they could talk to me alone. That really scared me - there had never been a time when that had happened. The doctor said Toni had a positive culture for MAI. I had never heard of it so I wasn't too concerned, after all, she'd had a number of infections. She went on to say that MAI is an opportunistic organism that ultimately affects all the organs and statistically people rarely live more than a year after becoming infected with it. I forced myself to listen and not become the hysterical parent. I tried to ask coherent questions but had a hard time thinking what to ask. I just felt numb. I couldn't bear to think about it. I was so sure that we were doing well at keeping the disease at bay and here they were telling me she would be dead soon. How could that be? My poor Toni! Poor me! What would I do without her? My first urge was to take her home and give her everything she wanted. I would spoil her and make sure she was having the happiest life she could. I would let her spend the rest of her life doing what she wanted so she would never be unhappy. Fortunately, that thought went away fairly soon.

I decided that the best life I could give her was one that was as normal as possible. She had a need and right to have the same expectations as other kids have. One of my favorite books as a child was *The Secret Garden*. I remembered what a tyrant Colin had become because he was expected to die and people spoiled him. I wanted people to like Toni and continue to be happy to see her. I didn't want to have people avoiding her because she was a brat. Security would come from knowing what was expected of her and what she could expect from the adults in her life. I continued to treat her the way I always had and expected the same from others. It was one of the best decisions I ever made.

I was worried that my plan wasn't going to work, when in December she started to do a lot of acting out. She would be very angry, have temper tantrums, and run away. No one could figure out what the problem was. She did have ADHD. She probably felt awful much of the time, she might have been scared because of the changes she was going through, and she certainly had been in the hospital a lot. In addition, she had constant thrush, both in her mouth and in her throat. She was on major amounts of drugs, had chronic diarrhea, and frequent vomiting. She had started to wet the bed after one of her many bouts of chicken pox. I am sure she was confused and scared, even though she never said anything about it. A Child Life Specialist started to do medical play with her, and I signed her up for counseling so she would have someone away from the family and the hospital to talk to. It was a rough time. I was torn between telling her about dying, in case she was worried, and not wanting to scare her because we didn't really know when. I decided not to tell her but have the experts look for signs that she was concerned about it. I spent endless hours worrying about whether it was the right decision. When I look back, I know I did the right thing for us, as the months passed, her behavior improved and nobody ever knew why she had been acting out.

In early January, Toni's vomiting turned to violent retching and severe abdominal pain. She was admitted to the hospital with acute pancreatitis. It was very frightening because she had such unbearable pain, with hours and hours of retching. She was so much sicker than she had ever been before, and everyone worried that we would lose her. She was heavily medicated and disorientated. I prayed frantically for her to get through it. I couldn't spend nights there because I had to go home and take care of my other kids. When I was home I couldn't sleep and called the hospital every few hours. If I wasn't able to reach someone (there weren't any Unit Coordinators at night), I was nervous that there was an emergency with her. I felt guilty that I wasn't there with her and desperate until I could be reassured she was OK.

I found myself angry with the staff when they didn't respond to her immediately or when they gave medications late. They let her do what she wanted and didn't give her a regular schedule, the very thing that kept her centered. If she could do what she wanted; stay up all night, be rude, and so on, the hospital might become a place where she would look forward to being rather than at home. I wanted her to dislike it enough to work to be healthy. The nurses avoided me when they could, and the CNAs were afraid to take care of her for fear I would be critical of them. It wasn't that I was mean or that I said hateful things, it was just that I needed to be in control all the time. It became so awful for us all that I decided one morning when her linens didn't get changed, to go to the Nurse Manager to complain. I went into the office and as I told her about my frustrations with the staff, I began to cry. As we talked, I realized that the real problem was my frustration with having no control over the disease. I was trying to stop the disease and blamed the staff for many things over which they had little control. We decided that it would help my frustrations with the quality of her care to pick some "primary" nurses so there would be people who knew her well and would get to know my expectations, too. I was surprised when, in looking at the staff, the RN I felt was the best suited to meet Toni's and my needs was the nurse who had made me angry enough to go to the manager in the first place. It was a perfect choice.

I made a list of the things Toni was not allowed to do and a schedule of naps, bedtimes, and so on, so she would have the same schedule and expectations at the hospital as she had at home. It worked beautifully. Life became better for all involved. One of the staff put all the rules on poster board, which was brought out and posted at each admission until one time between hospitalizations it disappeared. But by then everyone knew the way things were supposed to be, and I was a little less rigid.

The changes made it easier for me to not have to be at Toni's bedside all the time to make sure things were done the "right way." I knew that if her primary nurse was on, I could get things done at home. That didn't mean that I gave up control or that I wasn't frustrated and frustrating. I still got angry, but eventually they got to know me well enough to tell me when my expectations were too much.

Because Toni's condition was tenuous, we decided to it was important to tell the people at school about her having AIDS. We felt it was best to tell the school staff and then at a later date, tell the students. The HIV social worker; a representative from the school district, and I went to a staff meeting and discussed Toni's condition and answered questions. As at the other schools, they were curious but very supportive.

Toni, in her amazing way, bounced back; her pain got better and she went home. She was discharged on codeine but was pretty much her usual busy self. Because almost the only thing that can be done to treat pancreatitis is to rest the intestinal tract, Toni was sent home on TPN, concentrated IV nutrition. It had to be run continuously, so she carried it in a backpack and had to go to school with it. She obviously was different from the other kids because she went around the school beeping when something happened with the infusion pump. It didn't faze her a bit; she was so accepting of whatever she had to do.

One clinic visit threw me for a loop, though, when the Pain Management Team came in to talk to me about pain control for the future. I knew Toni's disease was expected to shorten her life, and I knew she was getting sick but had never ever thought that she would experience pain in the process. I had visions of her dying peacefully in my arms as we sat on the deck watching the sunset or something beautiful like that. Pain was not part of the picture! I was so scared that I had a difficult time listening to them. I think I may have been really short with them and possibly rude, too; I really don't remember, it was so surreal. I was angry that they brought me such awful news. When they talked about beginning to use some routine narcotic pain medication, like morphine, I wanted to scream and cry. It took all my strength to continue to listen to them. They talked about palliative care and hospice when I wasn't ready to think that this was more than a temporary setback. Toni seemed like the same kid I had before, so to think that she was expected to die in the near future was unbelievable! The Pain Team was patient and said they would be developing a plan for her present and future pain and that we would be talking again. I felt my heart would break, it hurt so much. I did my best to keep my fears and worry from Toni and continue to be as matter-of-fact about her illness as I could.

After Toni was back in school for about one month, we decided to tell the students about her illness. Some of the students were beginning to ask questions about Toni and why she had the backpack, and so on. A lot of thought and planning went into it. On the designated day, the school crisis team went from class to class and talked about AIDS and told the children about Toni, answering any questions they had. Amy went to the fourth and fifth grade classes with the team, to talk about Toni from a sister's standpoint. Toni was in the hospital, so she wasn't involved in person. A letter was sent to the parents, saying the kids might be discussing what they had been told, and a parent meeting was scheduled for the next week.

I was very apprehensive the night of the parent meeting. I didn't know what to expect—after all, there had been incidents of homes being firebombed and other forms of harassment against people with AIDS. When I arrived, there were 15 or 20 parents in the room, mostly women. The principal, the crisis team, the hospital social worker, and a representative from the school district were also there. After a brief description of what had been covered with the students and some basic HIV information. I was asked to talk about Toni. After that, there was an opportunity for discussion. I talked about Toni and what she was going through. I was amazed as each person spoke during the discussion period; they said were there to make sure that no one caused problems for Toni. I almost cried! I was so relieved!

By now, things had changed and life became a constant round of hospitalizations, IVs, medications, trips to the clinic and the Emergency Room, transfusions, vomiting, diarrhea, and varying amounts of pain. We worked closely with the pain team, and I found that it was actually one of my greatest sources of strength, control, and comfort to know she didn't have to have unbearable pain. I learned that there were various interventions that could be used to control her pain as well as many drugs that would help. There was now a plan that would automatically go into effect whenever Toni had to be admitted. She was put on routine doses of methadone because it was long acting. If she had "breakthrough" pain, she would get morphine.

Through all of this, Toni stayed surprisingly happy and accepting of it all. She had a growing list of fans. She knew all the caregivers' names and whether they had kids or not. No matter how awful she was feeling, she would ask others how they were and was genuinely interested in their answer She thanked the lab personnel when they drew blood, the IV Team when they had to start IVs, and the rest of the staff whenever they did anything for her. Volunteers loved her, and because she was in-house often, they knew her well and always were happy to see her. She still had to be on Ritalin or she was impulsive and made dangerous decisions. By then, the staff knew the importance of having her doses given on time.

I found myself alternating in hope and despair. I searched the news for any word of new medications being offered. I asked the HIV team regularly what was happening with clinical trials. I called the National AIDS hotline and signed up for newsletters and other types of information. I went to the White House with a group of other mothers to meet with the president to ask for increased AIDS funding.

I helped form a support group for parents of HIV-infected children. In the beginning, there were quite a few mothers coming but as Toni got sicker and a few other kids died, the parents of kids who were doing well faded away; they just didn't want to think about that future for their child (and in many cases, themselves). I found it a comfort to be able to rant and cry and have someone listen to how I felt. It was one place where I didn't have to put on a brave front; I could be scared and angry and speak honestly. I was sad that some of the other parents who worried about the future of their children didn't feel safe in going. I found myself with frequent pain in my chest and worried about having a heart attack; I had skipped beats. When I went to the doctor, he said it was stress. I did my best to be calm and positive around Toni and the rest of the family so they wouldn't worry.

When Toni was younger, Make-A-Wish Foundation granted her wish to go to Disneyland. She'd loved every minute of it and always wanted to go back. When one of her little friends from HIV Clinic chose Disneyland for her Wish, we all decided that it would be fun to have both families go at the same time. We got the tickets and were looking excitedly towards April and Spring Break so we could be on our way. Toni talked about it constantly and could hardly wait to see Mickey. Planning was complicated because we had to get special permission for my foster children to leave the state plus Toni was on the continuous IV feedings and medications that she carried in her backpack. We hoped it would all work out but knew it would be worth all the planning. We could hardly wait!

But at the end of March, Toni was rushed to the hospital with severe abdominal pain and retching and was again diagnosed with pancreatitis. She was sent to the Intensive Care Unit with pulmonary edema, renal insufficiency, and an enlarged heart. When she went up to the Unit, she was admitted to the same room where Kayla died. I was sure it was a bad omen; I was so scared, and all the feelings of Kayla's death came back. The pain Toni experienced was more frightening than ever and she was so very ill, I was sure she was dying! I was very relieved when she improved enough to be returned to the Medical Unit.

She still had excruciating pain and a long way to go to get through it; she wasn't out of the woods yet. She was given massive amounts of pain medication, and constant changes were made in treating the illness. It was difficult for the doctor on duty to get away from Toni's room for very long because she was so ill. The focus had become keeping Toni alive long enough to get to Disneyland.

As she improved a bit and became more aware of her surroundings, she became her social self again. She looked so sick and I know she felt awful much of the time, but she was still happy to see people. "The Lion King" came out on video; she watched it three or four times a day. Because of the medications or because she was still so sick, each time Toni saw it was as if she was seeing it for the first time. She would get so frustrated with me if I didn't look up every time she wanted me to look at a part of it. With each viewing, she would cry when the dad died and laugh about how dumb she thought Ed the hyena was. I was certainly glad when she improved enough to at least remember she had seen it before. "The Lion King" remained one of her favorite movies.

As the days progressed, her condition fluctuated from better to worse and back again. I feared any call from the hospital and on the occasions a nurse would call to say Toni wasn't doing well, I would jump in the car and pray frantically the whole way that she would be alive when I got there. Then, after a couple of weeks, she began to hold onto the improvements and make some headway. It looked like it might be possible to make it to California. She had a lot of visits from doctors and other staff that had taken care of her over the past years. They were so happy to see her improved and more like her old self. They would bring her gifts and play games or watch "The Lion King" with her. A number of times I went into her room and found one of the residents sitting there while she slept—amazed that she was still alive.

On April 17th, after enormous amounts of planning, Toni went on a pass from the hospital to Disneyland. It was quite an undertaking because we had to adjust her medications, take her drugs along, and have a place to go to give her IV infusions of antibiotics and other drugs throughout the day. It was such a relief to be on our way! The first evening, we met our friends at the Disneyland Hotel to have dinner at a restaurant that features Disney characters. She was so excited and the look on her face as she talked to them was so full of joy that every bit of money and work was worth it a hundred times over. That image of her is forever imprinted in my mind, and brings tears to my eyes when I think about it. It was pure happiness!

The next morning, we rented a wheelchair and went to the "Happiest Place on Earth." We were so glad that she was alive and having a good time. We had to make regular stops at the park's infirmary to do her infusions and to give her a rest because she would become exhausted, but we did see most of the park and rode many of the rides. We also watched the Lion King Parade twice a day; she was thrilled! The other family was generous in letting Toni go along when they had a private meeting with Jasmine and Jafar from "Aladdin." Toni was delighted as she carried on a private conversation with the characters. I found myself crying frequently in a combination of joy and sorrow. I felt complete joy that she was able to be there having a good time even as I realized we would never be doing it again. I wondered if we would ever have such a happy time again.

After 72 hours, we returned to Seattle, and Toni went back to her room at the hospital, exhausted but exhilarated! She stayed in the hospital another ten days, watching "The Lion King" with new enthusiasm and telling everyone she could about her wonderful trip. When she was discharged, we returned to the way of life that had become so normal: IVs, medications, clinic and ER visits, and so on. Toni went back to school and was welcomed with open arms. She was delighted to be back!

That July, Toni got to be a Sea Fair Junior Princess and ride in a parade with a crown, bouquet, sash, and trophy. She was selected through Make-a-Wish, along with another girl her age who had cancer. It was very exciting for her but difficult to find a dress that was pretty but at the same time didn't look funny on her. We eventually found the perfect one—made of blue denim with a lace collar. She looked lovely. There was a story on TV about it, and they got to meet the grown-up Sea Fair princesses, who made a big fuss over the girls, teaching them how to wave. She was in the hospital, so for a while it looked as she might not be able to be in the parade. But she was discharged the day before, so there she was, IV running, waving like a pro. I couldn't help weeping as did many of the other people watching the parade.

A few days after the parade was Toni's seventh birthday, and we had a huge party for her. It was a birthday I wasn't sure she would have, so it certainly was a celebration of her life. I couldn't overlook my fear that it might be her last, making it bittersweet. There were fifty or sixty people there to help in the festivities, all with the similar feelings. She had a wonderful time, surrounded by people who loved her.

One day around the time of her birthday, I realized Toni wasn't following instructions very well and seemed to have a hard time understanding things. The first thought I had was that she was suffering from AIDS dementia. I had known other infected kids who had gone through that before their deaths and had seen it frequently with adults. I was so alarmed and didn't know what I would do if it were true. After watching her for a few days I noticed that she did fine if she was looking at me but not if she wasn't. I realized she very rapidly was losing her hearing. I took her to the Audiology clinic, where they confirmed she had hearing losses in both ears.

They weren't sure if it was caused by a virus she was born with or by the antibiotics she received frequently; many were known to be ototoxic but there was no other choice but to use them. As time passed, her hearing continued to deteriorate. Within a few months, she had to use hearing aids in both ears. Later a special amplification system was used at school to help her hear the teacher in class. As usual, Toni took it all in stride and remained cheerful and happy most of the time.

Toni's mother, Martha, and I had a long conversation about what kind of services we should have after Toni died: it was extremely painful to even think about it. We both cried a lot but as difficult as it was, I am glad we did it then. It would have been so much more difficult to talk about later. Even though we all thought that Martha would outlive Toni, she died the following October, at 26 years of age.

The next spring, we had to move again. I bought a house in a suburb close to Seattle but it meant that we would again have to face the possibility that people might not accept Toni and her disease. So that she would have as little disruption as possible, we kept her in her old school until the end of the school year. It gave us a chance to develop a terrific plan for her schooling in the new district.

She had a wonderful, caring group of teachers at the new school, and Toni loved them all and adored going to school. We decided to follow the same model about telling this school her condition that we had used in her previous one; we would let them get to know her, then tell the teachers and later the students. The problem was that Toni was asked to do publicity for Northwest AIDS Foundation, so there were newspaper articles and TV stories about her. We sped up the plan and told the teachers in the end of September but didn't make any announcement to the students. We would wait to see if there would be any repercussions. A few students and bus drivers asked about her but there was no big problem, which was a relief.

I could see changes in Toni's condition and feared she knew she was really sick and would die. I regularly questioned the professionals involved to make sure Toni wasn't worried about it. Every indication showed she was OK, but I did talk to her frequently about how much I loved her, and that no matter where we were, we would always be in each other's hearts. We always sang a lot and her favorite songs were ones that talked about love. Whenever a song said, "I love you," Toni would look at me with a big smile and we would point at each other. She drew pictures that always had smiling faces, bright colors, and me and her. She learned to write, "I love you, Mom" and sent me frequent notes. Even now on occasion, I find a note or picture she gave me in a drawer or between the pages of a book. They are a sign to me that she is still around and wants me to know she still loves me.

The summer of Toni's eighth birthday was phenomenal! Like other kids, she spent a lot of time in our backyard pool. Her sister, Martha, spent time with us and the girls had a wonderful time together. Martha was so sweet and gentle but seemed sometimes to carry the weight of the world on her shoulders. It certainly had to be difficult to have her Mom, sister, and Dad infected with HIV. We all positively cherished her and felt like she was a part of our family. We hoped she knew how important she was and still is to us.

In late summer, Toni's hospitalizations got more frequent, and the side effects of so many of the drugs became more apparent. She had the Cushinoid changes in her body that came from the use of large doses of steroids: thin arms and legs, thick belly, and very puffy face; her hair fell out in clumps, and she continued to have violent retching.

Because of her chronic pancreatitis, she couldn't eat but the steroids made her hungry so occasionally we would find her sneaking food. One night, I found her with a croissant in bed with her. It was a combination of sad and funny. We looked for things that she could have that wouldn't cause a flare up of her symptoms. She was happy with that and would spend time reading the labels of foods to check the fat content—no fat, she could have it! It broke my heart to see how happy a little juice or Jell-O could make her.

October came and with it a new problem. Toni started to have pain in her legs. The medical team discovered she had osteomyelitis. After treatment with strong IV antibiotics, she still had to have surgery to remove the infection. The orthopedic surgeon did his best to remove all of it but was unsuccessful, so she had to continue on drugs to treat it. She was in a wheelchair for two months but took that in stride as she usually did.

December was a wonderful month! Toni was home the whole month, and Christmas was beautiful. We had a couple of toddlers living with us, and Toni had a great time with them. We went to see Santa, drove to see the Christmas lights, and went to parties. The highlight was going to see The Nutcracker performed by the Pacific NW Ballet Company. Toni almost burst with delight as she sat in the Opera House, watching the dancers. She loved the music; maybe because we had danced to it when she was a baby. We had a copy of the movie version, and she loved to dress up in long ballet costumes left from the days of Beth's dance recitals. Toni often "performed" using one of our wooden nutcrackers as a partner; I'm sure she saw herself as Clara, graceful and lovely. For the next few weeks, she wanted to watch the movie of The Nutcracker over and over. At least it wasn't "The Lion King"!

The day after New Year's, Toni became ill again and was in the hospital for a week. She came home for a few days and then went back again. It was that way for the months of January and February. She was cheerful but slower and still having frequent bouts of nausea and vomiting. She started to have problems producing enough of certain blood cells and became jaundiced. Her spleen needed to be removed but she couldn't have surgery safely because she didn't have enough platelets to keep her from bleeding excessively. All we could do was wait and hope things improved.

A lovely thing happened during one of her hospital stays in February when I got to go to court and have Toni's last name changed to mine. She was ecstatic and wore a nametag saying, "My name is Toni English" so everyone would know.

The afternoon of the clinic visit after one hospitalization, the doctor called to say Toni's labs had come back and were showing some alarming changes in her liver function tests; she needed to go in to be admitted. I wasn't too disturbed because she had problems with them before. She wasn't happy about being admitted, but we packed her things to head in. As usual, she chose the items that she wanted to take: the first things to go along were her stuffed Barney, a bag of videotapes, and the comforter from her bed with Disney characters on it. Those were the things that always went along to make her room as homelike as possible. She also took along a variety of other objects that struck her fancy this time: Tabitha, a stuffed cat and Sara, a pink fuzzy bear. We said, good-bye to everyone and left. No one paid much attention to her departure because it was not unusual.

As we drove along the lake toward the hospital, we played "Slugbug" and sang songs. Toni was happy and chatty even though she didn't feel well, frequently telling me that she loved me. We had taken that same trip to be admitted forty-one times before, and yet this is the only one I remember. It is as clear today as it was the day we drove it.

Toni settled in to a room and routine that was all too familiar to us: many of the staff dropping in to see her, setting up her hospital schooling, going to the playroom and doing the other things she did when she was there. February 27—it was just so very ordinary.

That night she developed a fever and more pain but the next day was feeling well enough to get out of bed to play in her room. The physicians did tests and procedures, including a trip to surgery to have a bone-marrow biopsy. She developed another fever and cough and slept more after the test; she also needed a transfusion. As usual, I wasn't very worried and was sure she would rebound as she had done so many times before.

The night of March third, I was called because Toni was having increased pain and high fever. When I got to the hospital, I was told her prognosis was grim and they doubted Toni would live more than a few days. It was so blunt that my first response was disbelief and shock. Then I went into a protective mode; I was going to make sure that Toni would be protected and given nothing to worry about. My initial impulse was to take her home. I remembered my vision of her dying peacefully on our deck, looking at the mountains and water, much like Barbara Hershey's character did in "Beaches." I cried and became angry when a nurse whom I thought wasn't capable was assigned to take care of her that night. I was so upset that I said I would take her home right then. A compromise was reached; another nurse was assigned for the night; and in the morning, I was able to talk to people who knew Toni well.

The staff and I discussed all the options: my taking her home and handling care of her alone, using Hospice, or having her stay in the hospital. Most people I spoke to thought hospice was the answer, but then I had a long conversation with the HIV nurse. She felt the hospital was filled with people Toni knew and loved. Many people loved her in return, and staying there would allow her to continue to see them. It was easier to bring home to the hospital than to bring the hospital home. She was right, and that is what we did. Toni was moved to a bigger room that was sunny and had a large window seat. I went there as soon as I got the other kids off to school and stayed until Toni went to bed at night. I would make a trip home to spend some time with the kids after school during the time Toni had a volunteer to occupy her. My son took care of the kids at home and was a lifesaver because he handled the day-to-day managing of the home. I just had to worry about Toni and make sure the other kids didn't feel forgotten during this time. Of course, I had lots of practice with that over those last three years.

Two days later, Toni was up and playing and singing. She was silly and loved to use the hand gestures for "you drive me crazy" whenever she could find an opportunity. I was back to thinking that this was one more of the close calls we had had so many times before. She was still happy and talkative, so I wasn't worried. She'd been sick so many times—I just assumed this was the same.

But this time, Toni continued to have bleeding problems from the insufficient platelet count. After a few days, she felt too tired to go to the playroom, and volunteers came to her room to play games. She spent a lot of time watching movies; her current favorite was "Matilda," the story of a child who had an absolutely awful life but who developed powers that gave her control over it and all the bad people in it. Toni loved the parts where the evil people got their due. As with "The Lion King," she would watch it more than once a day.

The doctors had regular meetings with me and kept me up to date on the latest information but were concerned that I just was in denial about the grim outlook. I could see the changes in Toni: she had less energy, she slept more, she suffered more jaundice, but at the same time, I saw that she still loved entertaining visitors, playing games, and having me there. I tried to keep a balance between hopeful optimism and despair. I wasn't giving up hope, but still knew this was very serious. I tried to be calm and not appear too delusional. I was so afraid that I would be taken less seriously if I was too far from the place where they were and was constantly doing checks to make sure I was seen as rational.

Toward the middle of the month, Toni was unable to go much farther than the bathroom. She would sit in a chair beside her bed to play and receive visitors. She was still alert and pleasant and played games. I still spent as much time with her as I could.

The meetings with the medical team became more difficult. They wanted to discontinue the aggressive treatment that was being done to manage Toni's blood counts. Her liver was failing rapidly, so she needed frequent transfusions of various blood products. They were also concerned about her pain. While I didn't want her to be in pain, it had been such a constant part of her life, I knew it was controllable. The Pain Management Team came twice a day and were very responsive to her needs. Most of the time the pain was pretty well-managed, although she was receiving large amounts of narcotics and the doses had to be changed frequently. Often the only time the HIV staff saw her was when she was having pain or in the morning when she was sleeping. They didn't see her interact with visitors and staff as I did. I felt they were making a horrible, permanent decision, based on a few minutes out of her day. I wasn't willing to cease anything at that time. I knew I would know when it was time to stop. They agreed to send her to surgery to have her spleen removed to see whether that would help the bleeding. The doctor who had done all of her other operations did the surgery and was hopeful that this would help; he also felt that because this was Toni, the "come-back kid," he wasn't giving up on her either.

I started having chest pains. I felt that there was a giant weight on my chest and I was on the verge of crying all the time. I tried to not cry when I was with Toni but as soon as I left the room, I would break down. I told her how much I loved her and that no matter what I would always be with her. I talked to the Child Life Specialist and hospice people about what to say to her. We decided that I should continue the way I had always done. Some of the staff related stories of children that "hung on" because their parents hadn't given "permission" for them to die, some who died immediately after the parent left the room. I found myself with a list of fears: that she would die when I wasn't there, that she would die alone, that she would be afraid and/or she would be in pain when she died. If I went home, I called numerous times to make sure she was OK. I ate in her room, rather than in the cafeteria. If I had to leave to go anywhere, I made sure the staff would check on her regularly or asked someone to stay with her. The pain in my chest increased the whole time I was away from her. I couldn't sleep at night and had frequent nightmares in which she needed me and I wasn't able to reach her. I had one especially awful one where she died without me and I wasn't allowed to see her body and hold her. I woke in a sweat, shaking with fear. I felt ice cold for hours.

She continued to sleep a lot but when someone came to visit, she would wake up and be her social and frequently silly self. She could walk to the bathroom with a lot of help and sat up to watch TV and play short games with volunteers or staff members. Other times she would cry in her sleep, and when we'd wake her to find out what the problem was, she would deny pain and say she "was just dreaming." I would ask her about her dreams later, but she didn't remember them. We held hands a lot and sang the songs we did so many of the times she was in the hospital. In many ways it was so ordinary, it was hard to think that she might soon not be with us. It was unbelievable and hard to reconcile myself to it. I felt torn between hope and despair.

March 20th, Toni started to throw up bright-red blood and had bloody stools. It was very frightening. Again, the doctors asked about not being aggressive in treatment. I found myself angry at the attending physician. She was the most vocal about whether we were doing the right thing for Toni. This doctor was always some-one for whom I had tremendous respect—I admired her— but she was saying things I didn't want to hear. I felt she was giving up too soon. I treated her rudely and argued about her view, even though she was just expressing her opinion and doing her job. She would have been remiss if she hadn't done as she did, but at that time I couldn't see it. I know this was a difficult time for her, too, as she had known Toni since she was small. If there were anything I could go back and do differently, it would be to treat that doctor better.

I started spending nights at the hospital. I had never done that because I felt that it was important to get away from the hospital to see what was going on in the rest of the world and to check on how things were at the house. But being with Toni was the most important thing and my friend would bring the rest of the kids up to see us. The HIV social worker stayed the night, too. Toni liked that and talked about it being a "sleep over". I wondered whether it worried her that we were staying, but she never said anything and was just so happy about it, I didn't care. Many of her primary nurses and staff members stayed after their shifts to spend extra time with her. We made a list of people who wanted to be called to come in if it looked like she was dying. We posted the list at the nurses' station, at her bedside, and in her chart; that way if anything happened, whoever was there, could start calling.

The night of the 23rd, Toni lost a tooth. In the past it had always been a happy thing with her looking forward from a visit from the tooth fairy. In this case it was disastrous! The bleeding wouldn't stop because her clotting was so far off. They called the oral surgeon in the middle of the night to find out whether there was anything that could be done. She packed it with some special clotting material, but that was only partially effective. They had Toni bite on wet tea bags to help with it. They suggested sending her to Intensive Care, but the nurses and I felt she would be better being left in the room she was in with one-on-one nursing. Fortunately, the nursing supervisor agreed. The tea bags had to be changed every hour or so, all night long. It broke my heart to think that such a normal childhood event could be life threatening.

The next day, there was a big care conference with all the HIV team, some of Toni's primary nurses, the medical team, and me.

The doctors told me they felt really uncomfortable with continuing treatment at the level they were doing, when it was futile. I felt they were giving up on her when I was sure she would give me a "sign" when it was time, something she hadn't done. While I was resigned to the fact that she was more than certainly dying, I wasn't sure that it was going to happen soon. I knew how dire things were but felt that she might have a bit more time; after all, they had said three weeks before that she had just a few days. We finally decided that they would continue to treat Toni with blood products until I said to stop. Her condition would be monitored by symptoms only. They would stop doing lab work and frequent vital signs, some of the more awful meds would be discontinued, and they would monitor her intake and output. Emphasis would on Toni's comfort and not on cure.

While I felt this was an acceptable compromise, I still wasn't feeling like it was time to give up. She was still so social and alert and enjoyed visitors and "Matilda." I was still angry at "them" for giving up on her. I had long talks with the Senior Resident about his Hindu beliefs of death and afterlife. I wished I had strong religious beliefs to draw comfort from and hope for a future in some other place. I allowed one of her nurse to pray over her every evening as she finished her shift. Although I don't truly believe in God or Heaven, having the nurse pray, couldn't hurt. And if I were wrong about God, then Toni would be better for it. The next night was especially hard for her, and there was concern because she was difficult to arouse. Everyone felt she was near the end and would die that night. At 2 a.m., the social worker and I took all of Toni's videotapes and donated them to the Emergency Room; I was sure because the tapes were gone, Toni would wake up and want to watch "Matilda" again. If they were in her room, she would die. It worked, and in the morning she opened her eyes and asked me to put the movie on. That is the kind of thing I felt I needed to do to keep her alive—not unlike the rituals sports fans use to bring their team luck.

Over the next few days, there were large numbers of visitors coming to see her. It made me angry in many ways because she had been in the hospital so many times when no one but two of my closest friends and I came to see her. I knew these visits were to meet their needs, not hers, and it made me sad that it was at a time when she didn't have the energy to really enjoy their visit as she would have done in the past. I had the nurse post a sign limiting the amount of time people could stay, and I asked her to come in to tell them when it was time to leave. Toni got many gifts, but she wasn't able to use or appreciate most of them.

Toni continued to bleed, and I continued to agree to the use of blood products to try to correct the problem. And it did slow down. Her pain was well controlled, so she was more alert when she had visitors. She was bothered by the steri-strips left from her surgery. The nurse and I tried to soak them off, but they wouldn't come off. We decided that a bath would be the best answer. She was so sick and it was midnight, but her primary night nurse didn't let that stop her. She recruited a whole host of helpers, including some of the medical residents who were taking care of Toni and even some who weren't. We were quite a parade as we went down the hall to the tub room pushing oxygen, IVs, and smiling, waving Toni. We put her into the huge tub and washed her hair and soaked her. She loved it! It amazed everyone that the young doctors would give up a chance to sleep just to give her a bath. It said a lot about them and a lot about how much she affected people.

On Wednesday afternoon, Toni's bleeding increased. I spoke to the HIV doctor about another transfusion. When I went back to her room, I went over to Toni and she just looked different. There was nothing I could describe—she just looked changed in some vague way. I knew at that moment that we had done all that we should do and it was time to let her go; it was the sign I was waiting for. I went out to the doctor, told her my decision, and we cried together. I went back to Toni's room and held her hand as I had done so many times over the last eight years.

Later, I sat with the senior resident and changed Toni's code status, which previously had been to do a full resuscitation if she had a cardiac or respiratory arrest. It would now be just bag and mask ventilation if she developed respiratory distress. That would help until they could give her drugs to ease the symptoms. He was very patient as he went over all the different things that are considered part of a code. Even though I am a nurse and had some training in that area, I didn't remember it all and was so thankful that he did it so thoroughly. Later I went through it again with the attending physician. I felt a strange peace and resolve. Having a plan helped.

As the evening passed, a few visitors came by. The social worker, Toni's three primary nurses, and I sat around and talked while Toni slept. She would wake up from time to time and look for me, say, "I love you, Mom" and then go back to sleep. I held her hand and watched her, trying to memorize everything about her. I felt her cheek on mine and memorized how soft it was. I touched her hair, remembering how pleased she was that it was long enough to braid. I tried to absorb every part of her so I would never forget anything about her.

At 1 a.m., the evening nurse said she needed to go home and wanted to go get something to eat before a hamburger place nearby closed. Everyone decided it would be a great idea for her to pick up something for everyone and each person gave her an order. As she started to leave, I called her back to pray as she had done for so many nights, she from a religious belief, I from a "ritual" need. Everyone gathered around Toni's bed and joined hands as she asked for Toni to find peace and have a painless and effortless death. As we dropped our hands and said "Amen" and people began to leave the room, Toni woke suddenly, sat up gasping, "I can't, I can't breathe!"

Everyone rushed into action; the doctors were called, the respiratory therapists began the bag and mask ventilation to lessen her distress. The charge nurse started calling the names on our list to come in. One of Toni's adored nursing assistants put on Toni's favorite music, Kenny Loggin's "Return to Pooh Corner." I held her hand and told her everything would be OK, not to be afraid, and we were there for her. After a moment, she pushed the mask away and said, "I like that!" Everyone laughed, and Toni got a huge grin on her face. After a few minutes, she put the mask back on her face but told the RT not to do it so hard. It was so typical of Toni to be in charge.

Soon the room began to fill with the doctors, nurses and friends who had asked to be called. Most of the staff were not on duty but had hurried in from home. Everyone was touching some part of Toni's body and crying. With tears rolling down my face, I continued to reassure her that everything would be OK; she would go to a place where she could eat anything she wanted, where she wouldn't have any pain and she would always be with us.

Over her bed were hanging various sizes of three-dimensional stars that I had made from paper and placed there a few days before. At one point, she looked up and said they looked "like fish, like starfish." Her words were coming in short sentences as the morphine was increased to relieve her distress. She became peaceful and her breathing relaxed. She pulled me down to her and kissed me and said, "I love you". A few minutes later she said, "I think I'm dying." I told her that I would be all right and she could go and not have to fight anymore; she had been brave and fought for a long time but it was OK to let go. I would always love her. Her breathing slowed, and shortly she took her last breath. She was gone

Forty-five minutes had passed since she woke. I sobbed and held her for a long time. She looked as if she was sleeping. I was overcome with pain and grief and yet comforted, knowing that my list of fears had not happened—she was not alone, not in pain, not afraid, and I was there. I couldn't have asked for more.

Other people began to come into the room to say their final good-byes and the others stayed, talking and reminiscing about Toni. We did hand and footprints on poster board, and someone brought a tin with plaster in it from the infant ICU to do a hand-print. We took pictures of her. We washed her body and brushed her hair. I cut her braids. They brought the plastic shroud used to wrap bodies, but I couldn't bear the thought of her being cold so we wrapped her in a sheet. When we put her on the gurney to take her to the morgue, I put a little pillow under her head; I wanted her to be comfortable. I put a paper crown on her head over the wrap so they would know how special she was to us. I wanted to go with her to the morgue, so they let me accompany them. I was amazed how calm I felt.

About 6 a.m., I left to go home. It was just getting light. I drove home thinking over Toni's life, wondering if there was anything I would have done differently. I was content with what we had done and decided if I had a chance to do it over, I would do the same things.

When I got to the house, my son was asleep on the couch. I woke him and told him about Toni and then went to bed. I didn't hear another thing until 10 a.m. I awoke and lay there for a second and then remembered she was gone; I cried for a long time. The next thing I knew, I was waking up and it was noon. I got up and made calls to people to notify them of Toni's death. I felt as if I was in a fog, moving like a robot. Chris took care of the household necessities and later a friend came to fix dinner. I just sat there absolutely numb and occasionally crying. I just couldn't do anything.

The next morning, I went to meet with a small group of friends from the hospital to plan Toni's memorial. I was amazed how well

I was able to function. While I still cried frequently, I was able to plan and take care of what needed to get done. I decided it was because I had known Toni was going to die and had done some of my grieving beforehand. Little did I know this was just the calm before the storm; the pain would come back with a vengeance.

The memorial service was lovely. We played a video of her life and music she loved; displayed photos and some items that portrayed her life; and to honor her Native American heritage, we had a Makah elder chant and tell about tribal beliefs on death and afterlife. At the last minute, I decided to have the service videotaped. Some people thought it strange but I am so glad we did because I have watched it many times, laughing and crying over the memories people shared about her. Close to 300 people attended the service, including teachers from each of the schools she attended, doctors, nurses, neighbors, and friends from the past and present. I met people who knew her as an infant when she still lived with Martha. Aunts, uncles, and cousins from both of her families were there as well as children from her school.

I was astonished at how peaceful I was and kept telling everyone that "this is workable; I know I will survive." But one morning after the memorial was over, the thank-you notes written, and the house back in some sort of order, I woke and was unable to do anything except sit on the edge of the bed. I couldn't think, and I couldn't function. It took me an hour to get dressed. I found that frequently over the next month time would pass as I sat there, sometimes thinking of Toni, sometimes thinking of nothing—just blank. I had a hard time concentrating and couldn't even pay enough attention to understand what I was reading, so the newspapers piled up. If I watched TV, I couldn't follow the plot. I thought I was losing my mind or at least my intelligence. I could take care of the necessities: cooking, laundry, and taking care of the kids' needs, but I just couldn't do anything extra. I was running on autopilot much of the time.

I saw children who looked like Toni everywhere I went. There were times when I could feel her presence or feel her cheek on mine and times when I couldn't even visualize her face. I felt for a long time that she would come through the door at any time and then be hit with the reality that she would never do that again.

I became concerned about how others perceived me and how I was grieving. I felt I was being judged at how much emotion I was or wasn't showing: if I cried, I was being overly emotional. If I didn't cry, I was holding it in and not dealing with things. I didn't know what was the "right way" to feel and was afraid to talk to others for fear I was doing it wrong. I wanted to talk about her all the time but was sure others felt I should be moving on with things and getting over her loss. I didn't know if I was crazy when I needed to sleep on the same pillow she died on with one of her shirts under it. Or whether I was crazy because I couldn't hang new toilet paper in the bathroom because she liked to do that or because I couldn't get rid of her toothbrush in the glass with mine over the sink or because I kept her ashes next to my bed and talked to her frequently or because I cried myself to sleep every night. I just didn't have anything to judge by.

Then one day I spoke to a friend about a group she attended to help deal with the death of her child. After thinking about it for a few weeks, I finally decided to go with her. It helped to talk with other women whose children had died. I found I wasn't crazy as they shared their feelings and methods of dealing with their grief. It was a safe place to be honest about my feelings. It was also scary because some women were dealing with sadness and loss many years after their child's death while I felt that a year was an eternity away, and I was sure by then I would be through it.

I attended the group fairly regularly for quite some time, and after three years I still go as often as I can. It has given me emotional support and a place to check my sanity. It has given me a place where I can talk about Toni and how much I miss her. It is a sisterhood of women who have dealt with a tragedy every mother fears and no one should have to bear. Without these women, I don't know how I could have gotten through her death and the feelings following it.

I judge myself less harshly and worry less about what others think. I gave up on the idea that I would sprinkle her ashes on the first anniversary of her death and still have Toni's ashes next to my bed. And I still talk to her. I still sleep on her pillow but don't have her shirt under it. I don't know if or when I will get rid of her toothbrush, but I don't care: I don't need to—it is a comfort for me to look at it every day, and that is all I care about. I will survive this and be a more loving and tolerant person because of it.

Hard to believe it has been fifteen years since Toni's death. Time is a strange thing, it seems like just yesterday she was here and eight but she would now be 23 if she were with us.

I spoke to our local high school on World AIDS Day and was surprised how many of the teens involved in their peer HIV education program went to school with Toni and spoke to me about her and their feelings about her. An award is given at her school each year in her name for students that show eagerness in learning. Many of the children we knew when she was at clinic are now entering their twenties and most are doing well and leading fairly normal lives. I see many of them a couple of times a year and love them so much. I still wonder why they lived and she didn't but am happy for them.

I think about her every day. I miss her awfully. I wonder what kind of an adult she would be. Her toothbrush still sits in the glass in my bathroom. Her ashes are on a shelf in my room and, indeed, I still talk to her. I can remember the feel of her face but not her "smell". The pillow is gone.

I was able to give away most of her clothes shortly after she died but saved her favorites and the ones that held special memories, like her Sea Fair Parade dress. A few years ago, I took them out of my closet and was able to eliminate a few more...so much for the quilt I was going to make. Over time the Pooh Corner CD disappeared and I was sad to find it isn't available anymore, though I bought some of the songs on iTunes so I can listen to them and sing along like we did together before. I cry about her still and don't judge myself because of it. For a number of years the doctor that I had been so awful to seemed to avoid me. I had an opportunity to apologize to her. I don't know if it helped her, but it helped me.

When my children are in the hospital I judge the caregivers less harshly and have been able to realize that most people are doing their best and that even I make mistakes...occasionally. I have been able to put that into perspective with some of those that I was angry with and had never "forgiven". When one of them died I realized that I had never given up the burden of that anger I had toward her and others so I gave it up...I forgave them in my heart and am amazed how much lighter I feel. They hadn't been affected by my feelings, but I certainly had been.

I have a tremendous affection for those special nurses and doctors that helped her during her illness and especially the ones that were with us that last night. I see many of them and are in contact with many that have moved out of the area. They still all talk about what that night meant to them.

My children have done well and have been deeply affected by her life and death, mostly in a positive way. I tried hard not to make Toni a "saint" after hear death so they wouldn't think they could never meet the expectations. They are compassionate and caring and my daughter, Amy, recommended to the hospital she worked for that they have a program to have volunteers available to sit with patients that are dying when they have no family or others to be with them so they don't die alone. They have put the program in place. I still go to my Mothers' Group but not as frequently as in the past. I continue to draw strength and comfort from the other women and know that the meetings are there if I need it.

What I've learned:

The lessons I take with me are that life is precious and there is no guarantee how long one gets so make sure those you love, know it. It is OK to cry and is often helpful. Be patient with others and forgive easily...the burden it gives is not worth it. Don't judge yourself too harshly. Knowing your child is going to die does not make it easier...you can't "pre-grieve. The pain of losing a child lessens but never goes away.

FRED
June 26, 1965 – December 28, 1996

Fred

Died in his Tent, Covered by an Avalanche

By Gail

I saw my son, Fred, alive for the last time three days after Christmas, 1996. Fred, Scott, and Tim left to climb Mr. Index. It was to be a three-day trip. They were all killed in their tents by an avalanche while they were sleeping.

Fred was happily married to his wife Lisa and had two little girls named Tabitha, age 2 ½ and little Gloria, 7 weeks old. He has two sisters, Lynne and Ellinor, and his Dad and me.

I sometimes climb the mountain to the place where Freddie died, but most of the time when I write, I am sitting at the base camp where we parents waited for 13 long days for word about our sons.

January 28, 1997

Dear God,

Freddie has been dead for one month today and I am still unable to keep it in my mind. I know it in my intelligent mind but my heart is having a very hard time with the pain.

At first I was so relieved to know he did not suffer. But now, God, I have times where I am so angry and lash out. People try to stop my anger and make me feel bad about it (and I do.) But God, my anger is there if I hide it inside – it is still with me. I can't get away from it. It is so painful and I cannot share it with anyone I love because they are hurting too. Please help my anger to pass.

Why did it all have to happen? I miss my son Fred so much. I love him with all my heart. God, why was it not me? My life has been full. I am an old woman and he was young – with so much to offer. He loved You so much, God, that he went up that mountain to find You. He knew not to be afraid of death. He has shown me not to fear death too.

God, please help me to accept the things I cannot change and change the things You want me to. May Freddie know I love him with all my heart and soul and that I would give my life for him if only I could.

Freddie once told me he had to be broken to find You. Lord, I am broken. Please help me. I have never been so broken.

May 2, 1997

On the Mountain

It is a beautiful sunny day and I sit in my quiet place at the base of the Mountain. It is the only quiet place in my life right now.

Fred has been dead for 16 weeks tomorrow, and the pain is so strong within me. It is different from in the beginning but still as strong.

I look at the trees, and they have new light-green leaves. The green moss on the trees is so beautiful. The birds are singing, and all is well here. Quiet, not like the raging winter before it. My life is not the same. It will never be the same and that is good and Bad.

I can't seem to fit in anymore. Things that were so important before don't matter to me now. Except if I forget what happened for a moment and start complaining about things that don't matter like sand on the driveway or dishes in the sink. I have been shown that it is unimportant but sometime don't get the message. What will it take – isn't losing a son enough? I know that life is so short and that loving people is what is important.

Thank you for my quiet place, God. I know people don't understand why I come here, but You do. It is the last place I saw my son and I feel much comfort and peace here with nature. "God never leaves us during our winters of the heart."

First Mother's Day letter   *May, 1997*

Dear God,

    Today being Mother's Day, it is so hard. I love my family so much, but one is missing and my heart is so broken. I hurt everywhere. I am in such pain, and I do not know what to do. I knew it was important to get away today for me. I did not want to hurt them as much as I hurt and I was—by being around. I feel so sick inside. I miss Freddie so much, and I need to cry. I feel so trapped and ashamed at home. I wanted to go to church and smile at everyone and go to lunch and smile, but my heart is not smiling—it is wrenched with heartache and pain. I miss my son so much. I feel so empty inside and so sad and yes, sometimes angry at the world for not understanding. But I know it's not the world's fault. It just is, and I can't change it.

    Every day is hard right now, but to set aside a day for mothers is too hard for me. I hurt too much. I have two wonderful daughters whom I love so much, but it is like the story of the lost lamb—I keep searching for him, and I know he is gone. It's too hard right now, it's just too hard. Please help me. I am so sad inside. Please.

    I am sitting at the base of the Mountain where I saw him for the very last time, and I miss him so.

    Two hikers passed by me and it is a beautiful day in a wonderful wooded place. For me though, all I can see is deep snow, rescue trucks, people and the helicopter with three boys in it. Freddie was in a zipped body bag the last time I saw him. He looked like he was sleeping. His face was as it was when he was a little child—peaceful and happy. I remember checking on all my children when they were small before going to bed each night, making sure that they were all tucked in and safe. Now I see him tucked in a black body bag. Oh God—it is so painful. It is.

My peace comes in knowing that he is with You and that is good, but I miss him so. Please help me to heal and be able to help the rest of my family. I am no good to them like this.

My Freddie had a very hard time on this earth. He searched his life to find meaning and happiness. He was struggling for many years, I believe. In the very last of his 31 years on earth, he had found a peace in You, Lord, that helped him to be the person he had always wanted to be. It was so comforting to me to see him happy. All moms wish the best for each of their children. Freddie had found his peace and wanted to share it with the whole world in a quiet way. I don't know if the world was all ready for Fred, but he shared where he could and did what he could to help people. Fred lived in the world but was never truly a part of this world again, but he was finally happy. I know he was ready to die and be with You, Lord, because he told me so the day before he left on this trip. That is not so say he wanted to die on their trip. He had a wonderful wife and two beautiful daughters he loved very much. He planned to be home in three days, but we both know that that was not to be. Freddie died mercifully in his sleep and I am thankful for that. He was spared the agony that he had had on this earth at many points in his life. Lord, I know he loves You with all his heart and soul and that he is now in heaven with you.

Please, Lord, give me—if it is Your will—understanding and respite from my pain.

Each Mother's Day, I go to the Mountain to write my Mother's Day letter. After I have written my letter, I read the letter from the previous year to see if life is changing for me.

May 21, 1997

I feel we are all a little low right now. Fred is at the computer a lot. I am feeling sad sometimes. The good weather has not helped. It made me miss him more. I wish he could be here to see the Spring. My heart is still in the cold winter of the Mountain.

May 22, 1997

After a very hard day, I headed for the Mountain to seek some peace and understanding. I was crying so hard and playing Freddie's music so loud. As I drove, the sun was setting behind me. It was a large, bright, orange ball in the sky. I watched it through my tears in my rearview mirror. As I approached the Mountain, there was still snow on the top. It was starting to get a little darker and grayer now. I arrived with more tears and very loud music. There was a black car there. It left about five minutes after I arrived. I was so glad to be alone on the Mountain. It's funny, I feel like it is my place and anyone else there is an intruder. The car was gone, and I was alone with my hurts and tears. I opened the sunroof and let the music blast and listened, prayed and cried. God, please help me understand what is happening to all of us.

First Father 's Day

It is Father's Day and we are not the same people this year now that Freddie is gone. To watch Tabitha and Gloria without a father is so hard. Tabitha is hurting in her little heart. Poor Taba, I love her so.

Dad is trying hard to not feel. I think if he allows himself to feel it will hurt so much, but he is still hurting anyhow. He just does not acknowledge it to himself or to us. We are all new people - the old died with Freddie. We are a bereaved Mom and Dad now and are starting again with the rest of our family on a new journey to life, as it will be for us without Freddie on earth (but in our hearts always.)

Happy Father's Day My Son. I will always love you, Mom

Sunday, June 22, 1997 On the Mountain
Dear God,

This week is especially hard for me. For on Thursday we will celebrate Freddie's birth, 32 years ago. For me, this brings back happy memories and painful reality, now that he is dead. His birth was such a joyous time for me. I loved him so much. I watched him grow to be a man, get married to a wonderful lady and have two beautiful children.

I know in my heart he is with You in heaven and at peace and I am comforted by this. I also know that my pain is so great. The pain is so unbearable I don 't think I can go on - but by your grace, I do. We are here to remember him and to learn that we are not in control, but You are - and that You will provide for us in Your special way. We have all been changed for the better, even though the pain. Happy Birthday, Son.

From the book, Praying our Good-byes:

`God we thank you for the gift of Freddie. You know what a treasure he has been for us. It is not an easy thing to part with him. The days are hard ones for us. The memories are there. Bless the hurt in our hearts as we move through each day. Please give us the energy and understanding that we need to live our lives well. Please do not allow us to move into bitterness and alienation with You or with one another. Help us to get through this painful time in our lives and to go on with Your strength to sustain us.

Thank you, Lord

The day of Freddie's first birthday after his death we put a stone engraved with the names of all the men who died with him on the mountain. It also said, "Jesus loves you." I can still hear Freddie saying these words to me.

Rabbi Harold Kushner

The candles in the churches are out; the stars have gone out in the sky. Blow on the coals of the heart and we'll see bye and bye.

What these words mean are that you will not find answers in Theology and science as to why bad things happen in the world and children die. Rather, the answers are in the coals of your heart. You can take the white heat that has been burned there by the terrible tragedy you have suffered and use it to warm the rest of the world. You can transform the world by your reaching out and in so doing make it a warmer and brighter place.

July 9, 1997 25 weeks have passed

The weeks are hard and different people want you to be ok now, but we are not. We are all struggling in our own separate ways. I find life so different now. I am in great pain a lot of the time and am trying to search for answers. Maybe that are right before me and I can't see them, or maybe I will not know until the day of my own death, but I know I need to continue to look until then. At times, I find myself drifting away from family and friends - out there alone I feel very alone in the midst of many people. I think at times that grieving is a journey that you take alone - like being born and dying. People all around, but you must ultimately do it alone.

July 13, 1997 Thirteen days till submission

As I now look back on our 13-day ordeal on Mt. Index, I believe it was as it should have been. God gave us the opportunity to exhaust all of our energy to try to save the three men He allowed us to give all of our guilt away because we were doing everything in our power to save our sons. I believe it was a gift God gave each of us. At the time it was happening, I would have told you it was just the opposite. Why was God not helping us? He was, but not in our way. Not in our control. That was my lesson. I was not in control. God was. He had a plan for each of us and I know each was tailored to fit our own journey. Mine began on that first Sunday morning when I awoke early with an uneasy feeling. I began taking down the Christmas tree. Pulling ornaments off it and then putting my coat on over my pajamas when no one believed me that the men were in trouble. I rushed out into the snow in my nightclothes and coat and started running for the golf course about 1/2 miles away. I was in direct opposition with God. He was not having my son, Fred. I fought with all that was in me. I cried, I begged, for his safe return. "God, he is mine. Don't take him."

Looking back, I know he was never mine - just a gift for a time. He was God's child, as I am and he was being called home and was already with God. But I was not able to relinquish my control. The pain was so great. I lay in the cold snow screaming to God to give him back, "please give him back." But that was not to be. As I lay there, I felt no cold - nothing but great waves of pain and fear that consumed me. When Lynne and Fred found me, they were so concerned about my lying in the wet snow for so long, but they did not understand I did not feel the cold. God was with me and is with me always.

That night the police and search and rescue were called when the men did not return home. The next morning, the search began. As the days passed and the search continued, we all fought to save the men. Everything seemed to be against us. The weather never seemed to be cooperating with us. When we had the helicopters, the visibility was poor, when we had hikers the conditions were sometimes too dangerous to go up the mountain. We were always struggling with search and rescue to please help us to find the men. As hard as we tried, it was of no use. We were not to succeed. For thirteen long days.

Each day we would think that we could not do it another day and each morning we would get up and we would have the strength to do it again.

During the time many miracles happened. People came to help and support us. Just regular people with hope and kindness. When search and rescue left us money came to help us pay for the private rescue teams. Food was always provided in our homes and on the mountain. Everything was provided by kind hearted people with much love and caring.

When we truly were unable to take another step, God gave us another miracle. Saturday January 11, 1997, Tim's brother was coming down the mountain and saw something. It was a tent stake. Tim's brother had found his brother and or sons. Of all the people on the mountain that had tried, his brother was privileged to be the one to save us all. My husband, Fred was up there as they began to dig out the men. They were brought down to the lower camp by helicopter where we were all waiting. I saw my son for the very last time in a black body bag. I am glad I was able to see him one last time. He looked like a little boy to me just asleep, just asleep. It had been raining and snowing most of the morning on the mountain, but as the helicopter took off the sun came out and there was a peace. It was as though the Lord was welcoming them into Heaven. Then we went home to begin our long journey.

July 26, 1997

Went up on the mountain again. I had a great longing to go to the mountain again - not realizing it was one month since I was last there on Fred's birthday. Most of the flowers we had planted were not there anymore, but by the stone was one red begonia. I thought how Fred had always loved red and how fitting it was that one little red flower still bloomed. (This begonia was still blooming in the Fall!) I will come again in the Fall and plant bulbs for the Spring. I feel close to God and my son up here - a peaceful place.

As we hiked down, we met a few hikers who said, "hello." One asked if we had seen the stone and we talked for a few moments and said our good-byes. It felt good to know that others had seen the stone and knew that Scott, Tim and Fred had lived. Fred and I sat at the base camp until the sun set. The birds sang and the mountain was beautiful and there was peace.

August 20, 1997 Thoughts about my Tabitha

Tabitha was two years old when her Daddy died. She has told me about and taught me many lessons.

"My Daddy told me how to eat an ice cream cone, Grandma." "How Taba?" "Just bite it, Grandma, just bite it."

"Grandma, do they have tuna in Heaven?" "Why, Taba?" "Because I like it."

One day, Tabitha drew a big green balloon. She said that it was all right if the balloon flew up to her Dad. "He always fixed my broken balloon. But now he just can't send them back anymore." We talked of how they played and how she knew he would be fixing her balloons for her.

A trip to the Hallmark store: Tabitha picked her colored balloons and gave them to the lady to inflate. She told the lady she wanted to send the purple one the Heaven to her Dad. The lady looked at me for an answer.

I nodded to tell her it was so. Taba picked each string to match so carefully. She watched as each was blown up. The lady curled all the strings and gave them to Taba. When we arrived at home, Taba pulled the purple one from the bouquet and let it go up to her Dad. We watched till it was out of sight. Now that little Gloria is older, Tabitha has taught Gloria to send balloons to her Dad, too. We do this on special days and also on days when they just want to touch their Dad for a moment.

Tabitha and the Hula Hoop: She thought she would bring it to Heaven to her Dad so that he could open it with his strong muscles and she could see what is in it.

Tabitha once said to me, "Daddy left and Gloria came." She came to comfort us all. To Tabitha, Gloria is her little sister and her healer. To all Gloria is our laughter. They are both our hope for the future.

One day, Tabitha told me she was afraid of forgetting her Daddy, and asked how she could hold on to him. She had a little medal and she thought if she held on to that, she would not forget him. "What do you think, Grandma?" I told her I had many pictures for her and that she could always ask her Mom and me and we could tell her stories about her Dad.

I tucked Tabitha into bed one night and she prayed, "Dear God, Please, I miss my Daddy so much. Please, please heal all the children. Please heal my tummy because it hurts so much." Her prayer spoke for all of our prayers. We miss Freddie so much. This little one says it so beautifully. *Thank you for her words.*

February 2, 1998
   Tabitha's lunch prayer: "Dear God, Thank you for the food. I miss my Daddy, but I know he is having fun with you."

February 25, 1998
   Tabitha came downstairs and said, "You know Grandma, some mornings when my Mommy was sleeping, my Daddy and I went downstairs and had soppy animal crackers and it was fun. Can we do that?" "Yes, we can do that."

November 5, 1997 Gloria's First Birthday
   It was Gloria's first birthday. One year ago, we were all so very happy. Fred and Lisa had a beautiful baby girl. Seven weeks later, we were so sad. Freddie was dead and Gloria and Tabitha had no Daddy on this earth anymore.
   I remember how happy Freddie was when he came out of Lisa's room smiling and saying, "Mom, Mom, it's a Lisa baby, it's a Lisa baby!" He was so glad she looked like Lisa. They now had one of each of them - for Tabitha looks so much like her Dad.

Thanksgiving Day, 1997

Fred and I got up early to go up the mountain. It was raining hard. I took three red roses with me. I knew it was important to spend time on the mountain remembering Fred. It was hard to leave because I knew the snow was coming and we probably would not be able to get up this high again until Spring.

December 2, 1997

Fred Sr.'s Birthday

Fred did not work this year on his birthday. He spent it with the children and me. In the afternoon Fred, Tabitha, Gloria and I went to find our first Christmas tree without Freddie. If it had not been for Tabitha and Gloria we would not have had a tree. It was so painful. One year after Fred's death we were here buying another tree. It did not seem real to me all that had happened. Tabitha had packed a special lunch with pretzels, marshmallows, fruit loops and juice boxes. She carefully packed many napkins to cover her basket. She said this would be our lunch under the Christmas tree before we cut it. Thank Heaven for Tabitha and Gloria - "a little child shall lead them." Fred drove the truck alone and the girls and I followed behind in the car. I tried to put some Christmas music on, but Tabitha said it hurt her ears. "Grandma, please turn it off." It hurt my heart too. We drove the direction of the mountain. The sun was shining and the mountains were beautiful that day. But the memory of the pain was with us. It was a windy day, looking for that first tree and Tabitha ran ahead holding her basket in one hand and her coat flying in the breeze. When we found the tree she opened her basked and spread her napkins and we ate. She was pleased.

The wind blew harder. Fred lay down to cut his first tree alone. After much sawing the tree fell. We had done it - the tree was ready to be pulled back to the truck. Poor Fred had to do this alone - not like last year when he and Freddie came smiling down the path together.

As we were driving down the hill from the tree farm, Little Gloria started saying "Da Da Da Da." Tabitha turned toward her and said, "Daddy is in our hearts, Baby. Daddy is in our heart and in Heaven and it's ok."

December 27, 1997

On the 27^t of December one year ago, I saw my son for the last time. Today, I awakened early and knew that I had to go to the mountain. When I go there, I gain strength that enables me to go back and face the world. I stopped at the little white church to pray and cry. I sent my three red balloons up to Heaven the way Tabitha taught me and then I could go home to my family. I love you, Freddie. God bless.

January 1, 1998 On the mountain

The first day of the New Year. I sit at the base camp looking back at the week. It has been so hard. I feel like the heavy snow is weighing me down. I ache everywhere, yet I know I am not ill with sickness but with grief. *My energy was drained away, but God, you gave me just enough. I have been sad, mad, not in control of my emotions. It has been a very d i f f i c u l t time. But God, I know You stand close beside me. God, I do not know how to think past today - the first day of this New Year. Please help me. I can 't do it on my own. May I ask the question old Morrie asked each day, "Little bird, Little bird, is this the day I die?" So that I live each day to the best as if there were no tomorrow. Only today. Dear God, thank You for the lesson I am trying to learn. I found much peace here today.*

January 11. 1998

It has been two weeks since Christmas. I have relived each day of the search day-by-day, as have others. Family members - even little Tabitha who didn't know the calendar dates had it on her heart.

Friends that had been with us on the mountain called and told us of similar feelings. Today I sit at base camp remembering last year. In one thought, I find it hard to believe one year has passed and in another, think how long it has been since I saw my son, Fred.

Life has such a different meaning for me now. It is short and we know that it will end. We did not ask for this knowledge, but it is part of us. Things, houses, cars, trinkets mean little. People are so important. Caring and loving each other is what life is all about.

Some days I dream of putting my arms around my son and telling him how much I love him. But then the dream ends and I know nothing will ever be as it was. I find it hard when people tell me to find closure and get on with life - there will never be closure for me. No one and nothing will ever replace Freddie. He was my son and I am so glad to have known him for 31 years. He will always be part of my journey.

End of January, 1998

Today was a warm, beautiful day. It felt like Spring is coming. I was able to get outside for the first time and plant some flowers in my pots. To work in the soil feels so healing to me. To see the new little green shoot coming - the new life.

March 6, 1998

The Mountain

Dear God

I have been waiting to be here alone with You. I felt as if I was standing on the land with a large river running under it. It is a river of pain and sadness. If it is pierced, up will spring the pain and suffering again. You never know just what will pierce the land and the pain comes again. In between, life goes on again.

March 10

Fred and I went to the mountain to the stone, where we spent time thinking about Freddie. When we arrived, I found someone had cleaned the winder leaves away. They had washed the two white angels I put there for Christmas and finished the rock circle I had started. It felt so good to know that someone else cares. The daffodils were starting to break through the ground.

I brought some primroses to plant (red ones.) I busied myself digging and cleaning for a while. Then it always hits me. He is gone and he is not coming back again. My heart breaks and I look at Fred and he feels it too. We stand for a while, then pray. I take a few pictures while Fred throws Jasper her stick. We start down from the top to where the men actually died. We stop again and stand in silence and wonder how and why this had to be. I looked over through the bushes and saw a little white ticket from the first primrose I brought to the mountain just one year ago. I picked it up and held it - then put it into my pocket. I don't know why, but I needed to take it home.

March 10, 1998

Today is Tuesday. It is a rather gray day and I am trying to keep up, but I feel so heavy and sad. I see new seeds coming through the ground and I know that Spring is coming. Ellie's birthday is this Friday and our anniversary is this Sunday. Thirty-four years and Freddie will not be with us. It is so hard to think about another Spring without him.

I remember as though it were yesterday when my son and his family moved into their first home. Fred cleaned the roof and stained his back porch. And yesterday, I was pressure-washing that porch - thinking that I was washing away all the stain he had so carefully put on. Just as his life is slowly washing away in people's memories. I don't want him to disappear from our lives. I miss him. I now know new people that have never known my son and they never will and that makes me sad.

March 17, 1998

Another good-bye. I was now saying "good-bye" to my dear friend, Janny - who is moving to Florida. Janny stood by and listened to me as I told her of my pain. She was there from the beginning and knew Freddie. She never tried to fix or tell me not to feel what I was feeling. She always sat quietly and lovingly just listening. Now she is gone. Before she left she asked, "Gail, do you ever think you will be happy again? Laughing and happy like we used to be?" I answered, "I don't know, but I don't think so." She said, "No, I don't think so either. I said, "Good-bye" and gave her a hug, as though I was going to see her the next day. I was unable to think about the next day when she would be gone.

March 20, 1998

Today has been such a nice day with the little ones. The weather has been beautiful. We spent the day at Bothell Village, feeding the ducks, having lunch outside, riding the merry-go-round. We collected some rocks and when we got home, we painted ladybugs and spiders on them. It is so wonderful to be with them. There is a magic that little people have that takes pain away - even for just a little while. *Thank you, God.*

March, 1998 At Gerri's in Oregon

We have been here for two days now and there is such a sense of love and trust among us. We have said what is in our hearts and been accepted as we are. We have affirmed each other's gifts and know that we are all special in God's eyes. It is really hard to hear the good about yourself and to have to tell what you like about yourself. We hear the negative so well and it is familiar - but to hear really nice things is sometimes hard to accept.

We are all very fragile, but very strong. We all bring different pains, but the same pain to this place. *God, I know you are with us and are teaching us to help each other and to go out and help in the world. We are so privileged to have this time away from the world to learn about each other. Our hopes and fears have been freed here. We are all different, but so alike. We all love, we all have pain, we all have fear, but to be honest and free to talk about it and to be unconditionally loved as we are is a gift from you, God. We all need love, but sometimes when we need it most, we are not too loveable. I know when I am angry, I need love - but it is hard for people to see past my anger and love me. It 's much easier to love someone that is lovable. Thank you, God, for loving me and giving me this experience of being with such special and wise women.*

Being at Gerri 's by the ocean has given us time to leave the world as we know it for a little while. It is as though you stopped time and gave us a safe place to feel our pain, to tell about it and then to be accepted and loved by others.

These ladies are so strong and wonderful and in such pain. They loved their children as I loved my Freddie and are so loving to each other. If asked to tell about my days at Gerri's, I would not be able to explain the miracles that happened here this weekend. I can only say that you were with us, God, in our pain and in our laughter. We cried so deeply and laughed - some of for the first time in a long, long time. Thank you for Gerri - she is so special to us all.

April, 1998

Dear God,

Thank you for a beautiful day in the tulip fields. Fred and I took the girls to see the tulips today. It was so beautiful. I said to Tabitha, "Look at that beautiful red field of tulips." It stretched as far as your eye could see. "If only your Dad could see those red tulips, he loved red so much!" Little Tabitha replied, "Grandma, he already sees it." Her little head was bent as her Father's used to be and she had a smile on her face like her Dad's. She is so wise for her almost four years! She made my day.

The children ran and played in the grass by the tulips. It was so nice to see. Thank you, Lord. After lunch, little Gloria bit her Papa in the shoulder. Maybe she didn't have enough to eat at lunch. We laughed and talked about what a comfort these little ones have been to us. It was a very happy day in La Conner.

April, 1998

Dear God,

It is almost Easter and I feel a sense of peace and a knowing that you are in control of the world - not the world in control of itself. Lord, help us to learn the hard lessons we need and to be faithful even if we do not understand.

I miss my son and I know you know this - and are by my side in my pain. I have learned so much from people this past year. And I would not have had this opportunity to learn if Fred had lived. I would give it all back to hold my son in my arms one more time - but that is not an option. I know I must learn from all you have given me and see the many gifts I have been blessed with. God, please help me with my pain.

Thank you, Freddie, for being my son and for teaching me so many things. It would have been good if I had listened harder when you were here. All I have is the here and now, and I hear words of the past and am understanding them in the present. You were a wise son. You gave me many things to deal with in your short years and I am still learning from you today. Thank you for being my son.

April 16, 1998

Dear God,

Easter is over and I am sitting in traffic on my way to the mountain. Lord, thank you for Easter and for Jesus. It was a happy morning. Fred and I got up early to go to the dawn service. As we sang, two geese flew over and I felt your presence so strongly there - and I knew all was well. After church, our daughters Lynne and Ellie went up the mountain with us to the stone. We stood together and prayed - hearts heavy because we felt the physical separation from Freddie. If only we could hold him in our arms and tell him once more how much we love him. Fred said a prayer that was so real and honest. We all spoke a few words to Freddie and then started down the mountain. You could feel the pain in our hearts. Our shoulders were slumped down. We did not stand too tall - we hurt so much.

Dear God, it is not our faith that we question, but the terrible pain of separation. I miss holding his hand and smiling at him. I know he is safe in your arms. Please give me strength to accept.

I see how much we are all connected to one another. We are responsible to each other. To help when it is possible to listen to the small voice within us and do Thy will. It seems so much clearer now. You are your brother's keeper and so are we.

At Gerri 's I felt unconditional love from the ladies and it was as though someone turned on a light - a spark in my heart and may it never go out. "To whom much is given much is expected." As a group we have been blessed. Through the pain we all suffer we were given a great gift of unconditional love and honesty and freedom to be real and to know we are loved with all our imperfections. God, I feel You with us as we spend time learning to heal and to give again. Thank you, God.

May 1, 1998

Dear God

Our little Tabitha is struggling this week. She told me she was having trouble remembering what her Daddy looked like. We talked about how she could always ask us and I told her we had many pictures to remind her of what he looked like. She seemed to be frightened and wanted to hold on to his memory. I gave her a picture of Fred in his? to take home with him. She was looking so hard into the face of her Daddy and trying not to forget. My heart was breaking for her. I was remembering the day she was born and how much her Daddy loved her - and the smile on his face!

May 9, 1998
Mother's Day gift through time for a grieving Mom

Last Sunday, my friend Sue was having Fred help her with some schoolwork. They needed a ruler. So I tried to find one for them. In my looking I found two very precious things - a picture of my Lynne and her handprints and a Mother's Day card from Freddie. It was a red tulip card tied with a yarn bow. Inside it read, "Happy Mother's Day" and "I wish you had a dishwasher so you wouldn't have to do dishes, Mom. Love, Fred". I felt so happy.

Later in the same week, I opened a large wooden drawer in the bathroom and put my hand in and took out a little green clay pot that a child had made many years ago. I had not seen it for many years, but I remembered that my Freddie made it for me and it is my gift. I handed it to his Dad and said, "Turn it over." On the underside was a little "F." Dear Freddie, thank you for my card and gift sent through time.

Mother's Day, 1998

At Base Camp Dear Lord,

I just finished reading last year's Mother's Day letter and I feel so many of the same feelings. I have been given many gifts from You this past year. You have placed many people in my life that were not there before and for this I am truly thankful. Lord, please help me to be patient with my pain. Today as last year, I am in such pain. I miss my Freddie so. Thank you for my Mother's Day gifts from past years - they meant so much to me.

The children are so precious to us. Lynne, Ellie, Lisa, Tabitha and Little Gloria. Thank You for their love and support during this last year and today. I was able to go to the front at church this year with all the other Mothers and I knew it was because You were standing with me, Lord. The girls were so kind with all their presents. I must admit I love my gifts. Lisa 's card was such a gift - more than her present, which I will always enjoy. But to read her words and to love her...Thank You for Lynne and Ellie's gift - it was beautiful too. They are so good to me.

Dear Dad took us all out to lunch at a very special place. He is being so good to me. I see his pain for his son today and for his own Mom. Lord, please be with him. Teach me how to help him. I don 't know how and I love him so. This family is so important to me. They are my gifts and I treasure them all more than anything.

Jasper and I went up the mountain to the stone. I had to get there today. Thank you for safe passage up and down. I know You are with me. I talked to the boys for a while and it always helps. I love my Freddie so. Please help my pain and teach me how to help others. I want to work for You.

May 22, 1998

On the mountain

Dear God,

Tonight I will meet a man that has come into our Lisa's life. I made a promise to Lisa then we were searching for Freddie to stand by her and I want to do that. I can 't do it without You, Lord. I am too weak. Please help me to give her my blessing and support.

May 30. 1998

On the mountain Lord,

Some days I feel like a loose cannon ready to explode and I do some-times! I wish I had more control over my emotions, but I don 't.

Lynne had her 31s' birthday last Monday and now she is as old as her brother was when he died. I wonder how Lynne feels, but she does not say too much. She wants so desperately for me to be happy again. I am trying as hard as I can. I love my Lynne.

June, 1998

Dear God,

    Thank you for a nice day yesterday with Fred. It was so nice to spend a whole Sunday with him. It was good to go to church together. After we walked the beach, talked and enjoyed the day together. I love him very much and hope we have many more good days like yesterday.

June, 1998

Lord,

    I was fixing muffins in the toaster for the girls. I was holding little Gloria in my arms and Tabitha said, "Grandma, I remember when my daddy held me and we went `Pop' when the toaster went `Pop.' Now I just jump by myself. " I was so sorry for her - she missed her Dad so. It has been asked, "When is a child old enough to grieve?" If she is old enough to love, then she is old enough to grieve. June 5, 1998

Dear God,

    This morning I was going through some of my papers and found a letter Freddie wrote to me in March 1991. I read it and he was so alive again in my heart. My stomach and heart ache for him. In reply to his letter, I am trying to be as strong as I can and yes, I am trying to sort out what is important to me. His letter could have been written just yesterday. Please help me to choose wisely about what is important.

    Freddie's birthday is coming closer. It is on my mind each day. I think of the day he was born and how happy we were and all our Happy Birthdays with Jell-O cake and fun. Now I will go to the mountain, plant flowers, and talk to you, God. I watch Tabitha and Gloria growing up so fast. Gloria was only seven weeks old and Tabitha was only 2 when he died. Next year, Tabitha will be starting school. Freddie, I wish you could see them - or as Tabitha said about the tulips, "He already does, Grandma. "

Our Lisa continues to see her young man I want the best for her and the girls. It is hard to walk two paths, but I know I need to. I must honor my broken heart and then bless Lisa on her way. Please help me, God.

June 7, 1998

Dear God

As I drove to the mountain today, I was remembering a robin that had built her nest in my dryer vent - many years ago. The repairman came and removed it. The eggs were gone, but the mother bird kept coming back to the spot where she last saw her eggs. I feel like that robin today. Maybe I will come until I am unable to get here anymore. Thank You for this quiet place to be alone and to reflect on this journey. I used to watch as Freddie as a child as he slept with his big purple rabbit. So peaceful, so peaceful.

June 13, 1998

Dear God,

I felt close to my Lynne and Ellie this week. Lynne was standing very close to me. She is so good to me. I sometimes forget because she is always here. I know I can always talk to her. She has a kind and gentle spirit.

Ellie and I worked on a moss chair together - it was so good to be with her.

June 26, 1998

Freddie's Birthday

It is a rainy day on the mountain - unlike Freddie's first birthday up here when it was hot and sunny and there were so many people with us. This year, we had only Fred, Lynne, Ellie and me. Fred and I are so glad the girls were with us. We had a few obstacles in our way, but we still made it up to the stone to plant our flowers, read and pray. We sang, "Happy Birthday" to Freddie and it was hard.

When we arrived, a gate closed across the road met us. It read, "Road Closed." We sat for a while and decided to open the road for ourselves. Two years ago, I would not have done this, but now I needed to be near the place where my son died. We started down a very bumpy, muddy road. I could see why they had closed the road, but we still needed to get up the mountain. As we rounded the last turn, the forest ranger was just ahead of us. Fred got out of the truck and explained why we were there. The ranger was a woman and she said that the road was closed, but that we could stay. A man stepped out of the other side of the car and approached us saying, "I remember you. I was on the mountain searching. I am so sorry." Dad shook his head. We gathered our flowers, soil and tools and started down the last part of the road leading to the place Freddie died.

Dear God,

I miss my son every day, but today my mind goes back to the day of his birth 33 years ago. It was such a special day. I only wish I had known just how wonderful it was and that things don 't last forever - and that sometimes our children die. I never thought my child would die before me. It is so unnatural. The children should bury their parents. In our case, that was not to be. It is raining so hard outside the windows of this truck and I am glad because my heart is raining too. I don 't think I would be able to stand the sun today.

Thank You, God, for the 31 years we had with Freddie. Happy Birthday, Freddie. I love you, Mom.

July 4, 1998

Happy Fourth of July!

I remember Freddie and his little green army men - blowing them up. I mentioned to Dianne and she said she remembers Scott dropping them off the steps. All we have now are memories of our children. No more hugs and kisses - just memories of what once was. And now we know how special memories are. When I look at a whole family walking down a street, I know how very special it is. Tabitha once said to me, "Life is changing right under your very own little feet, Grandma, and you don't even know it." "Yes, little girl, you are so wise. Yes, Tabitha, it is but we don't always see it if we resist it. We need to accept and walk through our journey. It is sometimes so hard and we fail time and time again. With your grace, God, someday we will learn.

July 6, 1998

Dear God,

Little Tabitha brought the tape player with her in the car today. She told me she was playing Twila Parish tape because it reminded her of her Daddy. She said, "My Daddy and I would put this on and dance and dance. He would throw me up into the air. I miss my Daddy." I was holding back my tears and told her I missed him too. She asked me if I would put up her tent so she could have private time.

I feel different as time goes on. I am not so numb anymore. The hole in my heart will never mend, just become different with each passing year. I feel pressure from people pushing, judging me, telling me to "...get better, get on with your life." They don 't want me to be sad around them. This adds to my pain because I try to fight now to give them what they want and still stay true to myself. I do not believe that they would tell a person to heal a cut on their hand, but they want me to heal the hole in my heart - right now.

July 10, 1998

Dear God,

Thank you for this beautiful day. Lord, I sit here again on the mountain listening to all of nature and I am blessed. I know that when I was here two nights ago I was filled with pain and hurt. I cried to You in my pain and You heard me as You always do and have given me a rest. Thank You, God.

July 12, 1998

Dear God,

I was thinking about why I want to continue to live and I believe it is because of the love of my family. Fred, Lynne, Elle, Lisa, Tabitha and Gloria. I know that living or dying not up to me, but at this point in my life they are my reasons for getting up in the morning and for being thankful in the evening.

July 17, 1998

Today, Fred and I hiked around Hurricane Ridge. It is so beautiful up here. The small purple flowers cover the mountainside with little white daisies sprinkled in between. We looked down into the deep green forest of evergreens and into the white fluffy clouds below as our hearts found rest and peace here. I understand why the men loved the mountains so much. Thank you for our blessing.

July 31, 1998

It has been 81 weeks since Freddie died. I wish I could hold him in my arms. I am so grateful, Lord that I can hold Tabitha and Gloria. They are my blessings sent from You.

Today is a rainy day on the mountain - cool and misty. I sit here looking at the path that Fred, Scott and Tim walked and think about how it was and then I think about how they never came down the path again. There is so much I would like to say to Freddie - to tell him how much he is missed, how much I love him - I wish we could just sit and talk about just anything.

August, 1998 Dear God,

I am so angry sometimes. I know anger is not acceptable with most people. It is not acceptable in my family not now or in my home as a child - and in most of open society. You can be happy or even sad if you have to, but not angry. You feel as if you have failed if you are angry. Isn't anger a real emotion too? Why do we have anger but are not allowed to express it? It need not be expressed in a destructive way. A very wise woman once told me that anger results from pain and fear. When I feel anger now, I try to decide why it is there. Why God can we not be angry sometimes? I wish people would let me be angry and not shame me for this feeling. I have much pain and some fear.

August 4, 1998

Thank you for a rest on the mountain. I walked the trail and it was so good for me. The trees were so beautiful and the sounds of the falling waters were so peaceful. As I arrived at the top, very tired, and still crying, it was so peaceful and quiet. The sun was behind the big moss-covered tree. I lay my head on the stone and fell asleep drying. I don 't know how long I slept, but as I awakened, I saw a leaf falling from a tree and thought of the story of Freddie the Leaf It was still summer and his leaf had fallen early. Then I saw two more and then two more. These are the leaves of the children that have left us early. God, it is so different on the mountain. I can be myself, so free of all the "shoulds" of the world. Thank you for today. It was so unexpected. We never know what is coming just around the next bend in the road.

Epilogue
Mother's Day, 1999 Monday morning at Base Camp

Dear God,
It is Monday morning the day after Mother's Day. I just finished reading last year's Mother's Day letter. Lord, mush has happened in this last year. Many changes have occurred in our lives. Our Lisa is now married and Tabitha and Gloria have a whole new family again. Lord, I can 't say this has been an easy year for any of us. We are all trying in our own ways to love and understand each other. Some days are much better than others are. Please stand by us and teach us to love each other. May we look into each other's eyes and see what You see in us, Lord.
Freddie will always be in our hearts, but help our hearts to allow new people to also have space in our lives.

Or Much has changed. I cannot say that my heart has mended, but I am beginning to see my family and friends and their hearts again. I still am very sensitive and fragile though. For the past two years, I had nothing in me to give. I was in so much pain and anguish. I now want to try to be there for my family and friends again. Thank you for all the patient people you have sent my way when I needed them so badly. Maybe not the ones I expected, but You knew who would be the best for me. Thank You, God. Jesus loves you my son. I love you, Mom

May, 1999

Life continues on. Freddie's birthday will be here again next month. I plan to go up to the mountain to do some planting and talk to you, Lord and to Freddie for a while. I will try to be open and faithful to what you have for me to do.

My son, I love you with all my heart and every fiber of my being. May I release you and give you back to God - who has always held you in his hands. May the angels take you home to Jesus for you loved him with all your soul. Mom

Sometimes the Lord calms the storm. Sometimes He lets the storm rage and calms His child.

Harsh Grief Gentle Hope
May White

Feb 9, 2001

On the Mountain
Dear Jesus

Thank you for your love and patience for the past four years as I sat here on this mountain. So many times in great pain and anguish I cried out to you "Take my pain away, tell me why my son Fred had to die". Why, Why and you were always there to answer me, but I did not hear. I sat on the mountain for hundreds of hours crying and asking and then crying again. You were so patient and kind and waited for me to hear you. You wiped away my tears and walked with me through my grief and helped me when I could not hold myself up.

I have seen many blessings and also things I do not understand. Lord you put the right people into my life to teach me how to live again. I am so blessed to have this special mountain where you and I sat as I grieved and now I see a new spring about to be born. It has been a long winter's journey and now I anticipate the beauty of spring. God I know you could have taken Fred and the pain from my heart at any time, but you are so patient and waited for me to give it and Fred to you.

God bless you my son, I love you and now can give you back to God. Thank you Lord for Freddie and the time we had together until we are together again.

What I have learned:

1. God was always walking with me, but I felt his greatest presence when I was walking in my greatest pain.
2. More compassion for other people.
3. We only have today, we were never promised tomorrow.

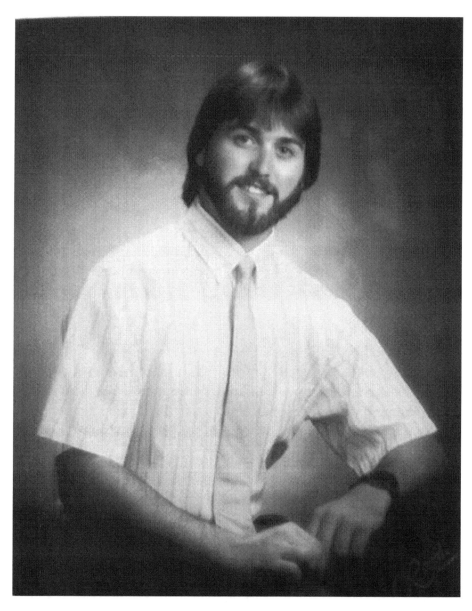

Chad
January 9, 1970 - July 29, 1991

Chad

Died in a Motor Vehicle Accident on the Freeway Near his Home

By Sue

Mother: Sue
Father: Roger
Siblings: Todd Michael, Kent Robert, and Melinda Sue

I have hesitated writing my story because I had hoped some-day to write my own book telling Chad's story and my place in it. However, wrestling with the whether to or not to, I decided that I, better than some, realize that today is all we have; and if Chad's story is to be told this may be the only opportunity placcd in my path. Therefore I will write, hoping that I do write again someday.

It was the last week in July of 1991. I had wanted a deck on the front of the house for a long time. I remember Chad in Roger's office, putting his arm around me and saying, "Come on dad, let's give her deck." That week was magnificent. Todd and Roger tore out all the moss-filled grass and leveled the earth. Chad de-livered the wood, and he and his father lay the groundwork for the deck. All of us were involved in hammering down the planks; even Mindy took her turn at a hammer. It was sad that Kent, who lived in Spanaway, wasn't closer to be a part of such a wonder-ful event. Everything was finished, and Chad had promised to bring me some of his planter boxes (he had his own little side company). He came in about noon, and we had lunch together:

turkey sandwiches; I remember it so well. He arranged the planter boxes on the deck just where I wanted them and nailed up some shutters I had just painted (his thumb print is still there). We were in the backyard cutting up some leftover wood, and he looked at his watch and said, "I gotta go, Mom." I answered, "Do you really have to?" and he answered in the affirmative, "Yeah, I gotta go." He bent down and I kissed his bearded cheek, I continued sawing wood and he turned around and left. That was the last time I saw my son alive.

At 3:30 a.m. July 30th, 1991, my doorbell rang. Being a light sleeper, I jumped out of bed and threw on a robe, thinking Chad had forgotten his key; you see he had moved back into the family home to save money for his marriage to Angela on May 2 the following year. There at the door was a round-faced man, with round glasses, asking me "Are you Mrs. Anderson, mother of Chad Anderson?" I answered, "Yes," then asked, "Why? Where is Chad, is he all right?" I called down the hall for my husband, "Roger, Chad's been in an accident." The rest of the time is pretty hazy for me. I do remember Roger at the kitchen sink pulling his hair and saying, "You are telling me my son is dead? My son is dead! My son is dead." The man, King County Medical Examiner, stayed with us answering questions. He told us that Chad had lost control of his truck while traveling at excessive speed on I-405 (five minutes from the safety of home) and had gone into the median and crashed into a cement pillar that supported a walkway over the freeway. He took the full brunt of the crash and was killed instantly, the boy next to him was hurt critically and airlifted to Harborview Hospital and survived. The boy sitting on the right side of the car (odd choice of words) received a broken arm and a small cut over his eyebrow. I don't remember much more of that horrible evening other than holding onto the M.E.'s hand not wanting him to leave and thanking him over and over for coming to our home. I guess if I didn't let him leave, "it" wouldn't be true. I don't know.

I hadn't shed a tear up to now; I was in shock! I went into a "robot mode" and went downstairs to tell my daughter, and called my other two children. They won't tell me what I said to them, I guess I was bluntly brutal. I don't know, I don't remember. We then got dressed and went to tell Angela and her family. I can remember feeling so strange, rocking back and forth on the couch with Angela vomiting and vomiting. We got back home, and I called my mom and dad and my brother in California; for some reason, I don't remember calling my sister. All this done, the reality of what had taken place hit and the tears began and didn't stop for two years.

All the next day, we went to the funeral home and the funeral was planned, I don't remember who did it. I just remember Angela wanted to have the same minister bury Chad as was going to marry then. There was only one problem, the big chapel wasn't available and we would have to use the smaller one; and that meant that Chad's body would have to stay outside the chapel. My sister, I remember this very clearly, said, "That is not acceptable." And we picked up and went somewhere else. That afternoon people came and came and came. We poured coffee and sliced meats, gave hugs and moved like robots, not feeling, not thinking, not realizing, just existing. Angela came and picked out the clothes Chad would be last seen in. They were the same clothes he wore when he proposed marriage to her. I was happy to relinquish this duty to her. She also requested that Chad wear the wedding ring she had picked out for him to wear the rest of his life as her husband, and she wanted the "wedding book" they had been filling out to be placed under his arm with a single red rose, the symbol he had given her many times expressing his love for her. She stayed at our home, sleeping in his bed, for the rest of the week.

The funeral day came. The limo picked us up, and we entered a chapel filled with our friends and Chad's friends. I remember Charles Jones coming up to me and hugging me and me saying, "It hurts so bad." and the tears began falling. The day was so hot, the chapel suffocating. At the end, people walked by my son and they cried. Then they all waited outside for me and all I wanted to do was to be with my Chad. I waited for all the people to leave and they waited for me to come to them so they could give me their condolences. I didn't go. I regret that now. But I thought they were going to take Chad away and I just had to see him one more time, touch him, love him, talk to him.

People came back to the house and mom and dad played their guitars and everyone sang. Imagine!! I had just buried my child, and everyone was singing. We even took a family picture with my brother and sister and mom and dad. Funny what you do when you are in the numbness of grief. Nothing is real. Nothing is real.

The bubble of shock was burst about two weeks later. I began crying and sobbing uncontrollable. So hysterically, my husband called his urologist to see if he could give me something to calm me down. Bless the man, Dr. Sood, he did; he gave me two Halcyon. I needed that medication that night because I couldn't bear what my mind was awakening to—my Chad was dead, he wasn't coming back, the pain burning constant in my heart was not going to go away soon. The most awful tragedy had befallen me, Roger, Todd, Kent, Mindy, Angela, Bob Tere, Mom and Dad, my brother and sister, my whole family. I, who I was, had died right along with Chad. The road ahead was dark, lonely, painful, erratic, and I had to walk it basically alone. I was hurting, angry, sad, and I didn't know how to do it.

Roger was trying so hard to help everyone. He went each day to see Angela and give her a rose, a red rose like Chad had given her and one to her mother Tere. One day she called and asked if I could gently tell him that that rose hurt her very much. She didn't want red roses from anyone but Chad. Then I got hysterical because he was stopping up at Angela's home each night and leaving me alone. We had the most loud screaming match. Well, I think I did all the screaming in the car one night and then realized that we needed some help. We wanted to get through this together, but we couldn't do it together.

I called a counselor that I, then Roger, then Chad, had seen in earlier years. I will never forget his voice when I told him Chad was dead and Roger raising his voice to me, "You told him he was dead?" But Paul Bestock gave us the phone number of Vicki, a member of The Compassionate Friends (TCF). Vicki spent an hour and one-half with me on the phone and through my tears I explained what had happened, how I was feeling, and my fear of going crazy. What was so helpful was that Vicki validated everything that I was saying and it was so helpful to know that she knew, she really "knew" what I was going through because she also was a bereaved mom. She shared with me that her son had died by suicide several years earlier and what had helped her the most was her attending support group meetings of The Compassionate Friends and a Mother's Group facilitated by a woman by the name of Gerri Haynes. Ironically enough Gerri's son, Craig, had been a playmate of my son Chad in elementary school. It was very difficult to plan to see her for the first time, but once in her presence, I felt that I was in the hands of an angel sent to help guide me through this trial here on earth. Gerri has been a guiding force in my life and very supportive of my efforts. I have since brought other mothers to her home, where she now holds the meetings, so they can benefit from her unconditional love and walk the walk as long as they feel the need.

My first TCF meeting was in Bellevue and it was only because of Roger that we found it. I know I wouldn't have had the strength to find it not only because it meant that I had a dead child, but its location was in an office complex at the back. I remember walking down this long, long, long, hallway (it's not so long now) and seeing people sitting around tables. There was no sign saying TCF, and I wanted to go back home. Roger, my dear husband, said, "Let's inquire if this is it." It was and I guess the rest is history.

I began attending TCF meetings twice a month and the Mom's Group twice a month. I read every book I could get my hands on (and there weren't many) about grief, how to survive the death of your child, and how to deal with a compromised spirituality. I also continued my training, which had begun months earlier at Evergreen Hospice, to be a bereavement volunteer. I believe this training helped me to learn more about the grief process as well as helping me do a lot of my grief work there.

I feel the "turning point" in my life came one night as we were leaving the Mom's Group at Gerri's. A dear friend named Phyllis Katz, whose daughter is buried in the same cemetery as Chad, came out of Gerri's and almost shouted, "I don't want to be this sad anymore." I answered, "I don't either." I think that was when I realized, really realized how much I was in control of how the rest of my life would be managed. Either I could remain bitter, angry, and broken, or I could use what I had learned and make a difference in the world and provide a legacy for my son.

It was shortly after that that I contacted Donna Riley Williams, a therapist. It was in her office that I could speak to the painful memories I held that I did not feel free to do in a group setting. There I could share life experiences I was not proud of that involved my son. I could share my misgivings about my parenting, the troubled marriage I had had, Chad's awful teen years, my concerns for my other children, and the poor self-concept I held of myself. It was here also, that Donna helped me understand that I had been depressed probably since the birth of my first child. She, over my protesting, got me to see a psychiatrist who prescribed a mild dose of antidepressant.

Being treated now for a simple chemical imbalance, I was able to forage ahead on my healing journey. Donna and I became friends and she invited me to speak, and perform rituals, at several workshops she was presenting on the grief journey. Donna also played a large part in my returning to school. She was one of the

individuals who wrote recommendations for me to get into graduate school. But I am jumping ahead.

Being in counseling with Donna, it became incredibly clear
how responsible I was for the direction my life was taking. She
helped me see what wasn't pointed out in support groups—that I
could be sad, angry, bitter for as long as I wanted to but at some
point, I would have to take charge and find the energy to reinvest
in life. She asked me, "If the roles were reversed, would I want
Chad to be sad forever?"

She played a song for me by Deanna Edwards entitled, "Walk
in the World for Me." It is a song to honor the life of a young
man named Eric who was dying of cancer. His mother, of course,
was distraught about what was happening to him and was pouring
her heart out to him. He grew frustrated, and to help her he told
her that she would now be the one to walk in the world for him.
Though saddened by her pain, she had a job to do. I will never
forget it and I have used it in some of my rituals.

That is where I want to go with this information. I do rituals for
the bereaved and I do workshops to teach people how to do rituals
for themselves. This is the privilege I have been given, the gift that
has been mine, since Chad died. It all began when I had gone to
Seabeck for a TCF grief retreat. The last evening we were there, we
sat around a campfire and we were told to throw a pinecone into
the fire with our pain in it. I remember how difficult that was for
me to do. I wanted to hang onto my pain and I resented having to
get up in front of people and to say what I was throwing into the
fire. I determined that next year I would be the person in charge of
the ritual. I volunteered to be on the committee for the next year
and that is how my journey changed direction and how my life has
been enhanced.

The next year, I worked for hours writing a ceremony that would
be healing and helpful to parents and not the least bit threatening.
It was beautiful, but I did not feel strong enough to read it myself,

so I had a dear friend read it. After the candle was set adrift in the lake and the parents all stood at the lakeside with tapers burning and Paul Alexander sang "Light a Candle," I burst into tears while Roger held me. I was overwhelmed with what I had accomplished and with the pain I felt in my heart, in my whole body, for my beloved Chad. But, I realized I had been able to give something to other parents—an opportunity to make something as intangible as grief, tangible in a ritual performed for them only to honor their children. I was "walking in the world for Chad."

That was the beginning. I loved the direction my life had taken, and shortly after that, Phyllis Katz, asked me to be with her on the third anniversary of Caryn's death. We would meet at the cemetery where Caryn and Chad were buried. I just felt I couldn't go without doing or having something, so I wrote a ritual for Caryn. Together, just the two of us (and the spirits of our children) sat on the lawn beside Caryn's grave, and I did my second ritual. Then Phyllis and I lay, each on one side of Caryn, and talked and cried. She was my biggest supporter and encouraged me to continue because she said it was so helpful to her.

I can't say enough how Phyllis has been a source of strength for me. She has been so free with her compliments and builds me up to the point I feel I can do anything. She is a true friend and I love her dearly.

I became more active in The Compassionate Friends. I made friends with whom I spent time with aside from meetings walking, golfing, playing Bunko, even walking a marathon. I did telephone work, speaking to brand-new bereaved parents and inviting them to meetings where I would be. I then took even a larger role by becoming the newsletter editor. I continued to do rituals both at Seabeck and during the holidays for TCF, began facilitating groups, taking minutes, setting up meeting places, chairing a raffle, a picnic and facilitator training, and so on. Later, my husband, Roger, became Chapter Leader, and together we worked diligently to give back to TCF in gratitude for the tremendous gift that we had been given.

It was about this time, also, that I decided to fulfill a dream I have always had—that of finishing up my Bachelor's Degree. I applied to the University of Washington and was admitted Fall quarter, but my father, who had been battling cancer for five years, died during finals and I withdrew from school. I gave myself another year to get stronger, to get some science credits at BCC, and enrolled again in the fall of 1994. I completed my BA in June 1996 and applied for graduate school at Seattle University in their counseling program. I graduated in 1999. During these years, I got a butterfly tattoo that symbolized my metamorphosis into another person, a bereaved mom yes, but a person whose mission would now be to help others through their transitions of life.

Presently, I am trying to establish a private practice and contin ue to do ritual workshops and rituals for bereaved parents whenever and wherever. I continue to be active in TCF primarily in an administrative role. My husband and I are undertaking the development of a new chapter on the Eastside to serve the parents in the fast-growing Redmond, Carnation, Duval, Monroe, Mill Creek, and North Bend areas. I facilitate six-week bereavement series at Evergreen Hospice, as well as a TCF in the north end of Seattle.

I have a full life with three wonderful surviving grown children, two grandchildren, and a fondness I share with Roger for golf. I love to read, attend professional workshops to assist me in my chosen field, and I treasure my relationship with my friends. I have changed. My innocence is gone. I know that children die, and I get scared sometimes that it might happen again to one of my children. I have a different relationship with God. My anger at Him has gone and instead I face the anger, guilt, and shame in myself upon which I continue to work. I do measure time by before and after Chad died, I know a part of me will always be missing. The hole in my heart has scarred closed but is tender to the touch.

I will never be "over" Chad's death, and I can't say as I want to be. Chad was born, he lived, he made a mark in this world. He loved and was loved and I hope to keep that love and his memory alive as long as I live.

As the years have passed, the pain has grown softer—it's different. I have learned that when I go down into the "black hole" as I called it, I could climb out again and I wouldn't stay there as long. I have learned moms and dads grieve differently and cannot be much help to each other until later. I learned what a wonderful husband I do have, and I am so glad that I have been able to do my grieving with Chad's dad. I learned that when I began cathartic crying, I would stop, and wasn't frightened of it anymore. I learned that it was okay to withdraw from some people who hurt me, and it's normal to fear investing in new relationships. I learned that the pain could surface at the most unlikely times (Roger calls them "land mines") even several years later. I also learned that the pain doesn't last as long as it did in the beginning. It hurt as much but not as long. I learned that letting go of my pain didn't mean I was letting go of Chad. I learned that Chad's physical presence—or the thoughts of his physical presence—still make me cry. At the same time, I feel Chad's spiritual presence in my heart whenever I want it to be there. I learned that holidays will always be bittersweet and to take the good from them. I have learned that others—people who are not bereaved parents—have no idea what we are going through, and I just have to remember that they mean well. (I can do that now!) I have learned that survival is a choice, and once we choose to survive, the quality of our lives is up to us. I have learned that rituals help at anniversary times, and going to the sea gives me peace. I have learned that heart-shaped rocks placed at Chad's tree give me comfort, and I feel loved by all the people who have sent them to me. I have learned that a sibling's death affects the other siblings in ways they won't discuss with mom and dad. I have also observed the strength it takes for a family to pull together after one of them has died. I have learned how suffocated children feel when mom tries to protect them after their sibling has died. I have learned how watching parents struggle through their grief gives siblings skills to face their own grief. Oh, the lessons I have learned that I didn't want to. Yet, the gifts, yes the gifts that have been bestowed upon me since my Chad died have been plentiful. I would give back in a heartbeat everything if I could have him back today, but I know that is not a choice. So I will rejoice that he was born and cherish the twenty-one years, six months, and twenty days we had together. And as my life on this earth comes to an end, I will reach out and grasp the hand of my child, who will pull me through to that land of rainbows, peace, love, joy, and sunshine where a mother's heart will again be made whole.

Here are my lessons.

1. I have learned that the way I grieved was <u>my way</u> and it was okay, in spite of what others may have said.
2. I have learned losing my child is the most difficult journey I will ever take because I am still walking the walk. However, I have found now after all these years it is "do-able" with help and support and the love of others.
3. I really have learned to experience "joy" again in my life, a feeling I thought I would never experience again.

Robin
10/4/82 – 3/13/08

Robin

Died by Suicide

My dearest Robin-

Oh, son, you were such a beautiful child! When you came along you quickly filled the empty place in our family. Our circle was complete. You immediately stole my heart—there was such a strong bond between us. That connection ran deep and never wavered.

You were the peace-maker in our family. Unable to tolerate arguments or anger, you became an entertainer, comedian, counselor, and the glue that held us all together. That must have been such a burden, although you were always happy, or so we thought.

As much as you totally idolized your older brother Woody and tried to follow in his footsteps, you developed your own sense of self. You loved dressing up in nice clothes, were an avid fan of movies, and could even recite much of the dialogue from your favorites. You kept us all balanced. I always expected you to find a career in counseling because you truly enjoyed helping family and friends. If anyone ever needed guidance, you were there with a compassionate, common-sense response and a reassuring smile. There must have been no one there for you when you needed a friend. I'm so very sorry. Any of your family or friends would have been at your side if we had only known you were having problems. Was it easier to hide your pain? Whatever trouble you were having, we could have found a way to fix it. Oh, how I wish you had let us try.

I wish you had known how very special you were. I wish you had known how very much you were loved. I wish you had thought about the huge hole you would leave in our hearts. I wish you were still here. I wish, I wish.

You gave so much love and happiness in the twenty-five years of your life. Now there is immense and overwhelming pain. When you took your own life, you also took a huge part of mine. Thoughts of you make me cry every day, and it's a mighty dark world that I live in now. I hope someday memories will not hurt so much and the pain will soften.

I'm so very grateful to have known you, and I'm grateful for the love we shared. It's too bad we didn't have more time.

All my love,   Mom

What I have learned:

1. Live each moment. Time should never be taken for granted and you can never get back the time you lose.
2. Be thankful and grateful for all the beautiful times I shared with my son.
3. Love is everything: tell those you love that they are so very special.

Heaven

It will be the past
and we'll live there together.

Not as it was to live
but as it is remembered.

It will be the past.
We'll all go back together.

Everyone we ever loved,
and lost, and must remember.

It will be the past.
And it will last forever.
Patrick Phillips

Scott
January 11, 1972 – September 15, 1998

Scott

Died from an accidental Drug Overdose

By Georgia

Scott's Gift

Dear Scott,

It's hard to believe 14 months have passed since I got that phone call from your wife. She was crying and said you were cold and blue and not breathing! I screamed for her to hang up and call 911. Dad waited by the phone, and I got into the shower in a daze. As I stood there with the water running over my head, a strange calm came over me. You were no longer suffering with your daily demons. You finally were at peace! I am happy for you because I know you are in a better place. God has called you home so you can now be happy there. I so wanted that for you here on earth!

Now comes the hard part. How do I go on with this hole in my heart? How do I go on without my only son? Our children are not supposed to leave before us. It's just not the right order of things. I know I have to remember the good times….and there were many! Your handsome smiling face that could light up a room, your wonderful sense of humor, your love of parties, candles, roses, classical music, dancing, family day, the sun, and Christmas lights. Your practical jokes. Your bravery at witnessing the birth of your niece. Your ability to be a much-loved Uncle Scott. Your artistic talent that was envied. Your "gift of gab" that started way before the age of two. Your unique way of doing things…..all things. Never by the book, always left or right of the norm. It was Scott's way. I loved your sensitivity. Your ability to articulate and express yourself never ceased to amaze me.

I keep thinking you are going to burst into the house saying, "Hi Mom!" and give me one of your special hugs. No one hugs like you. From the time you were born you loved to cuddle and it always came through in your hugs.

Scott, you've touched more lives than you'll ever know. You've brought happiness to so many people, but you never gave yourself the credit you deserved. I know that your bi-polar, anxiety disorder, and chemical imbalance were unbearable at times. I can't imagine living with the frustration of the doctors never finding the right medication for you. I know the times you tried to take your life and didn't succeed, you really wanted to live. You told me so afterwards. Isn't it ironic that just when we thought you were finally on the right medication….it's over. How can life be so cruel? We were told you had the flu and the autopsy showed a mixture of alcohol and your medication. To some, it looked like suicide, considering some failed attempts, but I knew in my heart it was not! You had too many plans for the future. I'm sure you were self-medicating trying to get a balance in your chemically unbalanced brain. I am so sorry the medical profession failed you!

Scott, I am trying to learn how to get through a day without tears. How to think of you and smile with warmth in my heart instead of a cold spot. You are helping me do that every day. Thank you. I miss you so much I think I am going crazy at times. I can't put a Christmas tree up for the second year in a row because that was our thing we did together. Maybe next year.

I want to thank you for the many, many "spiritual enlightenments" you have given to your family and friends. I knew if it were possible to communicate after you crossed over, you would certainly find a way. I want to thank you for the enormous amount of energy I know it must take for you to come through for us. I know you are doing it out of love to make us all aware that you never really die….your spirit lives on forever. What a gift you have given to us. My gift to you is to try as hard as I can not to grieve for you. I know that will make you sad. I love you so much I want you to be at peace. I promise to see the joy and beauty in life again. I know we will be together in another lifetime. Until then, I have my brightest star to look at and talk to. I'll love you always, Mom

A few years ago after reading "The Messengers," a story about Nick Bunick, my sister subscribed to their newsletter. In there, we learned of a psychic-medium named Atira. I finally got up the nerve to call and make an appointment in December of 1998. L left my phone number and first name on her answering machine. When she finally got back to me, we made an appointment for January 6th at 10:00 a.m. I was to call her that morning and have a reading on the phone. We were about to hang up when she said, "Oh honey, I feel such sadness!" I burst into tears. All she knew about me was my first name and phone number. Now she knew I was emotional. She said this is highly unusual, but she had someone there who wanted to talk to me. This wasn't even my appointment—that was set for January 6th. She went on to say a young man in his early 20s is there and she saw the letters S C O T. "Is his name Scott?" All I could do was sob. She said he wants to let me know his death was not a suicide. I already knew that! She said he was very sorry to see how sad we are. He told her some people believe it was suicide, and he wanted to let me know he was sick with the flu and he took his pills and couldn't sleep so he had some alcohol, and then forgot he took his pills and took them again. He wanted us to know that he is very happy and truly at peace with himself and God. He is experiencing true joy for the first time in his life. He no longer has a chemical imbalance, and his mind has been set free.

She said Scott chose us for parents because he needed to experience unconditional love in this lifetime. We had been together in other lifetimes as sister and brother in Rome, and I was his mother in Greece, but he had never experienced unconditional love. She said he tested us over and over and we always came through for him. She said he was asking about his blue car. She told me I have his picture in a wooden frame in the family room (I did), and to please put it in a metal frame. She said people who have crossed over have the ability to use their energy to move things and it's easier to move metal than wood. She said to start looking for coins and especially feathers. They are signs from the spirit world. She said they have the ability to make a phone ring, stop a clock, make static on a radio or TV, and make lights go on or off. She had me on the phone for 30 minutes, telling me things only Scott could have known. I said nothing, just muffled sobs. She said I could cancel my reading for the 6th of January since she's already talked to me, and I owe her nothing. I said I would like to keep my appointment for the 6th. I hung up and ran into my husband's home office and called my sister so she and my husband could hear what I had to say at the same time. My husband was brought up Catholic and really didn't believe in reincarnation or psychics, but when I was finished telling him everything he said, "Wow! She's made a believer out of me. How could she possibly know all those things unless Scott really was there?" My sister, daughter, daughter-in-law, and mom didn't have to be convinced. They just thought it was wonderful.

I had a different feeling about me. Since September 15, 1998, I had a knife in my heart. A constant pain that would not go away. From the moment I hung up with Atira, I noticed my pain in my heart was gone. I didn't know how long it would last, but for now it was gone. I am happy to report it has never come back. I still get a heavy heart when I am missing him, but that awful pain is gone.

I got a phone call from Atria on the 5th of January and she said she was sorry, but she had to change our appointment to the 11th. My heart started racing. That was Scott's 27th birthday! I didn't say anything to her about it. On the morning of the 11th she called and said she was very ill and wouldn't be able to do the reading. She changed it to the 19th, my granddaughter's 5th birthday. I called her on the 19th, and I had a wonderful hour hearing from Scott and learning about angels and spirit guides. I told her the significance of those dates and she said Scott had a lot to do with changing the dates. I believe it!

Our family and friends have had so many "spiritual enlighten-ments" from Scott. There are too many to list them all, some too personal to share, but I will tell you about a few. My sister got to see Scott and actually touch him. He hugged her and she felt her shoulders move. I am envious. She was on a spiritual high for days. My mom was in bed thinking about Scott and her radio gave sev-eral bursts of static then stopped. She said, "Scott, is that you?" It started again and stopped. Her radio wasn't even on.

On September 15, 1998, we had a houseguest visiting from Chicago, a special family friend for over 30 years. We had been tak-ing pictures and sightseeing for days. That morning at 8:00 a.m. as we walked down the hall to the kitchen, we glanced out the dining room window and ran for the camera. The sun was shining over the evergreens across the street through a mist, which gave the illusion of an angelic, heavenly picture. We were amazed and had never seen anything like that during the 9 years we lived in the house. The picture was taken at 8:00 a.m. on the 15th of September. We found out about Scott at 10:00 a.m. He had been dead for 8 hours by then. We had the film developed at a later date and gasped when we saw the date. I believe it was a sign. The next night we were all sitting around the kitchen table with broken hearts, and a bright light blinked outside and caught our attention. We went outside on the deck and looked up. The brightest star in the sky was actually blinking, like in Morse code. It was the same star Scott and I used when talking to my dad. I had never seen it that bright or blinking before. I got chills, and I knew Scott was sending me a message saying he's there with my dad and not to worry.

In late October of 1998, we took my mother, from Iowa, to Kona, Hawaii for some R & R. It's a common sight to see names and messages spelled out in white pebbles on the black lava all around the island. When our first grandchild was born, we spelled out her name and birth date and took a picture. This time, we spelled out "Aloha Scott 1-11-72 - 9-15-98." Aloha means hello, goodbye, and love. We took a picture and left it on the lava for the waves to wash away at a later date. Two days later, we were off for a 12-hour drive around the island to show Mom the sights. We talked about taking a 10-mile dirt road at the southern end of the island so we could say we've been to the southernmost point in the United States. We were talked out of going there by a man who lives on the island, saying it was no big deal. I was driving as that road neared, and at the last minute I turned and said, "Oh, let's do it so we can say we've been there." After driving several miles on a one-lane dirt road, you have to turn left or right. I decided to turn left. We drove to the end and got out of the car. The three of us stopped dead in our tracks…no names or messages anywhere on the lava except in big letters, "L U 2, SCOTT." We all took it to say, "Love you too, Scott." Now I know Scott didn't go there and write that, but the fact that we saw it 100 miles from where we wrote to him is amazing! We were definitely led there and meant to see it!

About three months after Scott died, our 2-year-old grandson announced from his car seat in the backseat, "Uncle Scott is in the car." My daughter turned around and said, "Did you say Uncle Scott is in the stars?" He replied, "No, I said Uncle Scott is in the car!" "Oh, do you see him now?" "No. He gave me a hug and left." He was very matter of fact about it. I really believe he saw him. I have since read books that say small children are still fresh from their spiritual lives and can see and hear people from the other side because they haven't learned to tune them out. That gift gets taught out of us, as we get older.

I now have a baggie with all of the feathers I have found since becoming "spiritually enlightened." It's absolutely amazing where and when I find feathers, just like Atira said. I'll be having a sad day thinking about Scott and all of a sudden a feather will be in a most unlikely place. I now take it as a sign and smile. My husband was having a sad Scott day leaving Denver airport heading home. He travels quite a bit for work. He landed in Seattle and when he got to his car in the parking lot, a beautiful two-inch feather was on his seat. He still has it in his car ashtray peeking out to remind him of Scott's message. You can't help but smile when you see it.

I was in our long-time family friend's powder room thinking about her daughter, who was in labor at the moment, wondering where her baby's birth angel was, and I saw a feather fall from the ceiling and land next to me. I learned from Atira we all come in with a birth angel who stays with us throughout life. I asked my friend if she ever had found feathers in her house. She said no, she doesn't even have a down pillow. That feather is now in the baby's baby book; who, by the way, is named after Scott.

My cousin was visiting from Idaho and we stayed up late talking about Scott and angels and beliefs. She had driven over in a terrible snowstorm and the pass had been closed most of the day. It opened right before she got there for a few minutes and closed right after she got through. She said, "do you think I had an angel watching over me?" At that very moment, two feathers came down from the ceiling between us. I said, "No, you have two."

It was Scott's job to replace our driveway post lights when they burned out, which was about twice a year. They were replaced about a month before Scott died. Since then they have been replaced about every two months. Lights all over our house have been burning out way before the normal time. Scott installed a dimmer switch sensitive to touch in our eating nook. About six months after his death it was off and as I walked by it got brighter and brighter. No one was near the switch.

Our phone rings a lot with no one on the other end. Now I just say, "Hi Scott. I love you too." We get a funny cracking on our TV and sometimes a ball of glowing red light is in the lower-right corner of the screen. We just smile and know he's giving us a sign. We put his digital clock in our bedroom and it would work then stop, work, then stop. I changed plugs, and the same thing happened. I plugged other things into that plug and they worked fine. The clock even had a new back-up battery. I finally moved it into Scott's old bedroom, and it works just fine.

We have had coins just drop from nowhere onto the floor. My husband has a battery-operated coin sorter in his office at home. It used to be a running joke that when it was empty, we knew Scott had "borrowed" the change. It's been empty and put away in a cupboard for quite a while. About nine months ago, my husband was working at his computer around 4:00 a.m. and the sorter turned on in the cupboard and started sorting a pile of change. Where did the change come from? We figured he found a way to put some back.

Scott's old TV got passed down to our grandkids for their bedroom. Our son-in-law says it has a mind of its own. It has turned on or off by itself so many times, the kids just say Uncle Scott is here.

Scott and our daughter-in-law had a nice apartment with a very large deck overlooking the University of Washington. They bought a huge market umbrella, which you could see from the University Bridge. The spring after Scott died, his wife had a reading with Atira and was very pleased. Atira told her Scott is moving things at the apartment and for her to be aware of this. She had wanted to have the table and umbrella moved two feet closer to the window, but it was way too heavy to move, even for two people. When she returned from work one day, the umbrella and table were exactly two feet closer to the window, right where she had wanted it. Scott always did like to put on a show.

I have had phone calls from several of our friends and family saying Scott has made his presence known to them in many different ways. My brother, who lives in Iowa, said he could never play the computer game called Myst again because Scott always walked him through tough spots over the phone and it would be too painful now. I told him to play it and he might be surprised at the help he got from the other side. A couple of months later, he was playing a game on the computer and words kept coming up on the screen saying things that Scott would say to my brother, kidding around. My brother couldn't believe what was happening and called my sister in Washington. She asked him if he had a picture of Scott. He said he did, and it was on top of the computer. She suggested moving it to another room. He did and the writing stopped. It has never happened again. Words don't ever come across the screen when you are in one of those games. This same brother has had a few conversations with Scott in the middle of the night. They were so real; he now keeps a pad of paper and pen by the bed so he can write down what Scott said.

Scott left one of his watches at a friend's house the week before he died. We told his friend he could keep the watch. He was talked into visiting a medium two weeks after Scott died to help him with his grief over losing a good friend. On the way to the reading, the watchband broke, and he placed it in his glove compartment. The medium said Scott was talking about his watch and the fact that it just broke. He also said Scott was talking about his driving and how he always kidded him about driving too fast. His friend said Scott always did say something about his driving. He brought the tape over for us to hear, not even knowing if we were open to such things.

Another friend of Scott's called me and said I would probably think she was crazy, but she had to share with me what had happened the night before. She was watching a movie about New York and the song, "How Bizarre" came on; she picked up a framed picture of Scott and danced around the room. She used to dance with Scott to that song at parties, and all his friends think of him when that song plays. It's an upbeat, quirky song and a lot of fun to dance to. When the movie was over she went to bed. At 3:00 a.m., she woke up to that song playing loudly in her living room. She doesn't have the song, and the TV and radio were not on. She went into the living room and Scott was dancing in two-piece flannel, hot pink, purple, and navy pajamas with three buttons at the neck, and navy cuffs on the wrists and ankles. She asked me if he had pjs like that and I said hardly, but you just described my pajamas to a tee! She had never been to our house, but when she came after Scott's one-year anniversary picnic, I showed her the pajamas, and she couldn't believe it. They were exactly what she saw. I was having a very bad "Scott Day" when she called, and I believe he sent that image to her, knowing she would share it with me and somehow cheer me up, picturing him in my pajamas.

Our daughter was driving home late one night on the freeway thinking about Scott and wondering why she hasn't had a sign or seen any feathers when all of a sudden her entire windshield was covered with white feathers. She had to turn the wipers on to see.

My teenage nephew was in a school play, "A Mid Summer's Night Dream." Opening night, all of the cast members forgot their lines and did a lot of adlibbing. The second night when we attended, they were all pretty nervous because of what happened the previous night. We were in the front row and when my nephew walked out, the first thing I noticed was he had Scott's boots on. I thought to myself Scott is with him tonight. About 20 minutes into the play, I nudged my sister and told her to look at his head. A white feather was on the side of his head. We couldn't keep our eyes off that feather. It stayed there until the actress reached up and flicked it away. After the play, he said he was amazed at how he remembered all his difficult lines. We smiled and told him Scott was helping him.

This year on September 15th, the year anniversary of Scott's death, some friends and family gathered for a picnic lunch at the same place where we had his memorial and celebration of his life. It's a beautiful spot in the mountains overlooking the valley. We were all walking around where the building used to be. It burned down four months after we used it. I walked over to the spot where we sprinkled his ashes a year before, and there was a rose bush with one beautiful rose on it. As I touched it, all the petals fell off in my hand. There was no rose bush there the year before. Scott's favorite flowers were red roses.

By now, I'm sure some of you are thinking I am one card short of a full deck. That's ok, because I am not here to convince you of anything. It's a terrible thing to lose a child, and I hope that by sharing some of my experiences with you, you will be left with food for thought and keep an open mind for your own spiritual awakenings on your journey to healing. Scott has taught me that death is only a spiritual transition, not the end.

James Stewart
November 13, 1976 – May 21, 1997

Stewart

Died by Suicide

Stewart was only hours old when I brought him to our home, where my mother was waiting to give us good care. Stewart's two brothers and two sisters burst in after school excited to welcome the new baby. How we loved this baby. I remember the joy of holding him. I remember rocking him, sometimes all night. Stewart had allergic asthma that kept us both awake.

Stewart was a fun little kid who liked to phone his neighborhood friends and get them together with his friends from church and school to play basketball in the park. By the end of elementary school, his friends had turned into a real basketball team with games in the school gym.

Stewart tested high academically, yet didn't want to be in advanced math. He had trouble following oral directions. By watching what the other kids were doing, he managed to do very well.

Stewart was funny and creative. In the fifth grade, he wrote these limericks:

> There once was a boy named Paul. .
> My sister wished he would call.
> The phone never rang.
> It drove her insane.
> And then she started to bawl.

> For dinner we all ate hash.
> After we all watched M.A.S.H.
> My homework is done.
> It wasn't much fun.
> I wish it could go in the trash.

Stewart reached out to kids who needed a little friendship. One morning when Stewart was in junior high, I found a kid sleeping on our front porch bench. He explained Stewart had told him he could sleep at our house any time.

Stewart's group of friends stuck together in junior high, giving me a chance to cheer for them in track and football. I was surprised when the principal called me to say Stewart had thrown a paper airplane in class. Stewart struggled to keep on top his academics because he had trouble with details like getting into his locker and keeping track of what was due when.

One day, Stewart told me he thought maybe he was from another planet because his brain didn't work the way other people's brains work.

Things got tough at Juanita High. Stewart was bright and struggled at the same time. His siblings had a lot of success at Juanita and some of the teachers expected the same from Stewart. A few made it harder for a kid already doing his best. A talented trumpet player, he could shine in music but the band teacher refused to let him move up in band with his grade level or play in jazz band. The band leader explained that Stewart's doctor-excused absences exceeded his attendance policy. Stewart always loved to read. The literature teacher wouldn't believe he read the Tom Clancy books and wouldn't accept his report. Stewart missed graduating with his friends.

Stewart did well in the community college classes he took during high school and got one of the highest scores on his GED the testing center had ever seen.

Stewart let me drag him to various doctors. Once when my grown kids were in town, I made an appointment with the psychiatrist at Group Health, hoping if he saw us all together he would see the big picture and give us some help. He offered no insight, just wrote a prescription.

Stewart and his buddies still had a wonderful time together. They would come with food, Nintendo's, and TVs and set up the big room with sleeping bags and pillows. They came with adventure in mind. They rappelled off roofs, trees, and a water tower, generating an ongoing saga.

Stewart got a neat job driving auto parts. He used the money to buy a Toyota Supra. He saw himself driving that cool sports car to go to college in another state, but it kept breaking down. Stewart was stuck.

Tuesday, May 20th 1997

I was doing some paperwork when I looked up to see my twenty-year-old son, tall, lean, muscular, with his short army-style haircut and blue, blue eyes with long lashes. "Wanna go for a walk?" he asked casually.

Sure I did. We walked a lot together. This day we drove over the hill into winery valley and parked by the gardens. Stewart seemed determined I should understand his views about responsibility. As we took the footpath, he pointed out that if someone drank beer and drove drunk, it was that person's responsibility, not the brewers' fault. I argued and talked about corporate and societal responsibility. While returning to the car, Stewart still tried to make his point clear, "Even if someone kills himself, it is his decision, and no one else should feel responsible."

I was silent. I had a strong feeling I should just not talk. If I could visit that moment again, I would throw my arms around him and say, "I love you more than breath. I would miss you if you died. It would break my heart. You are my joy, my son, my friend." Mostly, I would tell him he was needed. I would tell him that together we would leave town tomorrow and get him set up in college in another state.

It grew dark as we drove home. Stewart offered to drive a friend of mine to the airport to catch a late night plane so I could get some sleep before work the next day. I fell asleep and didn't even wake when Stewart returned.

Wednesday, May 21st 1997

I got ready for work and looked into the room where Stewart was sleeping. I felt impressed I should stay home. I overrode it and drove to work.

On the freeway, I was overwhelmed with the pain I'd felt in that room. There were layers of discouragement piled on Stewart. I begged out loud to God to end the pain. I had a huge urge to drive home but forced myself to keep driving, wishing I had a way to phone my boss. I wish I had turned around and driven home. Like a character in a Greek tragedy, I kept going.

After work, I walked into our house. It felt empty. I wondered where Stewart had stopped on his way home from work and kept looking at the clock as I worked in the kitchen. I had a calm feeling. My experience raising five children had been if I worried there was always a reason and if I didn't everything was alright. So I told myself Stewart was ok.

It was dark when a knock at the door made me hurry down the front hall. I opened the door. A policeman and a young woman stood there. They asked if I were Mrs. Jennings. I said "yes." I asked them how they found my house when the house number is hard to read. I wanted it to be the wrong house. I led them into the front hall and said, "It's Stewart?" They said, "Yes." I asked if he were dead or alive. They said, "Dead." I told them I thought they had a terrible job telling people their kids are dead. I asked how they could do it. The woman said they never had to—like me, the parents already know.

Still standing frozen in the front hall, I asked how it happened. They told me Stewart had driven to a patch of woods near our home, and a little after nine a.m., he had shot himself. County workers found him a few minutes later.

I wanted to be with him immediately. I needed to touch and hold and see him. They told me he was in the King County Coroner's office in Seattle's Harborview Hospital. I was desperate to go be with his body. They said it was locked at night.

I imagined my son in a cold, strange place alone. I longed to be with him. I imagined his spirit staying by his body. I wanted to go to Harborview.

I was incredulous that they found his body before ten A.M. and no one notified me. He was found with the rifle and his wallet with his ID in his hand.

The policeman asked where I planned to have him buried. I replied that I hadn't planned on having him die. He said he had to fill out the form. I chose a funeral home near my home. The policeman wrote it down.

The coroner recommended I consent to an autopsy even though this appeared in every way to be a suicide. He said it would close off questions that might arise later. My mind filled with thoughts of the invasion of the scalpel even as I made myself sign.

I asked them to leave because I wanted to be alone. The policeman and coroner said they couldn't leave until I phoned someone. I was stuck. Stewart was the one I would phone when I had a problem. He was my emergency number. My other children, siblings, and Mother all lived in other states. Stewart was my youngest child. We had lived in our big family house, just the two of us, for seven years since his brothers and sisters left home for school.

I hurt so badly that I couldn't imagine sharing this hurt. I didn't want to tell anybody. I thought that if nobody knew he was dead, maybe life would just go on. Finally, I relented so they would leave; I phoned a neighbor.

I couldn't make myself phone my children. The pain was wordlessly horrible and I knew sharing the news would break their hearts. I gave my neighbor my little black book and asked him to have my oldest son phone my other children and my mother and siblings.

My friends said one or both would spend the night. I told them to go. I wanted to scream and cry. They said they would stay downstairs, and I could scream all I wanted. I needed to be alone. To convince them, I told them when our neighbor's fourteen-year-old son was shot; his mother told me that no one understood how badly she needed to be alone. They believed me and left.

I walked upstairs, not believing I could move. Terrible pain pounded through each cell in my body. I had never felt every cell before. I couldn't believe such pain existed. I wanted it to count for every mother whose child died. I wanted it to count for everyone, even for people who had hurt me. I didn't want anyone ever to feel such agony.

Thursday, May 22nd 1997

I got up way too early to phone the coroner's office. Friends stopped by. I asked them to drive me to where Stewart died. He'd chosen a heavily wooded area with a little gravel road. At the end, was Stewart's green Supra. I touched it. I looked inside. It was a peaceful, beautiful place. The light filtered through tall fir trees. Peace settled over us as we stood on what to us was hallowed ground. I thought angels had surrounded Stewart and lifted him up.

I was still desperate to see my son. My daughter and I set out for Harborview Medical Center, where we entered the medical examiner's office. Stewart's body had already been picked up by the mortuary. I needed to see where he had been all night and where the autopsy occurred. The medical examiner showed us the big refrigerator where he had been overnight and the autopsy room. I asked questions about the autopsy. He answered. We walked downstairs.

I told him that I had questions about how Stewart died. He invited us into his office. He said, "If it were my child, I would want those questions answered, too." My need was validated, freeing me to ask exactly where the bullet entered and how much damage was done and how long it took to die and how much suffering he endured.

Each question was answered with respect. His clear answers provided information that I could ponder, filling the scary void of not knowing.

The coroner said if the bullet had gone a fraction to one side it would have injured a nerve but not killed him. He told of other cases where death was intended but the individual and family lived with permanent injury. I wanted every young person thinking of suicide to hear those stories. I wanted Stewart back alive but I didn't wish him or anyone the suffering of the young men in the stories. He told me bullet had hit a place in his head that brought death "about as quickly as death can come."

I am still grateful for the compassionate and professional way my questions were handled. We drove over Capitol Hill to the mortuary, where my precious son lay cold, wrapped in white. Finally, I was with his body.

Saturday, May 23rd 1997

The doorbell rang. Stewart's friends Mike, Andrew, Jeff, Michael, and one I hadn't met before came with Jeff's mom. They handed me my favorite ice cream. I was used to these young men being part of the house. We sat around the kitchen table. They were fine young men, each one. I asked if they would like to talk at the funeral. They seemed open to the idea. It was decided Jeff's mom and the young men would sit together and come up to the pulpit if they chose to talk. I thought they were brave.

We sat on Stewart's bed and his bedroom floor. They told stories I hadn't heard before. How I loved them.

The friend I hadn't met had hitchhiked from Portland. He told me Stewart encouraged him to join Kamiakin Junior High Football. It made a difference in his life.

Michael got leave from military duty and flew from Chicago. The others came from colleges all over, except Jeremy, who was serving out of the country on a mission.

They asked if they should talk about rappelling off the water tower at the funeral. I said, "Sure." I figured Stewart would like that. He was the leader of that adventure.

Memorial Day—Monday, May 26, 1997

I needed to type some notes for the funeral. I felt frustrated because someone kept turning off the computer and getting out of my programs, and Stewart wasn't there to help me with the computer.

I remembered the night I had been working on a paper and got up at four in the morning, turned on the computer, and there was one of Stewart's cartoon men with a bubble that said, "Go back to bed Mom and get some sleep."

I remembered coming home from work so tired that I went right from the car to my bed and found my favorite grapefruit drink waiting on the bedside table.

I remembered Stewart saying that there used to be five kids to do the yard work and now there was just as much work and only one kid doing it.

I remembered how Stewart could imitate anyone. He said, "Other people's mothers put their purses over their shoulders and walk like this. But you do it like this." And he quickly stuck a pretend purse under his arm and marched off.

I remembered holding my precious baby to the sky and bursting with joy at his arrival.

He was the infant who delighted my heart and the hearts of his siblings.

I had been warned that on Memorial Day few would probably come to the funeral. The church was filled to overflowing. Stewart had been a friend to many. There were people I didn't know who shared with me how he influenced them. His friend Dennis wrote a poem for Stewart and gave it to me. Friends from elementary school, basketball teams, work, lined up to say he had been a friend to them.

Afterwards

I returned from the burial to a big empty house. After work, I'd drive around the block three times before I made myself go in. One day a note on the front door invited me to phone a neighbor, Sue. I grabbed the note and phoned her number. She told me her son had died in a car accident. I hadn't even known. We walked. She talked of her feelings about her son's death. Some were similar to mine. I told her I was sad all the time. She said, "Things change." That sentence was a comfort as I felt great pain every minute every day and it helped to know it would change. Our walks often ended up in the woods where Stewart shot himself. Sue brought candles, or flowers, or seeds, and taught me the power of ritual.

Ritual gave me a simple thing to do when pain was overwhelming. I could walk to the grove of fir trees where Stewart died and plant a flower, I could keep a candle burning on the kitchen counter, and I could put rocks like the ones Stewart and I used to kick along on our walks, in a glass. These were all small things that symbolized and made real my pain and experience.

Living alone, I had the freedom to leave the house and walk when the pain was intense. It worked. Every hour or two, I'd walk. Sometimes I could walk off the pain going around the block. Sometimes I would walk and cry for hours.

Sue suggested I ask Gerri Haynes if I could go to her "Mom's Group." I did and found a place where I was "Stewart's Mother" again. I could talk about Stewart, pain, grave markers, family, everything. Gerri shared her insight as she listened to our grief. I lived from meeting to meeting, knowing I could deal with hard stuff there.

I learned from Gerri how to talk about something wordlessly sad and how to begin to wrap my mind around my son's death and my part in it not preventing it. When I look back, it is obvious what would happen, but in the moment it was not; I lived in crises. Every day I just kept rowing the boat. In Moms group, I could share the blinding 20-20 hind sight and longing for a do over.

Group gave us a place to talk about the ripple effects of our child's death on our families. I went to group as Christmas approached and was told by more than one other mother, "Remember, you have other children." I remembered and found joy in them.

One Sunday walking past Stewart's grove, I was dismayed to find it had become a yard-waste dumpsite for the county. Great piles of steaming debris covered the ground. Sometimes I walked past, and sometimes I climbed the piles. As the anniversary of Stewart's death date approached, I mentioned in the group, the change in his special grove.

On the anniversary of Stewart's death, I drove home from work in the rain. Sue and Gail, friends from group, knocked on my door and kidnapped my little granddaughter and me, taking us to Stewart's grove. I couldn't believe it. They had planted a garden, hauling in bags of topsoil, arranging old tree limbs between two tall fir trees. It was beautiful. It gave me a place to go to think about my precious son.

Each year we plant a rhododendron. Maybe someday there will be a forest of them.

Paul
October 24, 1976 – July 21, 1998

Paul

Died in a Motor Vehicle Accident

By Rosie

Our children are loaned to us. Life is fragile and can change in a moment. These are beliefs I have held for a long time. But in this last year, they have been severely tested Paul Glenn Davis was given to us on October 24, 1976. He returned to heaven on July 21, 1998. He was only 21.

Glenn and I had just returned from a fabulous trip to Hawaii, celebrating our 27th wedding anniversary. On Sunday when we got home, we called both of our children to say hello and let them know we had gotten home. I could not have asked or wanted anything more. We felt like we were "blooming." Our children were raised and functioning well as wonderful, responsible human beings. On Tuesday, our life as we knew it exploded instantly.

Tuesday was an ordinary July day, sunny and warm. Glenn, Jennifer (our daughter) and I all went to work. Jennifer and I both work at Harborview Medical Center, Seattle's Level One Trauma Center. I have been a Registered Nurse for almost 30 years and have always worked in intensive care or emergency. The last 11 years, I have worked at Harborview. I was told the Nursing Director wanted to see me. I thought this was unusual, and I had no idea what it was all about. As I walked down the hall, I saw Johasse in the hall crying. I got scared. When I walked into her office, the police were on the phone. I will never forget the words, *"there had been an accident, there were three fatalities and your son was one of them!"* I was frantic! *"What car"? "Who were the other Kids"?* They wouldn't tell me because the other parents hadn't been notified. There was one survivor and he was airlifted to us at Harborview. I didn't know him, there must be a mistake, and I can't fathom these awful words. We are trying to reach Glenn. *"Oh my God,"* I thought. My precious daughter Jennifer was called from the orthopedic clinic where she worked. *"This has to be a nightmare!"* Many people are here, I feel crazy! *"I can't believe this"! "I want to see Paul"! "I have to see Paul!"* I have survived my father's suicide, my younger sister's suicide, and my younger brother's death in a fire just two weeks after my sister's death. *"Haven't I had enough?" "I thought I had paid my dues!"* The Medical Examiner says I can't see Paul. He has to be seen at the mortuary. *"What mortuary, I don't know anything about mortuaries! I'll call Kay, my neighbor and best friend. She knows these things! I have to see Paul"!* Kay suggested Purdy's Mortuary. The chaplain and police agree it was a nice place. *"I have to see Paul!"* My dad, sister, and brother were all sudden deaths and were closed casket funerals. *"I have to see Paul!"* Glenn has arrived from work and Jennifer is here. Many people are around and there is a lot of chaos. I can't stand it! I'm frantic! *"I will not take another step until I see Paul!"* Finally I see Paul. It's true, he's dead. I can't stand it! *"What's going on?"*

The next three days are a blur. Relatives arrive from Minnesota. Purdy's Mortuary is nice to us. We have to make many fast decisions. I'm so overwhelmed. *"This can't be happening!"* I love Paul with my whole heart and soul. I see my beloved husband deeply sobbing. He says we should be planning a wedding, not a funeral! Four funerals are happening the same day, the three from my son's accident and a friend of Jennifer who had just died of Hodgkin' Disease. He was a youth minister. This is too much! After Paul's funeral, Glenn and I go to Scott's funeral, and Jennifer goes to

Chris' funeral. Megan's service was about the same time so, we couldn't attend it.

There is way too much going on. I can't eat; my heart is too swollen for the food to pass. ***"Someone help!"*** I want to die and be with Paul so bad.

I don't know how, but three weeks have passed. I can't stand it! Maybe if I go back to work, all of this will get out of my face for a while. Yes, work is a distraction. We are so busy that the thoughts of Paul, my beloved son, are off my mind for a few hours. This may be the answer, so I worked all the hours I could until I was exhausted.

Paul's birthday, my birthday, Halloween, Thanksgiving, Christmas, Jennifer and Glenn's birthdays pass. They are all very difficult without Paul being there. Now it is mid-January and I am in a deep, dark hole. My friends are calling. Cards are coming in. ***"Why don't people leave me alone, I just want to die!"*** I am amazed. Paul got over 400 cards and had 70 bouquets. What a lot of support, but I still want to be only with Paul! Exhausted, confused, suicidal, I land in the hospital trying to get some perspective. I take a week off of work and take some structured classes. I think the structure is a good thing for me now.

I am a robot trying to live! ***"Why me?"*** I know about the fragility of life and know Paul was lent to me but God, ***"did you have to take him no?"*** He was doing great. He had bought a house when he was only twenty years old. He had a steady job at Boeing. ***"Why can't he keep going?"*** We were all so happy and were not asking for anything more out of life. ***"What is the point to all this, is there a purpose?"*** I don't think God loves me, and I wonder what I have done that is so terrible that God does these things to me.

By April, I'm having some good days but I have some guilt over trying to be happy. I miss Paul so much. Maybe it is too early to have any happiness! I am struggling to live and find purpose in all this. I visit the doctor. I beg him to just kill me! I am seeing a counselor. ***"Is she helping me?"*** I don't know! So far, she hasn't fixed it yet! We are still getting phone calls and cards from family and friends. *"Why do people care so much?"* I am in great pain, my heart is swollen. It is broken and has a big hole in it. I feel mortally wounded.

It is now July 1999. The one-year anniversary of Paul's death is coming up in a few weeks. I don't think I can make it. I thought I'd be better by now, but I'm not! I have been seeing Gail (my counselor) and I have been going to a support group called Compassionate Friends with Glenn and Jenny. I have been put on several antidepressants by my doctor (too much, I think). I have also started attending a wonderful "Mom's" group, thanks to Gail, a friend who also lost her child whom I met at Compassionate Friends. Such love and support and compassion! I'm amazed, but nevertheless, I still am questioning my life. I'm exhausted. *"I can't go on!"* I land in the hospital again. This time for six days. I get out just in time for the anniversary of Paul's death.

With Paul's memorial fund, a grant from the Boeing Company, and the help of the staff at Harborview, we have made arrangements to refurbish two family counseling rooms in the emergency center at Harborview Medical Center as a memorial to Paul. We are hoping we can make things just a little more pleasant for other families who are waiting to hear if their loved ones are going to make it or not following an accident or some other type of trauma. We have a dedication ceremony, blessing the rooms and dedicating them in Paul's memory. A beautiful plaque, with Paul's picture and an inscription, is made up and will be hung in the area. The ceremony goes well. Paul's friends, our friends, my mother, my counselor, and many coworkers come for the dedication. Several Chaplains, the CEO of the hospital, and a representative from Boeing stop by and thank us for making this happen.

Well, it is now the end of July, and Glenn and I are spending several days at a beautiful resort on the Olympic Peninsula. I have received a book from someone called *Talking to Heaven* by James Van Praagh. I have plenty of time to read while Glenn is off doing things. Usually I don't read much, but with the quiet and serenity of this place, no phone ringing, no wash to do, nothing to cook, I read this book. I learn that Paul left because his journey is over and it is his time to leave. This whole thing isn't about me! It is not about God punishing me or not loving me! What I realize for the first time is, "this is about what Paul had to do!" I finally see a light in the tunnel and have hope. I also realize that I have a purpose, so therefore it is my job to stay on this earth to live out my destiny. I also figure out that if I should exit early, I will cut my journey and have to return to finish my stay on earth. The other point I learn is, if I leave early, I may not see Paul, or he may kick my ass for not doing the right thing! I want to arrive in heaven and be picked up and hugged by my son. I want him to be proud of me!

It is now August 1999. I am still feeling better, and I have hope. I will live out my life and die when I'm supposed to. In the meantime, I will love Jenny and Glenn with my whole heart and soul. Van Praagh said you are put on this earth to do two things: to love and to be responsible. I can do this, and I can be there for other people and continue my relationships with so many wonderful friends and family on this earth. I am committed to being whole and finding my purpose on earth in this journey called life.

Glenn and Jenny, I love you! Paul, I love you! I will stay here so you can be proud of me, so I can find my purpose, and see you again someday!

Final Note:

Initially, I said I'm not a writer. I cannot do this! But, with the help of Gerri and our Mom's group, I have written this story with my heart open. I hope this experience will help comfort someone in his or her overwhelming grief. I often felt crazy and out of control. But I know with help and time, I will be all right and my wonderful family will be all right too.

Scott
May 4, 1968 – December 28, 1996

Scott

Died in his Tent, Covered by an Estimated Ten Feet of Snow

By Dianne

As I sit here trying to find the will, the energy, the words, to write about my son I can feel cold pain emanating from the core of this body of mine. It radiates in waves like ripples in a pool. The pain is so intense—cold and yet burning and raw. My son, my first born and only son, Scott, who came into my life on a spring day in May and left in a freezing blizzard night in December. He was twenty-eight years old. It has been three years and three months since that December when he died on Mt. Index. He did not die alone; two good friends died beside him, shattering the lives of all their loved ones forever. They were on their annual winter hike. It was their sixth year and on Christmas day they laughed and assured each other that this time they would reach the summit. The day of their ascent was crystal clear, bright with sun and blue sky. I believe they did reach the summit that day. Late that same afternoon, the weather changed dramatically. A winter storm was blowing in, making their descent more difficult. Snow began falling thick by dark. They reached base camp by then, had a quick meal, and then snuggled in for the night—exhausted and pleased with their success. They lay sleeping in their arctic gear, unaware of the intensity of the storm. It reached blizzard conditions by midnight. Those who live on the mountain said they had never known such strong winds that howled and blew the thick falling snow into whirling, white curtains, obscuring everything. In their exhaustion, our sons slept deeply. The blowing snow began to drift and eventually encased them in their tent. Sometime in the wee hours, their oxygen was cut off and they went softly, gently home.

We spent 13 days searching for our sons. The night of the storm I watched and prayed. The snow was falling solidly all night. I knew they were in very great danger. I prayed over and over "God help them, please help them God. God help them, please, please help them," over and over until the words lost their form and became chant-like. God did help them. They did not endure any of the pain and suffering we had imagined during the endless days and nights we held hope and searched for them. During that time, each warm meal, hot coffee, warm bed, or blanket brought a shudder of guilt and pain through each of us, wondering about their need, their cold, their hunger. There was such relief to find them at last. It was the worst conclusion, but at last the search was over.

There was no strength to go on, but that did not matter. There was no alternative. Rebecca, Kirk (my daughter and son-in-law), Cindy (my son's fiancée), and I joined forces to remember as much as we could to celebrate Scott's life in a memorial service. On a cold, wet January afternoon, we gathered at a small country church. So many people came that the church neighbors called the police, who came and asked what was going on. How appropriate for Scott. His whole adult life, if there was a cop anywhere in the state giving out tickets, Scott would always be the recipient. I believe the service was a celebration of Scott's unique life. By God's grace, I was able to function, to share what a fine son Scott had always been and how very much I loved him. Rebecca poured her heart out on the piano in her loving tribute. Cindy read from

Scott's journal, written one summer when he and his trusty old dogs hiked from the Canadian Cascades to Stevens Pass. Kirk, Rebecca, and I read the poem "Stop all the Clocks" by W. H. Owen. A friend read from the Bible verses that had significant meaning to us—Romans 8:18-23 (LVB). I hired a piper to play *Amazing Grace* and *Goin' Home*.

I was surprised and unprepared for what I was to feel picking up Scott's ashes. I was handed a small, white, paper box. It was heavier than I expected. I stood staring at the box trying to take it in. This was all that was left of my beloved son's human body. In my mind flashed pictures of my golden boy, a toddler sitting on the grass with the summer sun shining through his white-blonde hair, blowing like down; another picture of him holding his baby sister for the first time; another leaving him on the playground his first day at school. Next, I could see him teaching Rebecca to row a boat and holding up his catch, and I could see him in junior high and high school. I could see his happy, laughing face. I could imagine I could still feel his silky white-blonde hair in the palm of my hand. I stood there trying to believe the impossible, but my heart was quite simply unable to take it in. How can this possibly be Scott?

In the weeks that followed, I don't remember much. I went back to work. I smiled at my customers and did my job. I felt I had to tell people that I had just lost my son. Because of the media coverage of the search, most people recognized our story. Looking back, I remember my mother saying she had seen news coverage in New Orleans of our search and our missing sons. Literally all across the country, people watched the news reports and many prayed that we would find them.

Ultimately, I took a leave of absence from work. Life was so hard. It was like trying to ignore that your heart had been torn from your chest, and you were putting one foot in front of the other but it simply did not work anymore. Having no income was terrifying but God provided one of his gracious miracles and I did not have to worry, at least for the moment.

I had not seen my sisters and my mother for a number of years. So in April, I flew down for five days. It was good to see my sisters, my mother, my niece and nephew, and their families. Much of the time was a joy. But I found when you have just lost your child, no matter how far you go the pain and confusion follow right along beside you. Your mind somehow slips away to some dark, unknown place. I could just sit and stare, unaware of time, unaware of even the thoughts I was thinking. Maybe it isn't like that for other mothers, but it certainly took up a large part of my days. Housework no longer mattered except for the basics—food, dishes, laundry, and bills. I watched things begin to pile up on my dresser, my coffee table, just about everywhere. I'd pull out the bills and leave the stack. I felt as though all my strength and energy had been sucked out. I found I had to meter out what I felt must be accomplished, and the rest would wait. The simplest task felt as if I were climbing through quick sand. If I dropped a tissue on the floor, I could walk over it for days. Things like that just didn't matter. I watched TV day and night. I even kept it on when I slept. Somehow I imagined that as long as it was on, I didn't have to think or feel or grieve. In truth, with my heart pulled from my body, I really didn't want to go on. I just hurt so much, I wanted to go somewhere that it would stop! But I owed my courageous, amazing daughter a better heritage. She was the wind beneath my wings. I know she was worried that I might sit and stare into space or the TV forever. But I knew I wouldn't. Whether I wanted to or not, I had to find some way, some direction. How could I honor Scott and his memory if I did not come out of this dark, thick limbo? Rebecca deserved only my very best because that is all she gave. She was unfailing, clear thinking, strong, and loving. To her fell the enormous task of settling Scott's far-flung estate. She had to gather the reins and steer it around, something most of us would have never come close to doing. She loved her brother so. All her life she had him to look up to and to laugh with, share with. Two years before Scott's death, Rebecca and Kirk had their first baby and they named him Colin Scott. As opposite as they were, they were always there for each other. One time, in a moment of heartache, Rebecca told me she felt she was dismantling all that Scott had worked his life to build. She had to make hard decisions, unpopular decisions, but she did them, she did them for me. I know Scott was always right beside her. I know he was finished with all the "things" of earth. I know he wished only to encourage her and help her know how proud he was of her. Rebecca's grief has been very controlled as it had to be for her. She has a lifetime to grieve. Why be overcome? – seems her means of coping and her philosophy.

I remember thinking of my own grief – how crazy CRAZY out of control I felt. Right from the beginning, I thought "I CAN'T TAKE THIS!!! MAKE IT STOP! I can't do this. It can't be happening. It can't be real." I wanted to <u>fly</u>, to run, to escape, to make this unbelievable thing <u>GO AWAY</u>. I felt I had no options and I didn't. I had to see, hear, feel, and endure this incredible nightmare. First that my son was missing and next my son was dead. Even now I feel the pulse in my throat hammering away. My mind searched and searched over and over but there was no escape. Years ago when my husband and Scott and Rebecca's father left me, I allowed myself to go crazy. I thought it would stop the pain, that it would help, <u>but it didn't</u>. GOING CRAZY ALWAYS MAKES THINGS MUCH WORSE. I do not recommend it anyway! I think part of allowing myself to "wing out" so to speak, was for someone to stop all this pain, this horror, but I learned no one comes to save you. No one tries to help you, NO ONE. You alone are the only one who can save "you" in your grief and sorrow. God is there for you too but when you are crazy you can't feel him. I cried and I cried until I threw up. I cried through boxes of tissue and rolls of T.P. I screamed at the top of my lungs and beat my chest and crawled on the floor whispering, "NO, NO, NO, IT CAN'T BE! MY GOLDEN BOY CAN'T BE DEAD! HE CAN'T BE DEAD!!! WHY WHY WHY?!! NOT SCOTT – NOT MY BOY!" I still do sometimes—when I must, or I think I will explode!

In May that first year after his death, we had to sell the land he had spent the last ten years of his life loving, building, clearing, gardening, mowing, and celebrating. Everywhere you looked, he was there. There also were our memories. The land had sold, and in four day it would no longer be ours. So on his 29th birthday, we gathered one last time on his beautiful land to scatter his ashes. We walked down to the river to the spot where he and Cindy hung their hammock between two moss-covered trees and where a dangling rope held a six pack in the cold, crisp water flowing down from Mt. Snow. I filled his pewter drinking horn (I had given him on his 18th birthday) with his ashes and a basket full of red rose petals, and each of us sprinkled his ashes with our hearts' good-byes. We prayed and listened to the rippling water and saw the bright green leaves budding in the stand of trees. This was the first spring that his beautiful eyes would not see. Cindy was the last to leave. She placed a long stemmed red rose on the mossy bend of their tree. It was so very hard. Maybe it was too soon, but for better or worse it was done.

During Scott's life, he had always pulled away from organized religion, but he was always quietly spiritual. He would tell me no one could feel closer to God than he did in the mountains. He would describe the tiny flowers that seemed to be only at a certain altitude, the birds, the mountain streams and pools, the sky and cloud formations—all the glory God had created and men had not yet touched. He loved it all so very much. I think he had the spirit of a Native American. I read this poem when I sprinkled his ashes. It was written by an unknown Native American.

> **Do not stand at my grave and weep.**
> *I am not there.*
> *I do not sleep.*
> *I am a thousand winds that blow.*
> *I am the diamond glint on the snow.*
> *I am the sunlight on ripened grain.*
> *I am the gentle autumn rain.*
> *When you wake in the morning hush*
> *I am the swift uplifting rush*
> *Of quiet birds in circling flight.*
> *I am the soft starlight at night.*
> *Do not stand at my grave and weep.*
> *I am not there.*
> *I do not sleep.*

The whole world seems empty without my Scott. He loved life so much more than I ever had! He filled every waking minute with either work or play. He rarely slept more than three or four hours. He just always had too much going on. He was well loved and appreciated by all different types of people. He had a wicked sense of humor and was always able to find something funny in almost any situation. He had a number of significant losses and trials already at twenty-eight. When his wife left him the second year of their marriage, I was very worried that he would stay hurt, angry and bitter, but his spirit was strong and true. He grew from his loss enough to fall in love and offer his heart and his love again. He and Cindy found each other, and after five years he bought her a diamond solitaire ring which he gave her three days before he died. Poor beautiful, tiny Cindy. She was as petite and cute as he was large and handsome. They were so cute together. He delighted in teasing, slightly ruffling her feathers in some comedic remarks.

I was so proud of his humor, his compassion, his strong sense of right and wrong, of his love of his country, his goals and dreams, his faith and his solid loyalty. I was also proud of the very sight of him. He was 6' 6", perfectly proportioned, lean but strong. He had white-blond hair, clear, grass-green eyes, and a red beard. I suppose all mothers believe their sons to be handsome but he was beautiful in my eyes, handsome to the rest of the world. I loved his tender side. His hugs were not to be forgotten. He made me feel small while he hugged me. He made me feel his love on the inside.

Scott and I had always shared a love of music but rarely the same "kind" of music. He was a rocker and I was not, but we both found music that we could play for each other and enjoy. During what was to be his last summer, he asked me to help him choose some classical music he would like. It was a pleasant surprise to see his taste widening and still growing. I knew it would be something we could really share. I so looked forward to it. It was as if he was becoming even more of the man I always knew I would be so proud of.

When you share with people, as I still feel compelled to do, that you've lost your child, you get all sorts of reactions. Some of them shock you, some make you angry, some wound you, and some give you comfort or at least acknowledge your pain. I talked with a woman who clung to her pets as if they were her children; she said, "Oh! I don't know what I'd do if my dog died, I just don't know what I'd do!" A frequent comment is "Well, at least you know he is in a better place now." I know people who say that are trying to comfort me. But it has made me angry and may always make me angry! I want to *scream*, "Yes, I know where he is, but that does little to nothing about my pain, my grief, my hunger to hear his voice, touch his hand, feel him in my arms." The death of a young man or a young woman is not the welcome release to a better place as it would be for the aged. I can never believe that it is right for a child to die before his or her mother or father. One woman I worked with had a son and a daughter similar in age to my children. When I told her I was trying to find my way back, to go on, learning somehow to live with the pain, her response was that she would never be able to go on with life if she lost either of her children. *She* loved them too much to even consider it. I felt like she had hit me. She seemed to be telling me that her love was deeper and that I must have loved Scott less because I was able to "go on." I have thought about this one woman and our conversation many times. I finally decided that going on, even as one of the "walking wounded," was the only way I could show my love for my son. I know he is out there rooting for me. I know he sees my pain, that he feels it. I believe he wants to help me.

I believe he left me a very clear picture of the peace he feels, the oneness with God and His universe. Christmas day, he left me the movie video *Immortal Beloved*. I did not watch it for months after he was killed. With the title and the day he left it with me—the last time I ever saw him—this movie had something Scott wanted me to hear or see. When I did get to watch it, the message was at the end. A young man escapes into the night, running and running. The background music was Beethoven's *Ode to Joy*. After running a long distance, he comes to a familiar pool. It is clear and warm and a perfect reflection of the stars and the heavens above. The young man slides into the water to lie on his back, looking up the night sky. The movie camera begins to pull back and upward over the young man in a pool, which has now become a pool of stars in the heaven. The higher the camera goes, the more they all become one, one with the universe. It is just a though Scott had drawn me that picture of his oneness with God, his peace, his joy. I try hard to keep that in front of me. I don't always succeed, but I am a very visual person. A picture *is* worth a thousand words.

Sometimes at night, when I'm driving and it's not raining, snowing or freezing, I open my sunroof and reach my hand up into the night and the stars with the wind pushing against my hand. I like to imagine the wind is Scott's hand holding mine.

Go sweep out the chambers of
Your heart
Make it ready to be the
Dwelling of the Beloved
When you depart
Love will enter
In you void of yourself
God will display her/his Beauty

Hafez

Shanda
July 23, 1969 – September 29, 1998

Shanda

Died in a Motor Vehicle Accident

By Barbara

I have probably experienced more emotions with Shanda than with any other person on this earth. She was born on July 23, 1969 and seemed so very tiny. She wasn't really as tiny as I felt she was, but knowing that I had all the responsibility to raise her from this point on, I was scared. I had thought I was ready for an infant but soon discovered that the work is far greater than one could ever imagine. I was determined to raise her with love; we began our journey together.

The feeling of being someone's mother was just short of a miracle. To hold her and smell her scent, to feel the warmth of her body next to mine, to feel her relax as she fell asleep while she was nursing in my arms was a feeling of total joy. As she grew, we were inseparable. To love and be loved by a child is a blessing.

Shanda was brilliant. She went through school in the gifted programs offered at the local school. She excelled but was still very shy. I was always proud of her. She was the youngest in her class. That was never a problem until junior high school, when she was no longer in the gifted programs that had been offered in elementary school. She became just a number in a very large school, and this was hard for her. She wasn't outspoken enough to let me know that she didn't know how to work with the system. She missed a lot of school and still kept up her grades but was falling away from what was expected of her.

Shanda was the eldest of my four children. She was my right-hand assistant, and I relied on her for help. She knew that I was busy, and so she didn't tell me what she needed often enough. At around age 14, she started to experiment with drugs. To this day, I don't know what she tried or didn't try, but I will tell you that the next three years were very hard on both Shanda and me.

She eventually met a young man named Jack and wanted to get married and start a family of her own. I told her to make certain that what she had taken during her teen years wouldn't harm the child she wanted to have. After dating and moving to Sacramento and back for a period of time, Jack and Shanda were married in September of 1992. They had been together off and on for nearly seven years. She was a very pretty bride and was so very excited.

They moved to Arizona after Jack's dad passed away. Jack thought this would be a good move for his mother, since she would be getting away from the pain of her loss. I couldn't stand the idea of Shanda being so far away, but I couldn't keep her from her happiness either. So they moved. She was working and they had been in Phoenix for about two years when one day she called me and said, "Mom, I'm pregnant! I am so excited! I have never been as happy as I am now and I can't wait until I can hold my own baby."

Her maternal instinct was very strong and she had done all the right things to get hold of what she wanted in life and for making decisions that were for her happiness and future.

On July 30, 1996, I received the call that should have been played around the world. Shanda called and said, "Mom, you have a granddaughter!" She was five weeks early, and that was surely because of the weather in Phoenix. The hot temperatures were very hard on Shanda and she went in and out of the swimming pool just to keep comfortable. The warmth of a mother's womb was a bit too warm for Jessica, so she decided to make an early arrival. She weighed a little over five pounds, but was healthy and totally beautiful. I called and made arrangements for the plane trip to Phoenix. I moved my vacation schedule closer by about three weeks and told my family I was on my way down.

When I arrived, Shanda handed me Jessica and said, "Here Mom, this is your granddaughter. Isn't she the most beautiful baby in the whole world?" Shanda was glowing! I had never seen her so happy and so much in love with her tiny angel. Her dream of having her own baby had come true. She was a mother and started to make plans for Jessica right away. She wanted the best for her. We shopped and got everything that she needed for her new baby and my new granddaughter.

From that day on, Shanda adored Jessica more than most mothers do or so it seemed from the perspective of a very proud and happy grandmother. She cherished her. She talked about her, sang to her, did everything for her, and was glad when each morning came and she would pick her up and start a new day! The one thing that was missing was that she didn't have her family or her lifelong friends around her to share Jessica with. She wanted to share her with everyone, and that was when she said she was coming home. She had been in Phoenix for four years and was bringing her baby home.

Her friends were so happy when Shanda came home with Jessica.

We began a renewed bond between mother, grandmother, and granddaughter. We went everywhere that we could together. I had a daily call that started "Hi Mom, it's me!" We would make arrangements to meet at Target to buy diapers, at Costco to have a hot dog, or to meet at a park to push Jesse in a swing. The three of us were together a lot of the time. We included Mandi, my other daughter a lot of the time too. The four of us would head to the mall or the grocery store or just home to sit and share the baby.

Jessica grew and we celebrated her second birthday. We were at Shanda's mobile home. It was a single wide, but she loved it. We had poured our time and energy into fixing it up to be just the way she wanted it. Cute, cozy, and all hers! We shopped for curtains and a new carpet for the baby's room. We painted the entire inside and decorated every corner. It was small, but we had a good time. We laughed and compared colors of fabric to paint and decided after many trips to the store on just the right one.

Jessica loved her mom and she was always into something. Shanda took a roll of pictures every week of Jessica. She was the only mother I know that had an up-to-date baby book. She also had a photo journal of every change that Jessica made.

It was nice, and it was summer. Shanda wanted to take Jessica on a boat ride, so one Saturday we hopped in the car and drove over to Seattle, got on a ferry, and headed for the Olympic Peninsula for the wild animal farm. It was an all day trip, but Shanda was so excited to take Jessica on a boat ride.

There were many other times that summer that we shared the baby and what she was doing that day!

September 29, 1998 was a Tuesday, and I was at work. I had a strong feeling to call Shanda and have her meet me, but there was a phone call and I was distracted. Then later, after lunch, I had the same strong feeling that I needed to call Shanda, but then two of my co-workers walked in and I forgot again.

After work, I went to the grocery store and figured I'd call her tomorrow. So I went home and made supper.

There was a knock at the door, and the dogs started barking. That is what they do when anyone comes near the house. Chris, my husband, went to the door and let this man wearing a dark-blue t-shirt come up the stairs toward the kitchen. I read the shirt and it said "Chaplain." I looked into his face, and he asked if I knew Shanda. Of course he pronounced it wrong, so I knew that he didn't know her. I said that I was Shanda's mother and he said that there had been an accident and Shanda didn't make it. I asked him "where she hadn't made it to?" However, from the look on his face I knew what he meant. I felt that there must have been some mistake, but the pain in my chest was so strong that I knew she was dead. I think I fainted for a moment, and remember him saying to Chris that there was a truck that had crossed the double-yellow line on Novelty Hill Road and hit Shanda's van head on. She had been killed instantly, and Jessica was in the hospital.

I have never felt so confused. I had hoped all my life that this type of call wouldn't come to my door. I felt time slow to almost a stop; the car traveling toward the hospital was certainly going five miles an hour or slower. There must be some mistake. This couldn't be happening.

I remember calling my mother in Michigan and telling her that Shanda was dead. My parents were there in what seemed like a matter of hours. I remember going to the hospital and seeing Jessica with a cast on her leg. She had a broken leg and the straps from the car seat had left bruises across her chest. She was crying and calling for her mom. The time from when the accident had occurred until we arrived at the hospital had been almost four hours. Jessica had been with strangers and in a lot of pain from the broken leg.

They transported Shanda to Seattle, and they were going to do an autopsy on Shanda the next day. They couldn't tell me where she had been taken after that. The need to be with her even though she was dead was tremendous. I needed to hold my baby again, for one last time. It took me three days to finally find out that she had been taken to the funeral home in Bellevue. I went there and asked to see her. I was told that she "wasn't ready" and I said that didn't matter, I want to see her now. They brought her in to a room wrapped in a plastic bag and covered with a sheet. Her eyes were closed and her hair was a mess, but I was finally in the same room with my baby. I was there alone with her and I held her close to me. I touched her hand and her cheek. I felt her hair and kissed her lips. She was cold and I knew that her soul was gone. But I still needed to be with her.

We made the arrangements for her service. Her casket was a soft mauve color, one I knew she would like. I bought four gravesites so that Shanda wouldn't be buried alone for all eternity and because I had to have two sites wide to place a bench near her. I wanted to have the option of having a bench someday just in case Jessica wants to sit and talk to her mother when she has those growing-up troubles: when she wants to share what is going on in her life or when she just wants to say "I love you, Mom, and I miss you."

It has been a year and a half since Shanda's death. I miss her every day, and I thought that I wouldn't ever wake up again without first thinking of her. The pain in my chest was so great that I thought I would surely die too. No one could live with a pain this strong.

What little sleep that I got for the first year was just bits and pieces. I don't remember being tired, but then I was always tired. I would cry driving home from work. I would cry at work. I would cry in the laundry room. I would cry in the grocery store, and so I quit going to the grocery store. It is still too painful to shop without her. Down every aisle there are foods that remind me of a conversation, a meal that we had, or something we had talked about.

There are so many things in my life that have changed and I can't think of any reason that I wouldn't go back to the day before her death and change all that has happened. I would have taken her place in a heartbeat. The "why" did this happen, and the "if I had only" done something else, she might still be alive. What if I had called her that day, she would have been at the other side of town. What if it had rained, like it always does in Seattle, she wouldn't have been taking Jessica to the park to play. She would have been home instead. There are no answers that make any sense and there is nothing that can be done that will change what has already happened. I have made it this far with the help of a very strong support group. They have all lost children. They are mothers that feel cheated too. They are asking "why my child?" just like I have. They want answers that will never come.

The pain is less and the elephant on my chest has moved to someone else. I hear of an accident and another child dies. The mother is in great pain. I know this. She will suffer for the rest of her life. She will never be the same again, but at some point she will start to live again. She will say to herself, if not out loud, "my child is gone, but my child would want me to go on with my life. My child would want me to laugh and appreciate the day. My child would want me to finish each day and know that there will come a day that we will be together once again."

Shanda is gone. Her memory lives on in my heart and many others that loved her too. Her legacy is Jessica, and she reminds me more and more of her mother every day.

She is a wonderful child and I hope that through the stories I tell her of her mother, she will feel as though she knows her too. She is the one that has been cheated the most. She won't have a mother there to share her dreams with. She asks me when we see other kids in the movie theatre or at a park, "Does she have a mother?"

She realizes even at three years old that most children have a mother. Since Jessica lost her mother when she was only two, and from what I have been told, she won't remember her. She will need to have someone else tell her who her mother was and what she was like.

Children adapt to their situations. Jesse doesn't have the longevity that I had with Shanda and all the memories. There isn't a day that passes that I don't pray I will wake up from a very bad nightmare and Shanda will come through the door or the phone will ring and I will hear, "Hi Mom, it's me!"

Susie
January 21, 1970-November 25, 1995

Susie

Died by Suicide in her Home

By Mary

It was the day after Thanksgiving and I was worried about Susie because I thought she was showing signs of depression when we were with her for Thanksgiving at her house. Mo, Susie's husband, called her about 3 o'clock to let her know that he was coming home early, and asked her if she wanted to go to a movie that night. She told him yes. By the time he got home, 10 or 15 minutes later, Susie had gone to her closet, which was her favorite hiding place, and fatally shot herself through the mouth.

It was after dark when I answered the door. I had seen the Lynnwood police car drive up our street and knew when I opened the door to see the officer and chaplain something had happened to Susie. I asked them to come in. They asked if I had a daughter named Susan. The policemen said he was very sorry to tell me that my daughter was dead. All I could think of was how in the world I would tell my son, Brian. My husband, Allen was in bed, but got up when he heard the people. I asked if I could go see Susie, I wanted so much to hold her, to talk to her one more time, but they told me the coroner wouldn't let me.

The police followed me to Brian's friend's house. I asked for Brian to come to the door and the policeman told him about Susie. He screamed at the top of his lungs that she wouldn't do that. We went into the apartment and he threw himself on the floor, crying and screaming.

After the police left, I stayed for a little while, and then went home to be with Allen. I called Pastor Bill when I got home, and he came right away. I also called my friends, Margaret and Debbie who also came right away.

I remember now that when we left Susie's on Thanksgiving Day, she hugged and kissed me several times. This was unusual for Susie.

I felt stunned, empty; like I have lost my best friend, my "partner in crime" who could do great damage with me at the mall, shopping. I thought, now what is going to happen. I felt angry with Susie for doing it and at the doctor for letting it happen, although in hindsight, I knew he couldn't make her take her medication.

Mostly, I was just angry that she was gone and she hadn't left a note so that I could somehow understand why she was gone. I was angry with God. I told Pastor that he could come and help the others, but NOT me.

I really think it was the "others" in Susie's mind that killed her.

The good times with Susie were when she was playing sports. Watching her with her friends felt good. She was always the counselor in her group, mending romantic squabbles and listening to her friends in need.

She played basketball from the third grade through her first year in college. She always looked so happy when she was playing, and in retrospect, it probably kept her well for a long time. It was disappointing for her when she went to college and got to play only during practice.

Shopping with Susie was quite an experience. She liked to shop and always knew exactly what she wanted. She "never had anything to wear," a common lament of young women, so shopping was always necessary. I remember when we bought her prom dress. We became intimately involved with every shopping mall in the area! She tried on what seemed like hundreds of dresses that all made her "look fat" until she found the perfect dress. It was a strapless sky-blue gown that she looked like a princess in.

Susie didn't go to beauty shops easily. Her grandmother took her to the beauty shop when she was about eight years old. Her hair was cut short and permed into a popular "afro" style. Susie never let me forget that escapade.

Susie was a wonderful big sister. Although she and Brian were typical fighting siblings as kids, once she left home for college, she and Brian were the best of friends. Susie lovingly accepted the children we brought into our home through adoption and foster care. Her relationship with her adopted brother, Mark, was remarkable. She became attached to him immediately. Although Mark has never been verbal, Susie had no trouble communicating with him. They played, sang, took car rides, and had their daily special treat—French fries at McDonalds!

We had eagerly anticipated Susie's birth. We had arranged with a doctor to adopt the baby of one of his patients. We knew when she was supposed to be delivered, so I stayed close to the phone, eagerly waiting for the magical call. It came at 9 a.m. January 21, 1970. The doctor said, "You have a baby girl." I wanted to know every detail about my baby girl and could hardly contain myself as I waited the three days to go through the court system before we could pick her up. we went into the nursery, watched the nurse dress her in her own little clothes and whisked her home to the safety of our little family. Her brother Jeff was waiting at home with Grandma. Although he was three and a half years old and was undergoing chemotherapy for leukemia, he joined in our joy for our little Susie.

Susie had a long history of mental illness that probably started in high school. I thought that she may have been involved with drugs or alcohol, but it was probably just the beginning. When she was in college, she would sleep her days away until she finally dropped out.

When she came home from college, she got a job and lived at home. She would sometimes stay in bed for days at a time. It made it very hard for her to keep a job.

Susie's biological father is in a mental institution in Oregon. Susie's biological mother came to her funeral. Susie had made contact with her in December 1993. She had been searching for her for a while. At first her mom did not want to make contact with her, but after a while finally consented. Susie was so thrilled to know she had a sister and niece. She and Mo went to Denver after they were married to visit her biological family. Her sister had planned a party to introduce her to family and friends. Susie's bio mom called everyone and told them the party was canceled. Susie and Mo packed up and left.

Susie was diagnosed as bipolar (manic-depressive). She never admitted to this diagnosis; she was always in denial.

The last time she was in the hospital, she was there after being missing for over a week. She usually drove when she was having a hard time. Mo and Brian went to Ellensburg to pick her up after being contacted by the police that she was there. The inside of her car was completely torn up. All of the pictures of herself from my house were torn up and on the floor of the car.

Susie had very supportive friends from her school years. They always showed concern for her and comforted us at the funeral. The last job she had at a shipping company was good. They were very fond of Susie and let her have time off when she needed it to get herself together.

I think each episode she had was worse than the one before. I think Susie knew that she would have to have longer, more intensive treatment.

I know that Susie isn't suffering anymore. I still dream that someday she will walk through the door as if she had been gone on a long trip.

This year, we left her favorite pink roses for her on the anniversary of her death.

Susie.... From Mom

Loving, caring, compassionate
Carefree, pretty....then
Empty longings to see you again.

Lily
August 29, 1983 – February 20, 2006

Lily

Died

By Joan

As the Amtrak train raced across the long Montana plains, I was reading a story written by Emily Carr. In the story, a Native American elderly woman recounts the loss of each of her 10 children. I read a little deeper into the story and then closed the book overcome with foreboding. It was then, as the train roared towards Seattle, that I fully considered the fact that my daughter, my only daughter, could die. And one week later, she did. My daughter, aged 22, with doctors rather than family gathered around her, died. Her liver and quickly after her organs, blood, muscle, and bone, failed. Everything failed.

That was three years ago.

My daughter's name is Lily, or more formally Lillian Jeanette. I hardly ever write her name or say it out loud because all the air rushes out of my lungs, and then I have to sit down and just concentrate on breathing. But I think about her always, sometimes I cry, sometimes I am enthralled by a memory that settles on my mind like a blessing. Sometimes I am numb because I see her again in the hospital, not even able to breathe on her own.

Most of the time now I go about my work; a person passing me on the street would never know that an invisible shroud of grief is always present. Still, I am grateful that I can participate in the world. After she died, there were many months when I was hopelessly lost. Here is a list I made just after she passed away—my to-do list:

Things I want to do:
- Walk one block without collapsing
- Complete one simple task such as doing the dishes
- Drink one cup of coffee without crying
- Drink a half bottle of wine a day
- Run away and change my name to Ginger

Things I don't want to do
- Run away and change my name to Stella
- Become cynical
- Drink a half bottle of wine a day
- Forget

Yes, I know the lists have some things in common, and it was meaningful at the time, but I can't remember why.

Like many mothers, I was able to occasionally rally in those early days. By the power of the universe or the grace of God or whatever superhuman power you may ascribe it to, I was able to get through my words of remembrance at Lily's funeral. I was able to hold my youngest son as he wept through the night. But mostly, I sat in my rocker and let the motion help regulate my breathing and heartbeat.

Also in the first two weeks, I decided to get a tattoo on my wrist, a lovely image of a lily for my Lily. I remember my girlfriends, all dressed in black in the tattoo parlor, like a coven of good witches. They were stunned by my decision because I had a 50-year needle phobia. Disbelieving though they were, they wanted to support me as I permanently marked my wrist with a flower perpetually in bloom. I didn't feel a thing, the needles didn't hurt—I felt nothing. Nothing.

On rough days, my tattoo is a symbol of surviving the devastation—the holocaust of my daughter. It is my death-camp mark. I can tell you the wrong person walked out alive. On better days, I look at the tattoo as a symbol that I carry my daughter with me, she is etched in my skin, and I feel my hand bloom with the memory of her.

Almost immediately after Lily's death, I began having dreams about her and so began my dream journal that has over 60 dreams. And I began writing poems. I don't know whether writing and dreaming helped me in the beginning of my grief. But they have stayed with me, and I now find some solace looking back over the journal and writing new poems.

I also read the obituaries now. I read the obituaries as if they are short stories about old friends. I love the folks who have lived long lives   decades on decades—and leave the earth with a hearty farewell and a smiling face. I notice that the accompanying pictures are almost always happy pictures, as if to say here is my happy life, come to an end. Even when the death is tragic, like that of a young person, the picture is most often one of a radiant smile. I have found hope in the pages of the obituaries, because of the pictures, the bright eyes, the tender smiles. Often, if the victim is a woman, there is a comment something like "her smile could light up the room." The departed are flawless. Flawless and happy. As if in departing they are remade—perfected.

Death of a young person isn't pretty. It is like a reversal of birth, complete with body fluids. It can be noisy like a car crash, or the pounding of doctors on an unresponsive chest with the sound of a ventilator wheezing in the background. After a birth, the baby is washed and swaddled and ready to face the world. The dead are also washed and made ready. Their smiling, happy pictures are put in the paper, and we see the best, no matter how they died, no matter the devastation left behind.

Coming and going are messy.

December 31, 2006
For Lily

Let this year end.
Let the sadness recede
but not the memories.

Ok, maybe some of the memories.
The cold hospital room
her little white toes.

The hospital cafeteria
where the surgeon found me at 11p.m.
He has on scrubs and a hat from the Australian outback.

He tells me he can fix what God left undone.
I tell him to start now.
He says he needs a liver first.
He doesn't want mine.

The waiting room with shell-shocked families
all staring into the aquarium,
wishing their lives could be an easy swim again.

Never again.
She is gone;
we buried her, toes and all.

My daughter, Lily, had struggles. She had juvenile diabetes and also an eating disorder. She was bright. When she died just months away from graduating from Carleton College with honors, she spoke three languages, French, Japanese, and Mandarin. She could read music in western and eastern scales. She played eight instruments. And after much turmoil in her life, she had found extreme happiness—she was about to be married to her high-school sweetheart.

We buried my daughter in her wedding dress with the smallest little diamond ring on her finger. How far away this was from our beginnings as a family. How I struggled to provide a safe home. The little things and big things you do for your children to help them be secure. How stupidly optimistic. How dead wrong. I forgot that there is a universe spinning out of control and that at any time our plans for safety can be like so much cosmic dust blown to smithereens.

Here is a poem I wrote soon after my daughter was born in 1983.

Late Nap

We sleep through the twilight
into the early dark.
On either side, their breaths
chorus my own. My boy child
and baby girl bundled in blankets
of many generations.

Beyond our room,
the dishes are stacked on the table,
my husband reads on the couch,
his rhythmic turning of pages slows time.

Outside, an occasional leaf
crackles to the earth,
a robin scratches across the porch
searching for cracker crumbs
and spilled birdseed.

When we wake, it will be
tents out of covers,
jelly and bread,

and dragon stories from dad
until we sleep again.

I wrote that over a quarter of century ago and just recently found it tucked in an old journal. It is so idyllic, so comfortable and safe. The children sleep while the parents stand watch, the mother watching her children sleep, the father reading quietly but there in a moment should something go wrong. Things go wrong. When my children were in preschool, I remember a mother saying to me the worst thing that could happen to her daughter would be to have a child out of wedlock. All the markers for failure seem so extravagant to me now. My empty arms wish my daughter had had a child out of wedlock—several. She might have graduated from high school with a brood of children, my grandchildren. But those grandchildren I might have held are gone too.

It is hard to describe grief: the way it can blanket a family and how it changes an individual. Everyone lives with grief differently—every member of my family has a private grief journey. I read a book recently that said the death of a child is so horrifying in our culture that it has no name. If you lose your parents, you are an orphan; if you lose your spouse, you are a widow or widower. But there is no word for the devastation losing a child visits on your soul and on your body.

I function, in the world, have a responsible job although I can no longer work full time. And lately, I drink more than I should. My former husband had to take a year off from teaching. My two sons both struggle. One struggles with anger that erupts in violence, and the other battles depression. My daughter's fiancé seems lost. I often think I could live with my grief if I didn't have to witness the pain of my family. If only I didn't have to watch the slow grind of never-ending grief on my family.

Grief is never ending but it is also ever changing. Now three years out, my large extended family is transforming. Our lives have gone on, we hold Lily in our hearts, we love each other more, we have a motto: "If you're breathing there's hope."

Early on, I started seeing young women on the street that looked like my daughter. Once I followed a young woman in Starbucks out to her car and asked her if she dropped the dollar I held in my hand. Is that stalking? I traveled to Europe a year after my daughter passed away and on Kampa Island in Prague came upon a marble statue that from one side was the image of my daughter. I wrote this poem.

You Can't See What Isn't There

When I walk into the basement
I expect to see ghosts,
Wisps of departed loved ones
Whose love for me has
Kept them captive

I think I hear whispers.
And sometimes pinwheels turn
When there isn't any wind

Is that a rock in my path
Or a sign?

Is it a coincidence that the
Beautiful statue in the park
On Kampa Island in Prague
Looks like you, daughter?

How did I end up in Prague
And happen to approach
The kneeling girl
From just the right angle?

Stone face, pretty cold toes,
Sweet marble smile on that sunny day,
With the Vistula River rolling by

The century old trees beginning to leaf,
And everywhere park goers
See evidence of spring
In the basement of winter

One day, walking through a park in our hometown, I spied a young student hurrying to the bus, focused on her journey, unaware that a middle-aged woman was struck by her familiar gait: a woman held suddenly in the grip of an overwhelming vacancy.

Girl with Backpack

There she goes,
Forward-leaning, as if to hand off a relay baton.
She is a pack horse.
The backpack is full and sways
with the heavy load as the girl
hurries toward the transit center.

She looks familiar.
I look for the heavy
calves, courtesy of her Polska grandmother.

Her hair is long, halfway down her back.
But it is black
not blond
the way I remember.

But she leans right.
She has a heavy load

and somewhere to go.
She has glasses
that stay perfectly poised
on the bridge of her nose.
She doesn't look to the left
or the right
but straight ahead
to the bus shelter
where no bus waits.

Writing helps organize my feelings. Sometimes I feel I am in a free fall of sorrow. But that isn't the right metaphor either. A free fall assumes there is a bottom, a place to fall to. Sometimes I spend days just thinking up metaphors of what it feels like to be tossed around by grief. For instance, take a pinball machine. Watch the journey of that silver metal ball. First, it is violently launched…it travels down the long shoot until it enters the field of bumpers, flippers, and traps that propel the ball helter skelter over the playing field. Finally, the ball rolls past the last pair of flippers and drops into the dark abbess of the machine. The last time I watched a pin ball slapped around, stunned by the bumpers, catapulted by hidden springs, I thought I was looking at the violence and futility of my sorrow. Lily is not coming back, and sometimes the magnitude of my grief spins, and catapults and slaps me around like a pinball machine.

I collect crazy metaphors: Not many people weep thinking about pinball machines. Crying over seemingly neutral things or events is another symptom of grief. Things can get a little silly when you break into tears over any of these:

- hotdogs served at picnics.
- hearing any Beatles song anywhere. (I might mention the sheer number of Beatles songs that are played in elevators. I have climbed so many flights of stairs avoiding the Beatles that I lost 30 pounds.)
- the word *bunny*.

Crying over hotdogs is just unacceptable. While weeping over a tofu dog at the health food store might be acceptable, wailing over an Oscar Meyer at an all-city picnic is not!

Sometimes I am transformed by grief as if I walked into a brilliant light. I can feel the sorrow remaking me, twisting my DNA, realigning my synaptic switches, and I change. I have become in my own way a shape shifter. I start to breathe deeply and can almost feel the exchange of oxygen and blood in my lungs. It is these rare times that I feel Lily's presence or I take a forward step in my own evolution. I move toward peace.

My life is like a piece of kinetic art

Here I am, all metal and hunks of glass
at the whim of the wind—
slave to seasonal gusts.
Anchored but arms flailing.

In the doldrums, I am quiet
and stasis surrounds me,
but I stand ready to react
to the slightest breeze.

I refract light given to me
but can't move an inch to
capture a glow.

Completely reactive,
I posture, depending
on what is sent my way.

Give me grief—I'll reflect it back.
Give me light—I will
divide it into colors.
Give me a breeze and
I will sway in the wind
but only so far.

I have a firm foundation,
Bolted to the ground and
with my standard in a cement vault,
I am not going anywhere.

But I long
to see the bolts unwind
and movable parts rust through
and with a last great gust
sent spinning off into the black sky.

Finally, here is a poem that uses Hollywood fan magazines as
a vehicle to try and explain how occasionally I get a glimpse of
something bigger than my grief.

The Stars—They Are Just Like Us
for Lily

In the magazine there is an article:
Stars—They Are Just Like Us.
Pictures of the latest Hollywood starlets
and heartthrobs doing everyday things.
caught:
actually pumping gas,

actually pushing a grocery cart,
actually building a sandcastle.

See where our lives intersect
our beautiful commonality?

Somewhere behind a bush
there is someone watching
even me
even you
waiting to catch us unaware.
Caught:
leaning over a stroller full of happiness,
blowing a kiss to no one in particular,
ordering a third glass of wine because maybe,
tomorrow is too much to hope for and today is just fine.

Overhead
at night the lights blink on, they whirl about the sky,
some are named and charted, some are not.
Look—They Are Just Like Us:
caught sloughing off wishes,
caught emitting light long after death,
caught disappearing into the break of day.

I don't know where my grief will take me. I hope it makes me better, I hope I can honor my daughter by living a good life. I know sometimes I have bad days and want to run away or drink myself into a stupor. Some days, I don't get out of bed; some days, I go outside and shake my fist at God and make terrible threats; some days, I cry so much I my face looks red and puffy as if I were beaten. But most days, I get up, do the things I need to do, try to do one thing extra well, try to make this lonely, broken world a better place, take special care to tell my family members I love them....every time I see them...every time. And on those rare days where a leaf on the breeze brushes by or a stranger smiles, or a mackerel sky makes me break out in a Joni Mitchell song, I remember Lily. Her short life, her struggles, and bravery. And I thank the universe for tender moments and remembrance of my girl. Lily Girl

Here is a poem I wrote after reading an article on an archeological find.

Still Life

In the Sahara, where once a thousand,
no, five thousand years ago, scientists think streams and
cool reflective pools basked amid ancient palms,
a grave was found.
The experts were able to discern the bleached bones
of a woman and two children with
their bone fingers intertwined and dusted with pollen.

The scientists think they were buried on a bed of flowers.
The archeologists think they might have drowned together.
The hydrologists think five thousand years ago there was a
lake nearby.
The curator thinks they were a mother and her two children.

This is not a subject of art...this is not a subject to arrange on a
wooden table with symbolic objects, a dairy, a half glass of
absinthe,
an over-ripened pear.

This is the old bone yard of no discernible relatives.
This might be the end of a dynasty

laid to rest on ancient and long-gone desert flowers.
This is the jaw bone of the adult woman in a permanent scream.
These are the two children, their skulls staged so that they gaze
toward the older woman,
their jaws closed, their bones tucked into the desert sand,
little finger bones intertwined.
And now uncovered
by old guys looking for dinosaur bones.

Sleep, old mother.
Rest, children in your sandy blanket.
Keep your story to yourselves.
Rest on your ancient flowers
that bloomed before we had a word for flower.
Cling to each other in this desolate land.

Unearthed, unnamed, unstoried
but shouting across the millennium
that even in our bones we reach for each other.

Three things I learned in the first three months of grief:

- That Lorazepam is not a long-term solution
- That walking three blocks to the coffee shop, standing in line and ordering a cup of coffee without falling to your knees and weeping is a gigantic victory
- That there are many seasons of grief.

THINKING OF YOU

IT BRINGS ME JOY BECAUSE I CAN

MARLEEN

Laura
July 18, 1986 – December 27, 2002

Laura

Died in a Motor Vehicle Accident

By Ruth

Laura is dead. My daughter is dead. She died. This is how I begin, go through every day and end my nights. Every day, every night. I will never see Laura again. I will never hear Laura's voice. I will never be able to hold Laura or hug her ever again. I miss Laura so much. I still can't believe she is dead. How could she be? I need and miss her so much. Someone told me that to lose your parents, you lose your past; if you lose your spouse, you lose your present; when you lose your child, you lose your future. I have lost my future. My little girl is dead. After Laura's death, I realized I had lived almost my whole life with her. As a child and young adult I grew up knowing I wanted to be a mother, Getting married, I knew I would have children and for the 16 years 5 months and 9 days that she was alive, I was her mother. I can't believe she is not here for me to take care of any longer, or that I will never see her grow up, graduate from school, date, get married, or have children of her own. How could this have happened? It is so unbelievably sad. We are not supposed to bury our children. I had to bury my little girl. I stood at Laura's bedside for nine long horrifying days and watched her die. We made decisions about surgeries, looked at results of tests that would give me nightmares for the rest of my life. Laura died. No one could save her. She was only 16 years old. How could this have happened to my Laura? We were talking about her going to college. She had just gotten her driving license, we were all so proud of her. She had so much to live for. She was beautiful and intelligent and she loved people. She had a heart so big that she felt for every one she knew. She had such a kindness and gentleness about her. She had a way of finding goodness in people. I was blessed that she chose to share her life and friends with me. We would talk about things in her life all the time. I knew almost everything that was going on in her life. In today's world where children are silent so much of the time, Laura opened her life to me and we were friends. I miss her friendship. I miss her.

I keep going back to the line in the e-mail I received that said I could write a letter addressing the judge and let him know how I have been impacted by Shayla's actions, and the death of my daughter. Those fourteen words put so short and sweet have an impact of ATOM BOMB that has gone off in my life, destroying everything in sight. Nothing is left of my life with Laura. After I buried Laura, I went back home and had to learn to breath, eat, walk and talk again. I did not believe I could ever do any of those things again without Laura. There is no greater impact on anyone then to take life away with no possible way to get even a tiny part of it back. The death of my only daughter has made my life real. I have no time for little insignificant problems in everyday life. I compare everything against the death of my Laura. Nothing comes close to the pain. Nothing comes close to the suffering I do every day because Laura is gone. Laura has died. I have saved stories about her as a child to share with her children. There will be no children from Laura, no one to share that she was two weeks late and delivered at a weight of ten pounds. She always liked this story. I always teased her—saying she walked out of the hospital in front of me as they wheeled me out in a wheel chair. There's no one to share what a sweet child she was. Her teachers all seemed to like her. Her cat that she loved so much and worried what she would do to keep him in her life when she went to college—I have him now. He still misses her. He is such a cling cat. She would carry him everywhere with her. From the point of Laura's death, there are no more memories. Nothing. She started to fade away from that time on. I only have the past to cling to. Nothing more. Laura had a good friend: they would tease each other by starting sentences with "remember when we did...." That is all there is left to my life with Laura. Remember when we... Only past memories remain. We are not supposed to bury our children. I belong to a group of people who do not wish any new members. It is such a sad group of people. We all live our lives waiting to die. We miss our children so much and need to be with them. I am the same. Who is taking care of Laura? Who holds her when she is sad? Whose bed does she crawl into when she is upset and can't sleep? Who does she sit and laugh with at the things that only she and I find funny? Who is going shopping with her? How can she be gone? She was only sixteen years old. She was my life.

I have a son, Thomas. He has become the "golden child". What a responsibility this has left on him. He has lost his best friend. He and Laura were so close. I now have fears about him that are at best unreasonable. That is another loss. The loss of letting your child grow up without fear that everything he does will take him always from me. With Thomas there is always fear. I now know that the loss of a child doesn't happen to someone else. It happened to me. I proudly watched my son sit at the hospital for those long nine days watching his sister die, losing also what he had of parents, as all sanity slipped away. He was so good about take care of us both. He made sure he took me to the cafeteria every day to see that I ate, even if it was nothing more than a banana. He comforted us both as best he could, and let us comfort him when we could. He, in that one impact of Shayla's actions, lost his past, his present, and his future. He became an only child. He also lost the parents he has grown up with. I feel Tom and I are just shadows of the parents he once knew. He has had to adjust to new parents, sometime unrealistic parents. I am so grateful for him, and so sad for him also. I could not have asked for a more understanding, compassionate, loving son.

Shayla, what do I say about Shayla? She was a friend of my daughter's for many years. I know Laura cared about her. What do I say about a child who came to the hospital with her parents wheeled in a wheelchair to get whatever sympathy she could, while my Laura lay dying? What do I say about her parents, who never once asked how Laura was? They only asked for updates on her condition, stating they had the right to know. The only thing I have heard from this family came in the form of notes on sympathy cards after Laura's death with words on every one of them stating Laura was now in a better place. How easy it is for Shayla to say this and feel better about killing Laura. How easy it is for her parents to say these words as their daughter stands next to them through life, every day. How so very nice for them. They are a sad family, I have watched the problems go on and on. I personal feel that Shayla has never taken personal responsibility for the turmoil she has caused in life. I understand she did not ask Laura into her car to kill her. But she did, just as she has done countless other thoughtless things. I would like for her just this once not be patted on the head, given her car and life back, and told to do better next time. This has not worked in the past. I do not see it working now. I would like to think she would give some of her time to serving the community, in a way of acting and being a responsible person, to show she understands what she has done is wrong and not just that she has moved Laura to a BETTER place. I would like her to show some kind of remorse for what she did to my daughter. Thank you for giving me this time to share what the impact of all this has made in my life.

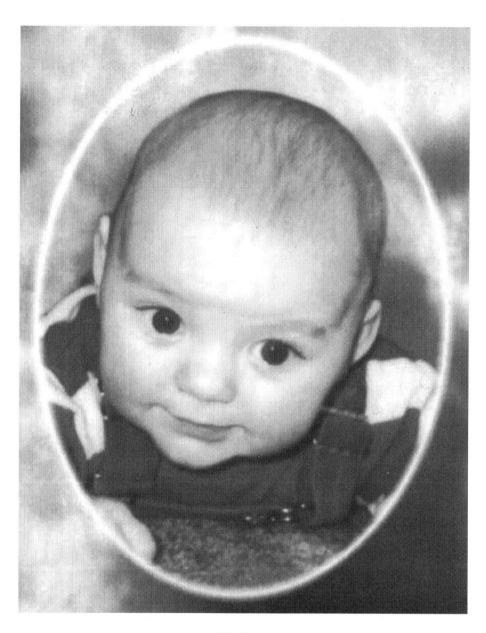

Nathan
October 1, 1999 – March 31, 2000

Nathan

Died of Injuries Following Being Shaken and Thrown by his Daycare Person

By Tammie

Let me introduce myself. My name is Nathan Lee Slater. I was brought into this world on October 1, 1999. It was a sunny day. I know, because it was 7:53 a.m. in the morning when I first saw the morning sun. Mommy was so happy to have it all over and have me in her arms. I had caused her back to ache the whole time and now I was enjoying the comfort of her belly. Daddy was just as excited as I was. I was his first baby and the second child to carry on his last name, out of 13 grandchildren. I knew just what to do; my lower lip went out and out came a cry. The nurse thought it was so cute, and they said I was going to break young girl's hearts. We all came home as a family the day after I was born. There were so many people there to visit and lots of pretty flowers and things for me to wear. I was a big boy; 8 pounds 8 ounces and 21 ½ inches long. I figured out right away how to get food and it stuck to my ribs and everywhere else it could, so my uncle called me the Michelin Baby. Mom and Dad loved all of the rolls on my legs and arms. It took an extra-long time to give me a bath, but I didn't complain because I loved being in the water. I could kick and get mom and brother all wet, but they must have liked it since they always laughed at me. I loved being my

Dad's first baby—he carried me everywhere. I knew that if Dad walked into the room, it wouldn't be long before I would be in his arms. Since it was close to the holidays after I arrived, I got to see so many relatives who (like Daddy) carried me everywhere. Mommy didn't think I would ever learn to walk with all the holding I got. When I had my first doctor's appointment, the doctor was just amazed at how I was growing. They asked mommy if she was feeding me steak and eggs for breakfast. They couldn't believe I was so healthy, just from nursing. I was a very verbal baby, and Mom and Dad said I would just babble on and on all day. I loved it when Jacob (my big brother) would play with me. It never failed—he could get me laughing in no time. I heard everyone commenting on what a great belly laugh I had. Mom loved it. All she had to do was say she was going to get me and I couldn't stand it, I would be laughing, even before she touched me. When Mom went back to work, I got to hang out with Daddy two days during the week and the other three days at a home daycare. During the time Daddy watched me, I rolled over for him first, but Mommy didn't believe him, so he taped it for her to watch. I was just getting into solid foods and Daddy couldn't understand how Mommy could feed me without a bib and not get me messy. Dad used a bib and still got food all over me. By the time I was ready for my 4-month checkup, I was really healthy, the doctor told my Mom I was almost 20 pounds and 26 ½ inches long. Mom said that I was wearing clothes that Jacob was wearing when he was 12 months old. My last couple of months of my life seemed busy, and I was trying to crawl. Mom and Dad said I looked like a beached whale when my arms and legs moved but my belly wasn't going anywhere, no matter how hard I tried. I was working on getting my first tooth, and everything I saw looked good enough to chew on and that is what I did. The day before I was killed, I went to Jacob's tee ball practice wearing my baseball cap and holding my favorite blanket. I tried my hardest to cheer him on, but all that came out was just a bunch of babbling. All I remember was that everyone said I was so cute. We did our usual that night as I helped Mom and Dad read Jacob a story. I had a bedtime snack and went off to bed, happy and full. Mom woke me up the next morning to feed me and she went off to work. She always called in the mornings to tell her boys to have a good day and Jacob told her I was watching Telly Tubbies and she just laughed, because she could hear me laughing at the TV. That was the last she heard from me that day and for the rest of her life. Daddy took me to daycare that morning and waited while the lady made me a bottle because I was hungry, which was very common, then he kissed me good bye and told me he would see me that night. I never made it to that night. I will now pass the rest of my life story on to my Mommy.

Nathan came into our lives on October 1, 1999 and was taken away from us March 31, 2000. Let me back up and tell you about Nathan before he even came into the world of ours. I could tell right away that the baby we were going to have was going to be different from my older son. I wanted chocolate and everything I craved was not good for me, or should I say, I did not crave fruit and healthy foods. He was very active inside all of the time. He also did not want to come out; maybe that should have told us something—he knew that he wanted to enjoy the comfort for as long as possible. They had to help my body get prepared as I was already one week overdue and showing no signs of even being close to having Nathan. He finally made his grand appearance bright and early at 7:53 a.m. on Friday the 1st of October. He was 8 pounds, 8 ounces and 21 ½ inches long. The first thing he did after letting his lungs tell us a story was put his lower lip out hoping to get the attention of the nurses there were caring for him, he had quite a few since he had his first meconium in vitro and he did get their attention. They said that he would be a heart breaker. That he was. His eyes were big, round, and crystal blue with long lashes—definite lady catchers. Nathan was very verbal in all that he did. He could do the deepest belly giggle and at a very early age of 2 months there was not a moment that he was not moving his body in some way or verbally expressing his feelings.

The day came when I had to go back to work when Nathan was just over 4 months old. I did the daycare search because Nathan could not go to the same day care as Jacob; they took only school-age children. I had the booklet from child-care referral in hand, which included all the questions and things you do when searching for that special place to place your child. I made phone call after phone call to many area home daycares, looking for that special one that stood out as the right place. I wanted a home daycare since Jacob had been in one for such a long time and it was more inti-mate than a daycare center where the turnover rate of employees is always high. I found one and did more research, calling referrals, making unannounced visits, feeling out what the environment of the home was like and getting to know the lady that would be car-ing for our precious one, Nathan. The daycare owner had two chil-dren of her own, the same ages as my 2 boys, home-schooled her oldest, and fed her baby organic foods and also nursed him. She had worked in her church daycare for a number of years and had her business for just shy of three years and had no reports of any incidents. Nathan would only spend at the most eight hours a day for just three days a week in the care of this lady. I worked an early shift at work and my husband shifted his work schedule around so that he could spend two days at home with Nathan. In the end, Nathan would spend only a total of 21 days going to this day care before his life ended.

On his final day, I got up to get ready for work around 4:30 a.m. Just before I left, I would always nurse Nathan and spent time rocking him in his rocker, I would then tuck him back in his crib and kiss him goodbye. Nathan was dropped off at the day care around 8:00 a.m. He was acting normal, and he was happy. He was hungry, so my husband waited until the lady fixed him a bottle before he left for work. Later that day, my husband received a call from the lady saying that Nathan was sick. He asked, what do you mean sick? (Dale worked in Renton, and we lived in Everett, a good 45-minute drive on a normal day and this was a Friday afternoon it could be a two-hour drive home.) She said, well, he is not breathing and the paramedics are here with him right now.

She had called 911 at 2:30 to report a child had stopped breathing. According to reports, the aid crew observed Nathan was unresponsive. Nathan was transported to Stevens Hospital in Edmonds, WA where at approximately 3:15 p.m. on March 31, 2000, he was pronounced dead by emergency-room doctors. I never once received a call from anyone about any of this going on. I had been going about my day as any other day!

So that afternoon, I went home to pick up my older son Jacob so that he could go with me to pick up Nathan. He had always wanted Nathan to go to the same place as he did, but it could not work out. We were going to go pick out a new car seat for Nathan since he was such a big boy. He had already outgrown his infant seat. Jacob was very excited to see where Nathan went. We made that final turn onto the street and what came into view were two Snohomish County Sheriff cars.

The first thing I felt was instant sickness in my stomach because they were parked right in front of the house that Nathan was at. We pulled up and we were greeted by a Sheriff asking who I was. I told him I was there to pick up my son Nathan and could I just get him and be on my way. He responded by saying that there had been an accident and that Nathan was on his way to the hospital and was being well taken care of. All they told me during what seemed like an eternity was that he was being well taken care of and that I should go to the hospital. My thoughts were how am I going to drive myself to the hospital not knowing what is going on; again, this is all going on a Friday afternoon where traffic is at its worst. The hospital was on the other side of town and I did not want to take any more time than I needed getting there so I told them I was going to speed to get there as fast as I could. They, of course, did not want me doing that, so they said that they could drive me there but again I would have to wait for a deputy to get there, again Jacob is with me and I have no idea what to say to him.

We were put in the back of a sheriff car, and boy did it seem like it took forever to get there, plus this whole time I still had not talked to my husband. He did not have a cell phone, and I had no idea where he was or if he even knew what was going on. The whole way there, I kept trying to call anyone who would answer a phone to let them know what was going on which still I just thought that Nathan was going to be just fine since he was being well taken care of, that is what they told me.

After we got to the hospital, I was escorted by a person toward a door with the words "Quiet Room" on it. They opened the door and there sat my husband, who was completely shaken up. All he said to me was that our baby was "DEAD." What do you say to those kinds of words when the last time I had seen Nathan he was very much alive? I instantly denied what he said and turned around and walked back out the door to ask them to take me to see my baby. The lady keep telling me to go sit down. No, I said I want to see my baby and you will take me to see him right now. It took plenty of times of me asking for her to finally take me to him. They opened the door to the emergency room, and there he lay. He was just lying there all by himself on a table, no movement, no color, tubes in his nose and mouth, a needle in his little leg, blood around his nostrils, and freezing cold to the touch. I wanted to scream but no words came out when I tried. I wanted them to take the tubes out and make him wake up. I went numb and I felt like falling down but I wanted to hold him to make him warm because he was so cold. It was a dream, and if I kept telling myself that, then he would wake up. But he was so cold, the nurses brought me some warm blankets for him and again I felt that once he warmed up he would wake up, wake up Nathan!

It felt like we were in that small room forever and I had forgotten that I had shown up with Jacob, where was he? The paramedics who had brought Nathan to the hospital had taken Jacob and given him a teddy bear and sat with him until we could come out and get him. We didn't know what was the right thing to do or what was the wrong thing to do. I knew Jacob would want to see Nathan one last time to say good bye. Jacob came into the room and he asked what was wrong with Nathan and why was he sleeping. We told him he was not sleeping, that he had died and that he was not there in spirit. Jacob asked where Nathan was if he was not there. I remembered back to when Jacob was about three and he lost a balloon out the car door when it opened. He was very upset about losing that balloon and he asked if it went to Heaven for God to hold for him. So what I told him was that Nathan had gone to Heaven to hold his balloon for him. (At Nathan's service, we asked everyone to bring a balloon instead of flowers. At the end of the service, there were over 400 hundred balloons let off in Nathan's honor. He will never be without a balloon to hold. One special thing that happened with the balloons that were released is that the group of balloons that Jacob let go for Nathan went a whole different way in the sky. It was like Nathan was pulling them up with him.)

A doctor came into the hospital room that night to talk to us to tell us that from what they could tell until the autopsy was performed, Nathan had died from SIDS. I could not understand or hear anything he was saying and asked to be left along with my son I just wanted to lay down with him and hold him forever. After the doctor left, the medical investigator came in and began to ask all kinds of questions going all the way back to how I took care of myself when I was pregnant with Nathan to how he was the night before. Questions I still did not understand as to how they were going to bring my son back to life. I felt that they were being very rude asking all of those questions while we were sitting there holding Nathan, wondering "WHY US, WHY NATHAN". Those questions are all just a blur in my mind, I could not understand how they could ask those things when we were going through such a horrible thing. We stayed with Nathan for as long as they would allow us to, they then had to take him away I was concerned with him being cold so I asked if they could keep him wrapped in his favorite blanket. I had to hand him over to the medical investigator who was taking him away from us to take him back to the morgue. We then had to leave the hospital that night, the same hospital that just over six months earlier we had left to bring our precious baby home. The home where he would be well taken care of and loved deeply by us as parents and by Jacob, the big brother who patiently waited for 9 months and one week, which according to Jacob was way too long. Going home was another nightmare waiting for us—his room, his toys; his being was everywhere you turned. I spent a good time on the phone calling who I could and remember having one friend ask if I was pulling an April fool's joke on her, since it was the next day. When we finally went to bed, I heard his cries throughout the night and kept getting up to check his crib. My chest was telling me that it was time for him to nurse; my whole body ached to hold him and touch him. I kept telling myself that when we woke up, he would be there. It did not happened the next morning or all of the mornings that soon followed.

When you lose a person, you don't begin to realize what you still have to go through as far as the funeral is concerned. Who would think that you would have to pick out that favorite outfit, that special song, write an obituary, who is going to talk or who can talk, what kind of service, open casket, closed casket? The list goes on. The whole time, you are numb to it all and wonder how it will ever end.

They were due to perform the autopsy on Nathan the Monday following his death on April 3, 2000. We told the medical examiner's office that we wanted to know the results as soon as they found out so that we could continue on with what we needed to do. I had spent the whole weekend researching everything I could about SIDS. I wanted to know all I could and more about it. The daycare lady called that weekend also to talk to my husband to say she was sorry, that she wishes it had not happened. We would later learn why she called to say that. We had an appointment at the funeral home that same day as the autopsy and we informed the medical examiner where we were. While we were making the decision on what kind of casket in which we wanted to bury Nathan, we got the phone call from the Snohomish County Chief Medical Examiner Dr. Thiersch. I asked Dr. Thiersch if I could put him on speaker phone since we had a lot of family there with us in the room waiting with us to learn of the results. Dr. Thiersch advised me over the phone that the autopsy revealed that Nathan had not died from SIDS; it revealed that he had died from a diffuse subdural hemorrhage. This means that blood was underneath the dura and over the brain. Such an injury is usually caused when a child is violently shaken and small veins in the head break, leaking blood into the area. Dr. Thiersch had concluded that Nathan died as a result of inflicted injury of blunt-force trauma. Where do my thoughts go now, what do I do as my sister screams and I wonder how can I possible even continue on with my life or my world? Something has happened to my baby and it was completely not necessary. Again, my body goes numb and all of my feeling go away; now I am just a body, just like Nathan is now. My spirit has floated away, and I wonder if I will ever get it back. After getting the phone call, we had to still finish with making the funeral arrangements, and the funeral home, Floral Hills at Purdy Walters went above and beyond to comfort us. There was a Snohomish county detective waiting for us when we got home to go over everything that we would have questions on, but the one they could not answer was "WHY!"

The defendant told police, in a detailed interview, that in the early afternoon she became frustrated with Nathan because he was crying. She said she tried to quiet him, she told investigators. At one point she "slammed" him against her knee, and police have indicated that she demonstrated how his head would have struck her knee. After that, she explained, she placed Nathan in his playpen where he took his naps. Nathan apparently continued to cry, however. To try to stop the crying, the defendant according to the statement, tried to feed him. As she fed him, he spit up some food on her (a severe brain injury causes a person/child to throw up). This apparently angered or frustrated the defendant. According to her statement to police, the defendant then "tossed" Nathan into the playpen. A shaking followed by the substantial deceleration of his head as might be caused when Nathan hit the mattress of the playpen, could have caused the brain injuries observed by Dr. Thiersch during the autopsy.

I spent the rest of the week in a state that is hard for me to describe. My body was moving but I did not seem to be controlling the movement. I would forget who I talked to and about what. I did not know who was coming or who had been here. I did not eat unless someone forced me to, and I could not sleep unless I had help. I had been nursing Nathan when he died, and that was another constant reminder of him being gone. You have children so that you can experience life to the fullest. We will greatly miss the life Nathan would have had. Now you can only look forward to what your life will be now, which is so beyond what you would have planned. I will never get to see the milestones in the walk of life that Nathan would have taken. I can only wonder how it could have been and wonder what he would have grown up to become. I feel that when I look at pictures of Nathan, it is of a person who comes with the picture frame you get when you buy it, not of a baby that was once yours just a short time ago. The feelings are so hard to explain and when someone asks how are you doing and I say "just ok" they don't seem to understand why you are "just ok" and not great! Most of the time I want to tell them I am doing horrible and nothing could be worse, but my heart tells me to say I am doing "just ok." I wonder what my reply will be in a year, 5 years, maybe 10. Will I still say that I am "just ok"?

I think about what the defendant did to Nathan all of the time. It is always in my mind, and it plays over and over again. I wonder only because I can't seem to understand how someone can harm a baby in any way, especially when he was doing what God created him to do. Babies cry when they want to express themselves. I wonder how someone can live with herself when she looks at what she did; she harmed a baby, a being that relied on her to take care of him, a person who is far more powerful than he was. A baby, a being that in no way can defend himself or respond to this evil person who is harming him. A person who to me is so cowardly to have to take her anger and frustration out on a baby who can't say anything other than to cry. I hope that all she did haunts her for the rest of her life and that she is not able to hold or care for another child for the rest of her living life. I wonder about the other babies or children this person may have cared for: did she harm them in any way and did she get away with it? I wonder if this person knew about this about herself, and if so why did she continue caring for other children or keep her daycare open? I ask myself over and over again the same kind of things and I cannot seem to find an answer. The only person who can answer the question is the person who killed Nathan—and God. I wonder if either one of them will be able to tell me why it happened. I look at my other son Jacob and am thankful that he is healthy and he is what keeps me going with his daily activities and excitement. He also is looking for an answer, and I ask myself how can I answer his many questions as to why someone killed Nathan when I can' t even answer them for myself? I look at him to see how he is now afraid to go to sleep by himself and wakes up numerous times scared. How many nights he goes to sleep crying and missing his baby brother that he will never get to play with or fight with. I wonder how this will affect him in the future that lies ahead of him. He came home one day saying a part of his heart is gone, and I asked what he meant. He said that when Nathan died, he took a part of his heart with him. I have to tell him constantly that if and when we have another baby that we cannot name it Nathan and he does not understand that. I grew up not fearing death; now I do because it happened in our home so suddenly at a time that was so unexpected. Now I wonder every day, "Is today my day?" I kiss Jacob on his cheek and tell him I love him and that I will see him later. I kissed Nathan that day this all happened and told him mommy would see him later. My husband wrote something, and I will remember it always: he wrote, "that no parent should have to kiss a cold cheek goodbye." We had to do that the night of March 31, 2000.

It is hard for me to look ahead now. It seems so scary to know what can happen and does happen when what you have done seemed all so right. I fear what the future will bring for me, my family, and the rest of the world that experiences a parent's worst nightmare: "losing a child before they even had a chance to experience them and their life."

I wrote this letter just a few months after Nathan was killed, and I still live in fear of life. The person who did this to Nathan did plead guilty to 1st degree manslaughter and was sentenced to just a short 8 ½ years in a woman's correctional facility in the state of Washington a day after what would have been Nathan's first birthday in October, 2000. She was paroled November of 2007, short of her 8 ½ sentence. They said she got out on "good behavior." What is good behavior? I ask myself ever since I got the letter from the State of Washington. Of course she will be on probation for the next two years, but again I ask myself, do they really watch these people? You see it on the news all of the time, people who commit the crime again. I worried about running into her at the local grocery store when she got out, but they released her to a county in California, so now I worry that no one will know about what she did down there and what if she ends up watching kids again?

My life since has had many ups and downs, since Nathan, my husband and I have had two more children. One I had a little over a year after Nathan was killed, and it was a boy. I wondered how I would feel if he looked just like Nathan, so we did not find out what we were having until he was born. The other child is a girl, and I believe a part of Nathan came back in her—she is full of spirit, just like Nathan was. I never did go back to work outside the home until just recently. I work in the evening, just to get out and mingle with adults. I found it hard to leave my children with anyone other than close family and friends and still have issues with them being away from me. I feel out of control when I am not around them, but all the same, want to be away from them. It is getting better since they are much older now, and I find myself letting them go more and more. The thoughts are still in the back of my mind every day; it was just the other day when we lost Nathan, and nothing warned us of what was to happen that horrible day. I live and feel differently than I know I would have if Nathan were still in our lives. I find that the happy times are far apart compared to the unhappy times. I wonder what kind of parent I would have turned out to be if this had not happened. Are my living kids suffering because of what I went through? For my children born after Nathan's death, I wonder every day how I can keep his memory alive for them since they never knew him.

"OH, NORMAL DAY, LET ME BE AWARE OF THE TREASURE YOU ARE.
LET ME LEARN FROM YOU, LOVE YOU, BLESS YOU BEFORE YOU DEPART.
LET ME NOT PASS YOU BY IN QUEST OF SOME RARE
AND PERFECT TOMORROW.
LET ME HOLD YOU WHILE I MAY, FOR IT MAY NOT ALWAYS BE SO.
ONE DAY, I SHALL DIG MY NAILS INTO THE EARTH, OR BURY
MY FACE IN THE PILLOW, OR
STRETCH MYSELF TAUT, OR RAISE MY HANDS TO THE SKY
AND WANT, MORE THAN ALL THE
WORLD, YOUR RETURN."

BRADLEY THOMAS

AUGUST 3, 1985 - MARCH 15, 2010

Bradley Thomas

Cause of Death: Prescription Interaction

By Carole

Brad was the youngest child in a family of four, with one brother. His mother was a Homemaker and his father was a traveling sales manager. During the time period before his death, he had been attending college classes and living at home with his dad. Brad was being treated for anxiety and panic attacks, when methadone was added and became lethal, causing him to stop breathing in his sleep. He was completely healthy and had no warning.

Our son Paul was two years old when his little brother Brad was born. The boys grew up in Woodinville, Washington, which is a suburb of Seattle. When Brad was a baby, he had so many ear infections, that his hearing was very poor. Because of this, he didn't start talking until he was about a year old. When the words finally started to flow, in his excitement, he would sometimes stutter, as if trying to make up for lost time. That kind of excitement about life followed him through his early years, as he watched for bugs, frogs, snakes or anything in nature. He and his brother had many pets over the years, including a turtle that used to swim in the kitchen sink while I did housework. Brad kept our lives full of smiles and laughter with his funny expressions and easy- going temperament. His older brother, Paul, was everything to him and Brad always looked up to Paul throughout his life. Paul was always trying to protect Brad and keep him out of trouble, as only an older brother could. While they were growing up, I think Brad felt as though he was living in Paul's shadow, because he thought Paul was perfect and couldn't do anything wrong. In fact, we all saw Paul being very responsible and mature for his age, almost like a little adult. Brad, on the other hand, learned life's lessons the hard way and had a habit of pushing the limits in almost everything he did. He was also somewhat clumsy and accident prone, when playing sports or just riding his bike around the neighborhood. It was normal for Brad to have a couple of band-aids on him all the time. His awkwardness could have been attributed to the huge growth spurts he had, making him twice the size of his classmates. He was an affectionate child and liked holding hands with us, even when he was a very large 10 year old!

Brad was always ready to go shopping and would try every tactic he knew to convince us to buy things he wanted. This was especially true when he was with his Grandma Nebinger. She dearly loves both boys and always enjoyed spoiling them.

When our children were in middle school, their father and I divorced and both sons took it very hard. As parents often do, we underestimated the toll that divorce would take on our children. Brad never seemed to fully recover from the loss of his emotional security. Even though he appeared to be confident and in control, he still felt somewhat insecure. From the ages of 14 to 18, he had serious problems with alcohol use and the whole family was extremely concerned about him. John's parents made it possible for Brad to go to a wonderful treatment program for teenagers called Wilderness Quest, located in Utah. That experience turned out to be an answer to prayer because we had spent many sleepless nights worrying about getting help for him. After completing all of the outdoor skills he learned while living in the wilderness and with the incredible support of the staff, he came home with a new perspective about himself and his life. He was very grateful for the experience and had a goal of one day returning to Wilderness Quest and "giving back" to the program by helping other teenagers.

After Brad's death, I went back to Utah and cried with the program director, who had known my Son very well. Both she and the original founder of the program were heartbroken with the news of our family's loss. I feel a strong connection with the place where Brad had been, just a few years earlier. Going back there will always be painful, but also a tender reminder of our beautiful boy who struggled and tried so hard to overcome his problems.

Because of Brad's wilderness experience, he was changed from the inside-out. We all returned to Seattle, after picking him up at the conclusion of his treatment program. We had the Brad we used to know back in our family. But we could not have known the challenges that were ahead of him. He started having severe anxiety and panic attacks that were so debilitating, our family doctor tried to control the symptoms with medication. It was a long and complex process, because of the side-effects that made Brad feel exhausted, "foggy" headed or wanting to sleep all the time. He struggled for years trying to find a balance with work, college classes, and his medications. Things were never easy for him, but he always had a sincere smile and sense of humor about it all. It was during this time that Brad met Hailey, who became his first (and only) real love. She was by his side through all the trials and tribulations he went through, and was his greatest emotional supporter. I thank God she was in his life.

It took Brad a while, but he completed his college classes and was one final exam away from receiving his two year degree at Bellevue College, although he already had enough credits to graduate.

At that time, both our children were doing well and we had every confidence that Brad was going to live a full life and become the person he was meant to be. He had come so far on his journey and still had his whole life ahead of him-or so we thought...

Brad was a good friend to many people and always loved us with his whole heart. He was very thoughtful about giving cards and gifts to us on special occasions or just calling to say, "I love you". There was tenderness that came out of him, you wouldn't expect from a young man so big and strong. Sometimes he would spontaneously pick me up and carry me around, just to be playful. People asked him constantly if he played basketball, because he was so tall. At around 6 feet 6 inches, he literally towered over everyone who stood next to him. He was also very handsome and girls used to stare at him everywhere he went.

Brad liked to spend much of his time at home. He would wait expectantly for his dad to come back from work or a business trip, and thrived on lots of quality time with him. He referred to his dad proudly as, "My best friend." He lived with him also, but would often call me at work or home to say, "I'm hungry" because Brad could empty the refrigerator faster than anyone I knew!

In their twenties, Brad and Paul became closer and started repairing the friendship that had become strained during Brad's teenage years. Paul learned to accept his brother and let go of the past and the mistakes that Brad had made. During Brad's difficult years, so much of the focus in our family was on him, because of the challenges he had. The stress on all of us was intense and at times felt overwhelming. Even now, the focus is still on Brad, because of the pain we all feel over losing him and the hole that is left in our family.

Just a couple of days before he died, Brad and his Dad went to Costco with me. The three of us had not gone shopping together since before the divorce, over 10 years earlier. I now see it as a gift to me in preparation for what was to come. It seemed like an ordinary day in so many ways, but since then, has been burned into my memory. It was the last time I saw my Son alive.

During the last month of his life, Brad had been taking time off from the restaurant where he worked, because of a work-related accident involving an injury to his leg. It was during this time that another doctor (not his family doctor) prescribed Methadone, as a pain medicine. Very shortly after that, the most horrible thing happened.

On the dreadful morning of March 15th, 2010, at about 6:30 AM, I received a panicked phone call from John, telling me that Brad wasn't breathing and that the paramedics were at the house, trying to get his heart going. That phone call brought sheer terror to my heart. My Son was in terrible danger or dying and all I could do was go to him as fast as I could.

I arrived at Brad's house and my heart sank down into the darkest place when I saw the medical personnel packing up to leave. It was then that I knew something truly horrible had happened to my Son. All I wanted to do was run as fast as I could to his side. At the door of the house, a very kind man informed me that my child had died. The medical team did everything they could to save him, but his heart never started beating again. I saw Brad lying there and asked for the sheet to be removed from his face. Our youngest child was gone from us, leaving his young and hopeful life on earth, to be in the presence of God. There would be no goodbyes from us, just tears, shock, and disbelief.

Our Brad had left us so suddenly and we didn't know what to do. I thought, "Oh God, help me". I sat on the floor, talking to him softly and crying, while I held his arm and looked into his peaceful face. He looked almost like he was sleeping, but in a very still way. His brother, Paul, and sister-in-law, Corey, were there with him and no one could make any sense out of what had just happened. We all stayed with Brad until the coroner came, which I think was about 2 or 3 hours later. I had lost all sense of time at that point. His dad told me later, that when we lost Brad that day, a part of him died too. I understand what he meant. I will always be thankful though, that we had those last moments alone with our Son, before they took him away. Many parents don't have the opportunity to be with their child who has died, because of distance or other circumstances that prevented it.

After Brad's body was taken, an autopsy was ordered and initially they thought it was an overdose of Methadone. (Since then, we have learned from another report, that the Methadone interacted with another prescription he was taking.) I asked the doctor, "How could this have happened?" The doctor who performed Brad's autopsy told us that Methadone is a very powerful and unpredictable drug that can cause a young, healthy 24 year old to stop breathing in his sleep. In fact, he told us he had seen it happen to other people. Of course, we didn't know this was a possible danger, and Brad had only been taking it for a few days when he died. Tragically, that's all the time it took to build up in his body and do its evil deed.

We were so trusting and believed the doctors wouldn't give our child something that would harm or kill him. The doctor had prescribed Methadone for Brad's knee pain and we thought it was o.k. for him to take it. Looking back, there are things we wish we could have known or done differently, but that is always what a parent goes through. We desperately wished there could have been a way to save him. My mind knows there will be no second chances, but my heart doesn't want to accept it. My mind and heart started fighting each other for a new reality. Life without our Brad is completely unthinkable! How can I live with this knowledge? How can I accept that we won't EVER see or hug or talk to him again in this life? I don't know.

As I reflect back on Brad's life and my experience of him, I get a wonderfully warm feeling that reminds me of being in his presence. That sincere friendliness and caring that followed him wherever he went and his ready smile that was completely genuine and heartfelt. Everyone remembers his big "bear" hugs. Brad was practically famous for his world class hugs. That's how he got the nickname Brad Bear. He was quick to look on the lighter side of things or find humor in everyday mundane things. I think it was this ability that kept his spirit up when things in his life didn't go well. Sadly, he had a lot of disappointments, many of which were caused by his struggles with alcohol, while others were just circumstantial.

He loved animals and adored his faithful dogs, T Bone and Zeus. He liked unique breeds that were very sturdy and good watch dogs, so he chose a Staffordshire bull terrier and an Italian Mastiff. Both dogs were very sweet, unruly and untrained. No one in the family could get them to sit or stay! Both of his dogs died accidentally and tragically, which broke Brad's heart. He cried when he lost his furry companions, because they meant so much to him. Each one died at a different time, about 2 years apart. It still seems so unfair to me. Brad tried very hard to accomplish goals in his life and always had a plan of how he was going to make himself successful. He loved bubble gum flavored ice cream and wanted to produce a line of food and beverages in that flavor, because he believed there was an untapped market for the products.

He challenged the way things have "always been done" and prided himself on being a creative thinker. He enjoyed debating his point of view and especially loved philosophy classes, as well as art and drawing. Thankfully, his Dad and I have some of his college drawings and artwork from his younger years. He was comfortable with his Christian beliefs, and easy- going about religion in general. He didn't expect other people to agree with his views and had a vast array of colorful friends. For the last 2 years of his life, he had been attending a Catholic church with his friend Rian, and found peace and comfort there. He believed in the Bible and the message Jesus taught of forgiveness for all who seek it. His faith was real and uncomplicated.

Just 5 days before he died, during the time he was taking a class on Mexican Indian culture, Brad wrote these words on his Face book page. "Interesting that the Aztecs believed in over ten gods (through faith) so much, they would sacrifice themselves, and some of us today cannot even have enough faith to believe in one God, Jesus Christ." We printed this quote on the program at his Memorial service. Brad was interested in everything and thought deeply about what he was learning. In his writings, he would often blend religion, history, and philosophy together to open up a wider perspective on life. He also had a natural quest for truth that compelled him to ask questions and try to find answers for himself.

When I close my eyes and picture Brad in my mind now, I see him the way his friend, David, often describes. Brad is laughing and playing with his dogs in Heaven. He will always be young and he will always be our lovable "Brad Bear". We miss him so much.

What have I learned from living with such a huge loss?

For one thing, we never know ahead of time which of our friends or family will "be there for us" and which ones will pull away in a tragedy. Some people feel awkward talking about Brad now. Others feel fearful of even thinking about a child dying, because it could happen to anybody. Certain people don't call anymore or ask me to get together with them. It hurts me, but I understand, because I'm human too and have responded in similar ways to people without intending to. I now understand the intense emotional pain that comes from losing a child, no matter what their age. My world has permanently shifted and it will never be the same again. Sometimes friends or family will assume that we are "moving on" in our lives, because they have already moved on. After a year, I can tell you that the pain doesn't go away, but it does change somewhat. I don't sit and stare into space for hours like I used to, but I'm not back to my "old self" either. I'll never be back to where I was before we lost Brad. I have less energy now and my memory is very short. I quit my job that I really enjoyed and can stay in the house for days looking at family pictures or organizing the closets and doing quiet things. I have changed from the busy, energetic woman I used to be and I don't care as much about what people think. I have a measure of peace about the future, but only because I believe in a plan for our lives that is bigger than we can humanly understand. This is how I find hope in the midst of such a horrible thing. I believe that one day I will see Brad again in heaven. Sometimes I hold onto that belief with the grip of a drowning person holding onto a life raft.

A few weeks after his brother died, Paul gave us a precious memory to hold in our hearts forever. On the day that would have been Brad's graduation from Bellevue College, Paul walked down in a cap and gown and received his brother's diploma: an Associate of Arts degree in General Studies. It was a very moving tribute and demonstration of the love Paul has for his Brother. Paul was brave and humble, honoring his brother's life and achievement on that day. The other graduates and their families were joyful and excited, but we couldn't share in their happiness, since our Son's dreams and our dreams for him had abruptly ended. Still, we saw it as an opportunity to celebrate Brad's life and express our love for him. I am so proud of both of our Sons, and Paul became my hero that day!

One year has passed since Brad's death. I don't cry every day like I used to, but I do feel incredibly sad and heartbroken on the inside. It's better for me not to try and explain how I feel to people very often, since they can't make the hurt go away. Still, the comfort they offer is needed and I appreciate the hugs and sympathetic words very much. Their kindness gives me emotional strength to keep looking past this tragedy and not get stuck in the sadness of it. As time goes by, I am better able to have moments of joy and thankfulness. I still love talking about my Brad and welcome any mention of his name. It makes my heart leap in my chest with happiness thinking of the boy I raised who will always be so dear to me - that will never go away.

Now I need to find a new way of looking at life; one that is hopeful. I don't want to live in fear of bad things happening, so I choose to believe in the goodness of life. I also choose to believe in the kindness of people and the tender care of God.

None of us in the family are ready to face any decisions about spreading his ashes. It's all we have left of our wonderful Son, who was totally unique in every way. I have Brad's ashes with me at the house and parting with them is just too much for me to bare. Since none of us had a chance to say goodbye, maybe someday, we will be able to express what we would have wanted to say to him…if only there had been time.

All through his life, Brad's heart remained tender and somewhat childlike. This little poem was written when he was 6 years old and I keep it in a frame on my desk at home. The words have shown me, through the eyes of my little boy, how personally the Lord cares about each one of us when we are hurting and going through hard times. I have been fortunate enough to experience this incredible peace that goes beyond my own understanding.

Jesus

By Bradley Nebinger

He helps me not to be afraid.
He wipes my eyes with a tissue.
He's always with me when I'm sad.
He gives me everything I need.

"NEVER APOLOGIZE FOR SHOWING FEELING. WHEN YOU DO SO, YOU APOLOGIZE FOR THE TRUTH." BENJAMIN DISRAELI

CPL Nicholas James
4/10/1985 - 9/06/2009

Nick

Died of Undetermined Causes

By Patricia

This is very hard for me to do as it brings up so much sadness and grief. However, I strongly believe that Nick's story has to be told so others will know what is going on over there in Iraq and Afghanistan.

My son, CPL Nicholas Wrobel, loved being a Marine and did not experience PTSD as a consequence of his two back-to-back tours of duty in Al Anbar Province, Iraq. After Iraq, he was stationed in Okinawa for a year. By the time he returned from Okinawa in May 2009, he was ready to start his life as a civilian.

Nick enlisted in the Marines in January 2005. He received his basic training at San Diego Marine Depot and Camp Pendleton, California. He was initially trained to work in electronics, specifically radio communications. That skill was not needed in Iraq at the time he completed his classes. Nick was then chosen to participate in additional training at Fort Lejeune, North Carolina where he was trained to work in civil affairs. My son was a tall, handsome, very articulate and well-written young man with the abilities needed to work in civil affairs. He was one of a few enlisted men who were picked to interface with the locals and tribal chieftains in an effort to rebuild their infrastructure, schools, post offices, and other edifices which were destroyed when their villages were under siege.

Nick worked with a body guard and an interpreter who accompanied him as he knocked on the doors of the villagers, never knowing whether he would be blown away when the door opened. He arranged meetings with the local tribal chieftains in which he helped broker deals worth thousands and thousands of dollars to rebuild their villages.

Nick had other duties as a Marine stationed in Al Anbar Province. His patrol was ambushed by terrorists firing on them from a hill above the valley they were guarding. His living quarters came under mortar attack many times. He spent his share of nights and days on guard duty whether at a huge strategic dam in the area, out in the countryside, or at his base. He experienced the fear of driving down Iraqi roads in a Humvee - never knowing if an IED would take him and his comrades out.

Nick was also required to take his turn tending to the burn pits which were used to dispose of waste that included raw sewage, spent ordinance byproducts and chemicals known and unknown to be carcinogenic. On a daily basis, my son and countless other soldiers and Marines were exposed to toxic smoke, ash and fumes generated by disposal of waste in open air burn pits.

Nick survived two back-to-back tours of duty in Iraq. He was proud of his participation in Operation Iraqi Freedom. He came home on leave and spent happy times with his family and friends. He then spent a year at the Marine Base in Okinawa. He returned to the U.S. at the beginning of June 2009. He was so happy to be home, knowing that he had only one more assignment at Miramar Marine Air Base in San Diego County to complete his five years of duty in the USMC.

During that month he was home on leave he told me, "Mom, I finally know what I want to do when I complete my service next year. I want to be a K-9 police officer. The police force prefers guys who have been in the armed forces, especially Marines. They recruit right at the bases. This is what I want to do." I was happy for him, because I know he had spent a lot of time pondering what he wanted to do once he left the Marines.

Nick decided to report to duty one week early at Mira Mar Marine Air Base. He arrived late in the day June 23, 2009. He was not yet completely checked in at the Marine Base. He was put up in a hotel next to the base that night and was to complete check-in the next day. That night at the hotel, my son, for no known reason, had a full respiratory arrest. He was able to call 911 and was transported to a local hospital.

After about two weeks at the first hospital, he was admitted to the ICU at San Diego Naval Medical Center in San Diego. He was on a ventilator for more than two weeks, experienced organ failure, blood infections, constant fevers, and required dialysis for kidney failure. Eventually, his lungs appeared to be healing. He had a tracheostomy and was given oxygen through the trach tube. He continued to have fevers and it became apparent that something was wrong with his heart. Tests revealed that the infections raging in his body had caused a hole to develop in his heart. He remained in heart failure and because of this his circulation was severely compromised.

He had several heart attacks, each one causing more damage to his body. The goal was to get him strong enough to undergo open heart surgery to repair the hole in his heart. He suffered like this for nearly two and one-half months. Tragically, he had another heart attack the last week of August that left him brain dead. On September 6th 2009, the decision was made "let him go" (according to Nick's wishes that should something like this ever happen to him, that he not be maintained on life support).

My beloved son, died with his family at his side, and my hand holding his for the six hours it took for his soul to leave his body. My heart is broken and there are days when I don't know how I can go on without him. Farewell my beloved son, you are loved now and on into eternity.

No known cause was ever isolated or determined to be the reason for Nick's fatal illness. Since the time of his death I have met other parents who have lost a son or daughter in the military in ways similar to my son's death. These young military men and women survived Iraq only to come home and die on American soil from terrible and devastating illnesses (very likely caused by exposure to the burn pits in Iraq). I continue to receive grief and loss counseling at a Vet Center here in Oregon. I was told by my counselor at the Vet Center that they are seeing many young men and women who have been in Iraq and come home with weakened lungs, asthma, chronic bronchitis, allergic bronchitis and frequent bouts of pneumonia.

The media and the general public need to be informed about this tragic loss of life due to a preventable cause. Toxic exposure to the burn pits needs to be eliminated so that others will not endure the same tragic fate as my son and many other military men and women because of their time in the wars in Iraq and Afghanistan.

What I have learned-

- There is nothing worse in this world than for a parent to lose their child.
- Life can be shockingly short for some.

- It is so important to always speak love to those who you care for, to make amends, to forgive, and to tell them you love them always.

Patricia, B.A. RN, M.A.

Tyler
May 2, 1986 – November 8, 2013

Tyler

Died of an Accidental drug Overdose

"For I know the plans I have for you, plans to prosper you and not to bring you harm, " declares the Lord, "plans to bring you hope and a future." Jeremiah 20:11

These are the words my son texted to me the night before he died of an accidental drug overdose.

Tyler had been sober for several months after 12 years of using Adderall on and off, being in different treatment centers and programs – some of which worked temporarily and others that either didn't work or he didn't complete.

That night, he was hopeful, in a good positive place, had a lovely sober girlfriend, and good relationships with family and friends. He called me to talk about God, his plans for the week and for the upcoming month. He talked about when he thought he would see his girlfriend again. He told me he believed in God and that God had a plan. After we hung up, he texted me the bible verse.

The next evening, we had a call from his roommate that upon arrival home from work, he found Tyler cold and not breathing on the couch and had called 911. Tyler passed from an accidental overdose of some sleeping pills and Adderall. He didn't take many –a total of 6 pills - just a small amount compared to the copious amounts of drugs he had previously taken during his addiction.

According to Tyler's psychiatrist, it is common for recovering addicts that relapse to die. They believe that if they take a small amount of drugs as compared to what they used to take, their body will tolerate it just like it used to when they were in the midst of their addiction. However, the human body does not react the same way. It cannot tolerate the drug as it's not used to it anymore. The heart will work extra hard to keep the body going as the lungs will fill with fluid. Breathing slows and they then pass quietly in their sleep.

The only redeeming thought to me immediately was that Tyler didn't suffer as he passed. For some reason, this was all I could think about as I heard the heartbreaking news. *Did my son suffer?*

Tyler used to tell us during his addiction that he should have died several times from taking so many drugs. He couldn't imagine why he hadn't so far. He knew that there was a risk of dying each time he took drugs but the disease for him outweighed the common sense. He fought and fought this disease but had never managed to keep it at bay. But each day, each week, each month, he never ever gave up trying to beat it. He tried so hard and I, his Mom, was helpless in the face of HIS disease. I couldn't fight this battle for him. There isn't a more difficult thing for a parent to accept. It wasn't my disease. I know in my heart and mind that we did everything in our power to help him beat it. That knowledge released me of any guilt or thoughts that I could have saved him somehow, someway.

One week prior to this tragedy, I was in the hospital following major surgery. I was now home recuperating and not able to move much without assistance and certainly couldn't fly on a plan anywhere.

Tyler's body was in TX, where he lived, many states and many miles away from where we lived. It wasn't possible for us to go identify the body, and my husband couldn't leave me alone to take care of myself. Tyler's older brother offered to go identify the body and bring him home to us. What a blessing and source of strength this was to my husband and me. It was the first time that we realized how wonderful a son could be that was now a true adult.

The only way I made it through the next week was that my family flew out to be with us the following days, and our church family immediately surrounded us in love and support from that moment on. Without that, I don't know how I would have survived the searing grief that came over me.

Nobody can tell you how horrible it is to lose a piece of your own body that had sheltered and grew this child for 40 weeks that I still considered my "baby". For days I went to bed crying, slept little, and woke up with my eyes glued shut from tears that came while sleeping.

Not a day passes by that I don't feel that grief within me. I do believe and know that time will heal us. It already has helped the acute sharpness of pain even after only 8 months. However thoughts of him are always around and in me. Then the pain stabs deep within, refreshed anew.

Loneliness now has a new meaning: not hearing his special ring on my phone calling me, not being able to discuss a movie or meal with him, not being able to feel his check on mine or the strength of his body hugging me and think about how amazed I am that he came from my husband and me.

I opened a magazine the other day and I immediately smelled his cologne. There was an ad within that contained his cologne smell and it smelled just like him! For a moment I could close my eyes and think that he was with me, close by.

Tears do help heal. I used to pride myself that I used to hardly ever cry. My older son was just like me in that respect. The week he passed and through his memorial service, we both cried like babies. My husband, who I had never heard cry, joined us. These are not pretty tears and are wrenching and painful. However it is a release for the sorrow contained in us all.

It is true that unless you have had a child of yours die, you cannot know this pain. My father passed away unexpectedly. The pain of a father passing did not even compare with this pain. Nothing had prepared me for this. I used to think that I would be prepared if this should ever happen. I had read the books on addiction, I had heard Tyler say that he could die from his addiction, I had heard doctors say it about him. I knew that there was a chance. But nothing prepared me for this.

I can tell you that family and friends do help. I can tell you that time helps. I can tell you that talking to other Moms who have lost their children helps – as only they truly can understand the pain. But life goes on for others and Tyler isn't the first and foremost thing in someone else's mind.

For me, the best thing is the knowledge that Tyler is in heaven waiting for me and that I WILL see him again someday soon. Knowing that my Dad is there, caring for him, along with Tyler's guardian angels, helps me. The thought that he is up to his usual good-hearted mischief helps me. For me, he comes alive when I think of him in heaven.

I do not believe, even for moment, that it was an accident that he sent me the text with the bible verse the evening before he died. I do believe that he wanted me to really understand how hopeful he was and how good he felt about the future. We just didn't know what the future held. I know that he would have been SO angry knowing that this had happened and that he was definitely NOT ready to go. But God holds us in his hands and he gets the last word. It was Tyler's time. I never ever thought my prayers for him to heal would be this way, but I try to realize that God does know best. He wants the good guys in heaven too.

Tyler, I look forward to seeing you in heaven when my time comes too and we will be reunited together as a family! Praise be to God.

Reference Materials

Over time, with the review and consultation of many people who have experienced the death of a loved one, these pages were developed. They are intended to be used as reference materials for those who experience grief directly and those who company with a grieving person.

Note: **Each person, depending on their history, their present, and their personal interpretation of life and the meaning of life, experiences death in a unique way. These generalizations of experience are meant to help normalize what may feel frightening or confusing. Physical symptoms can be warnings of problems that deserve medical care. Seeking professional counsel/evaluation/assistance is often wise. The syndrome of "broken heart" is known in medical literature.**

What can help? Again, generalizations are difficult. Some mothers find relief in further education, some in physical exercise, some in volunteer work. Talking with other mothers, counseling, singing, painting, meditating, praying, finding purposeful work – the healing options are many. Because the reality of this death will not go away, finding ways to keep learning and living purposefully can help.

Gerri Haynes

Family Systems Response to the Death of a Family Member

Family responses to grief vary widely and depend on a multitude of factors. Some of these factors may be obvious, some less apparent, but all influence how individual family members cope with the pain of a death.

1. Where the family is in the life cycle
   a. Time of reaching out and integrating members into the larger society...teen-age years of the family's children, new marriage of children, elderly years. (The Centrifugal Time) Vs.:
   b. Time of consolidating...young marriage with small children, time of early retirement, family maintained in this phase due to nature of child's illness. (The Centripetal Time)

2. Role in the family of the person who died
   a. Chronological place in family (eldest, parent, eldest-middle-youngest child)
   b. Tasks, (social, spiritual, physical) customarily accomplished by this person
   c. Conflictual or non-conflictual relationships between the person and other family members (associated longing, guilt, anger)
   d. How this person defined the roles of other family members (mother, father, big sister, little brother, etc.)

3. Emotional position of the person in this family
   a. Perception partially based on the ethnic background of family: Are there prescribed rituals that will assist the

family in marking the death of this person? Are there pre-scribed rituals that assist the family in feeling the reality of the death? Are there established family patterns of assumption of roles following death? (Noting and describing the differences is not the same as judging the differences.)

b. Centrality of the person to family function -- may be a positive or negative position - the person as a focal point of all family concerns when a life-long or long-term illness has required emotional and or financial resources over time or when the family has grown through relationship with this person.

c. Intensity of the emotional relationship of the family members to this person -- long-awaited child, unwanted child, central parent.

4. Nature of the death or illness
    a. Sudden, unexpected, traumatic, prenatal, suicide, violent
    b. Following long illness (stage of life-cycle - more or less continuous or discontinuous)
    c. Short illness, short time of preparation
    d. Stigmatized death

5. Previous deaths in the family and learned response to loss
    a. Other deaths of a similar nature in this family, i.e. multiple deaths through related genetic troubles.
    b. How previous generations dealt with loss through death
    c. Number of deaths experienced by this generation, and the nature of those deaths.

6. Spiritual/religious beliefs of family
    a. May give comfort, but carry risk of masking resolution of grief
    b. May offer focusing rituals which assist process of grief

7. Open- vs. closed-system families
   a. Open-system families understand their roles and have ability to freely and safely discuss their feelings.
   b. Closed-system families have confusion about their places in the family system and do not feel safe in discussing their feelings.

Consider that the intersect between the nature of the illness and the nature of the relationship is relevant as it affects the following: the intensity of the emotional response, the time required to resolve the loss and disruption of the family system

The Grief of Children: a Mirror for the Grief of Adults

Many authors have documented the responses of children to the death of a loved one. Adults do not lose their "inner child", and adult responses to death frequently mirror those of children. A sketch of the relationship between children's grief and that of adult grief follows:

Age 0 - 1: The lesson of trust

Children must learn to trust before they can learn to love. When the primary caregiver leaves the room, an infant does not know that the person will ever return. Repeated experiences of trustworthy behavior, over time, create security, trust and (ultimately) love in the child. This is a complex process, including the development of feelings of self-worth in the child (the feeling of being lovable) and the feelings that another is worthwhile. The death of a parent or a close sibling during this period requires significant work on the part of adult survivors to provide security and to promote renewed growth toward trust for the child.

Reference to adult grief:

An adult may suffer a significant decrease in his/her sense of self-esteem following the death of close relative or friend (or pet). This loss of self-esteem is probably related to the feeling that people we love are supposed to "be there" for us or that we were supposed to "be there" for them. When someone close to us dies, there is frequently a sense that we were not "enough" or did not "do enough" to keep them alive. This may result in a loss of trust, or a feeling of fear - often a fear that has an "unknown" source or direction.

Age 1 - 3 or 4: Death is temporary: magic changes anything

During this time, most children believe anything they are told by the people they love. Questions from these children can be very instructive - they will ask just what they want to know - not necessarily what you want to tell them! The permanence of death is not a reality for children in this age group. Frequently, it is only after about six months following a death that a child will begin to accept that the person who died is not coming back. In approaching a death, children in this age group may have a sense of power over the death, and may believe that if they do certain things (magic), the death will be avoided or reversed. In this age, the fear of losing a second parent may appear, and reassurance regarding some continuity in their life is often necessary.

Reference to adult grief:

Approximately six months following a death, an adult may suddenly feel an increase in the pain of the loss. An adult may say, "I'm just beginning to accept he/she isn't coming back," or "I hurt even more than in the beginning." Typically, immediately following a death, adults participate in a process called "searching" - looking for their loved one as they drive or work or shop - wishing that "wishing" could bring an end to the nightmare of the death. Often, particularly following a traumatic death, there is a wish that things could have been changed just before the traumatic event - a wish for the magic of turning back the clock.

Age 4 or 5 - 6: The inner judge and jury system

Having begun to develop a conscience, children in this age range will look for reasons to be responsible for a death, or for keeping someone alive. They continue feelings of being powerful and believe their magic should work "if I am good enough." Children may carry intense guilt after a death, judging themselves to be responsible for not having prevented their loved one from dying. In this age group, as with children in the 1- 3 or 4 group, it is important to use clear language about death.

Reference to adult grief:

Following the death of a loved one for whom an adult perceives a responsibility relationship, there may be a period of intense guilt and many thoughts which begin, "If only I had..." or "Why didn't I...?" There is a feeling that enough love will cure any ill - a combination of magic and responsibility. These reactions are normal and may reflect a strong sense of personal power and/or a longing for resolution that did not occur prior to the death. Giving expression to these feelings may be the prelude to self-forgiveness, but reassurances from others are seldom helpful. The inner judge is the important agent of self-forgiveness.

Age 7 - 12: The need to know facts and details

During this period, children begin to use factual information to bring reality to death. Stories involving vivid details of a death are often not as frightening as they are fascinating in this age range. Knowing details may be a way of bringing order to death - an order that may give a sense of control over the events. Questions may require sequential and complete answers. Guilt persists in this age range - particularly for things undone.

Reference to adult grief:

Typically, adults continue to require mastery of complete details about a death. Immediately following a death, an individual may not want to know the details, but as the beginning of acceptance of the loss occurs, the same individual may require details as an aide to accepting reality. Sometimes, immediately following a loss, an individual may need to tell the details from their perspective over and over. Later, this same person may need to hear the details from the perspective of others.

Age 13 - 21: The need to be like everyone else

In the teenage years, the job of the child is to be a teenager. This means constant comparison to peers and a need to be as much like everyone else as possible. The loss of a close loved one (father, mother, sister, brother, etc.) means a separation, a difference, between the teenager and his or her peers. Often, following an immediate period of grief, the teenager will chose to return to "normalcy" - putting grief away, delaying the full process of grief and healing until later when it will be less noticeable. It may be important for teenagers to be told that with the passage of time (five to ten years), they may experience periods when they need to "revisit" this loss and to complete the process of grieving. Teenagers can romanticize death. They accept that death is final for everyone except themselves (this is particularly notable with regard to teenage suicide.)

Reference to adult grief:

Adults may "put off' grieving in a manner similar to that of teenagers. Returning to work immediately, participating in frenetic activities - the ways of holding grief "away" are many and varied. This "putting off' is a coping mechanism - sometimes allowing enough time to pass that the painful reality of a life and/or a death can be processed. When the time of delay passes, the process of active healing can begin. Grief waits.

With thanks to Margarita Suarez

Normal Manifestations of Grief

* Loss of appetite, nausea, diarrhea
* Feeling of emptiness in the stomach
* Experience a "lump" in the throat
* Have tightness in the chest
* Feeling of weakness or no energy
* Palpitations of the heart
* Inability to sleep, early morning awakening, extreme fatigue
* Grinding the teeth during sleep
* Dryness of the mouth
* Inability to concentrate, forgetfulness regarding what is being done in the middle of a task, forgetfulness about what is being said in the middle of a sentence
* Loss of time perception
* Difficulty with remembering or maintaining a schedule
* Have intense sense of loneliness and feeling of social isolation
* Overwhelming sense of sadness
* Longing for life to return to the way it was
* Crying at unanticipated times
* Heightened sensitivity to noise
* Breathlessness, frequent sighing
* Restlessness, inability to complete normal tasks, such as reading a book or newspaper
* Experience resentment that 'life goes on' for others
* Hear, smell, see loved one, particularly in familiar settings
* Need to retell the details of the loss again and again
* Experience a feeling of anger at the loved one for dying
* Temporarily try to preserve life 'as it was' for the loved one
* Have recurrent feelings of guilt or remorse

* Assume the characteristics, mannerisms of the loved one
* Have a sense of unreality about life and about the death of loved one
* Irritability, feeling 'on edge' – sometimes feel "explosive"
* At approximately three month intervals, experience intensified feelings of sadness and loss
* May have a heightened sense of sexuality
* Confusion over the place of laughter and enjoyable activities

Normal Manifestations of Grief for Teens

1. Don't like to talk about it a lot
2. Confusion -- don't know what to feel
3. Want to do a regular activity -- wish life could return to "normal"
4. Great frustration -- feel situation (life) out of control
5. Short temper -- want to strike out
6. Feel raw
7. Take refuge in sleep
8. Sleeplessness
9. Cry over "little" things
10. Inability to concentrate
11. Memory of time around death may be confused
12. Loss of time -- sense of unreality about time
13. Difficulty with remembering or maintaining a schedule
14. Loss of appetite, change in eating habits
15. Grades in school may drop
16. Lack of caring about performance in any setting
17. Friends may change -- feel "different" or "changed"
18. Sense of guilt over the death
18. Worry about other close loved ones dying
19. Wonder if the child that died should have been the one to live
20. Assume some of the roles of the one who died
21. Physical problems: heart palpitations, colds, stomach aches
22. Don't feel like participating in any activity with others, especially parents (when a sibling dies)
23. Loss of interest in life and in school -- loss of sense of purpose

24. Anger over missing life with the one who died
25. Anger at Mom or Dad for the living circumstances leading to the death
26. When pain is too great to cope with, may develop a "whatever" attitude
27. Resist "processing" a death
28. May take ten years before they have the life skills to evaluate the meaning of a death for their life

For All Parents Everywhere:

"TO BE HOPEFUL in bad times is not just foolishly romantic. It is based on the fact that human history is a history not only of cruelty, but also of compassion, sacrifice, courage, kindness.

What we choose to emphasize in this complex history will determine our lives. If we see only the worst, it destroys our capacity to do something. If we remember those times and places—and there are so many—where people have behaved magnificently, this gives us the energy to act, and at least the possibility of sending this spinning top of a world in a different direction.

And if we do act, in however small a way, we don't have to wait for some grand utopian future. The future is an infinite succession of presents, and to live now as we think human beings should live, in defiance of all that is bad around us, is itself a marvelous victory."

Howard Zinn

Made in the USA
San Bernardino, CA
11 February 2016